FAIRY IN *THE FAERIE QUEENE*

For my father
For Gareth Roberts

Fairy in *The Faerie Queene*

Renaissance Elf-Fashioning and Elizabethan Myth-Making

MATTHEW WOODCOCK
University of East Anglia

ASHGATE

Published by
Ashgate Publishing Limited
Gower House
Croft Road
Aldershot
Hants GU11 3HR
England

Ashgate Publishing Company
Suite 420
101 Cherry Street
Burlington, VT 05401-4405
USA

Ashgate website: http://www.ashgate.com

British Library Cataloguing in Publication Data
Woodcock, Matthew
    Fairy in the Faerie Queene : Renaissance elf-fashioning and
    Elizabethan myth-making
    1.Elizabeth, I, Queen of England, 1533–1603 – In literature
    2.Spenser, Edmund, 1552?–1599. Faerie Queene 3.Epic poetry,
    English – History and criticism 4.Fairies in literature
    5.Myth in literature
    I.Title
    821.3

Library of Congress Cataloging-in-Publication Data
Woodcock, Matthew, 1973–
    Fairy in The faerie queene : Renaissance elf-fashioning and Elizabethan myth-making / Matthew Woodcock.
        p. cm.
    Includes bibliographical references and index.
    ISBN 0-7546-3439-6 (alk. paper)
    1. Spenser, Edmund, 1552?–1599. Faerie queene. 2. Spenser, Edmund, 1552?–1599–Characters–Fairies. 3. Fairy tales–England–History and criticism. 4. Epic poetry, English–History and criticism. 5. Renaissance–England. 6. Fairies in literature. 7. Myth in literature. I. Title.

PR2358.W66 2004
821'3–dc21

2003052346

ISBN 0 7546 3439 6

Printed and bound in Great Britain by MPG Books Ltd, Bodmin, Cornwall

Contents

Preface

With the exception of Isabel Rathborne's 1937 *The Meaning of Spenser's Fairyland*, scholarship has consistently failed to engage in detailed analysis of Spenser's employment of fairy mythology in *The Faerie Queene*. This book sets out to reassert the importance of fairy in *The Faerie Queene* by demonstrating how Spenser places fairy at the very centre of his mythopœic project, and is the first comprehensive examination of the poem to locate Spenser's work within the context of early modern conceptions and representations of fairy and to discuss the representation of Elizabeth as the fairy queen in relation to the vast range of studies on Elizabethan myth-making.

After establishing a methodological framework for studying the use and presentation of fairies within early modern texts, the literary and political background to Spenser's employment of fairy as a panegyric device is examined in order to address the question as to why in particular Spenser should use fairy mythology in the celebration and glorification of Elizabeth. It is then demonstrated that Spenser comments upon the myth-making project with which he is engaged through constructing and maintaining a fictional scenario in the poem's framing narrative whereby the narrator figure is engaged in setting forth a fairy story for the queen. Individual chapters discuss how Spenser's presentation of fairyland, fairy knights, the fairy chronicle, and the fairy queen herself repeatedly draw attention back to the framing narrative and the mythopœic enterprise that is modelled therein.

Spenser does not present a straightforward, unmediated representation of Elizabeth as Gloriana, but offers instead a more reflexive commentary on the process of using fairy to represent the queen, and in doing so foregrounds his own role within this process. Spenser's 'elf-fashioning' is therefore a vital part of his authorial self-fashioning.

I should like to acknowledge financial assistance and academic support from the following institutions: University College, Oxford; the Oxford University Chest; the British Academy; the Bodleian Library; the libraries of the English and History faculties at Oxford; the British Library; the libraries of Emory University and Washington and Lee University. I am grateful to Ashgate Publishing for permission to use elements in chapters two and five here that appear in a revised form in my essay 'The Fairy Queen Figure in Elizabethan Entertainments', published in Carole Levin, Debra Barrett-Graves, and Jo Eldridge-Carney, eds, *Elizabeth I: Always Her Own Free Woman*, (Aldershot: Ashgate, 2003). I would like to thank the estate of T. Heath-Robinson for kindly giving me their permission to reproduce the illustration of Arthur and Gloriana on the dust-jacket of this book. I am also very grateful to Erika Gaffney and Ann Donahue of Ashgate Publishing for their help and patience during the course of this project.

Sincerest thanks go to Helen Cooper for the characteristic combination of kindness, patience, erudition, and attention to detail that she has shown at each stage of supervising the doctoral thesis upon which the present study is based. I would like to thank my thesis examiners, Richard McCabe and Elizabeth Heale, for their comments and suggestions regarding the overall shape of my argument, and acknowledge the support and guidance of Diane Purkiss in the earlier stages of my project. I must also thank the late Gareth Roberts for first introducing me to Spenser, and for the inspiration that he provided for my studies. For reading over successive versions of my work I am indebted to Matthew C. Hansen, Andrew King, and Matthew Steggle. I am grateful to Lisa Richardson and Emma J. Wilby for allowing me access to their theses, and to James Mawby of Glasgow University for an extensive correspondence on all matters elven. Thanks also go to friends and colleagues at Birkbeck College, London and University College Cork, particularly Andrew King, who on many occasions in discussing interpretations of Spenserian allegory has reminded me that - to use Freud's famous line - sometimes a cigar is just a cigar. I must especially thank Sethina Watson for providing immeasurable help in this project: suggesting new ways of structuring my argument in several chapters, vigilantly ensuring (or at least imploring) that my discussion remain adequately focused, and reading over the manuscript with both intelligence and rigour. My thanks also go to my family, in particular my father, whose financial support allowed me to continue my research, and to Amy Gasper for her sweet distractions and kindness.

List of Abbreviations

All quotations and references from *The Faerie Queene* are taken from Edmund Spenser, *The Faerie Queene*, ed. A. C. Hamilton. 2nd edn (London: Longman, 2001). Quotations from the 'Letter to Raleigh' are from this edition, pp. 714-18.

Shorter Poems   Edmund Spenser, *The Shorter Poems*, ed. Richard A. McCabe (Harmondsworth: Penguin, 1999).

CV	Commendatory Verses
EETS	Early English Text Society
ELH	*English Literary History*
ELR	*English Literary Renaissance*
ES	Extra Series (EETS)
HLQ	*Huntingdon Library Quarterly*
IUR	*Irish University Review*
JEGP	*Journal of English and Germanic Philology*
JWCI	*Journal of the Warburg and Courtauld Institutes*
MLN	*Modern Language Notes*
MLQ	*Modern Language Quarterly*
MLR	*Modern Language Review*
MP	*Modern Philology*
NM	*Neuphilologische Mitteilungen*
N&Q	*Notes and Queries*
n. s.	New Series
OED	*The Oxford English Dictionary*
OS	Original Series (EETS)
P&P	*Past and Present*
PBA	*Proceedings of the British Academy*
PMLA	*Publications of the Modern Language Association*
PQ	*Philology Quarterly*
RenQ	*Renaissance Quarterly*
RES	*Review of English Studies*
RS	Rolls Series
SCJ	*Sixteenth Century Journal*
SEL	*Studies in English Literature*

SP	*Studies in Philology*
SQ	*Shakespeare Quarterly*
SS	Supplementary Series (EETS)
SSt	*Spenser Studies*
TLS	*Times Literary Supplement*
TSLL	*Texas Studies in Language and Literature*
UTQ	*University of Toronto Quarterly*
Variorum	*The Works of Edmund Spenser: A Variorum Edition*, ed. Edwin Greenlaw, et al., 11 vols. (Baltimore: Johns Hopkins University Press, 1932-57).

Introduction

This book sets out to examine Spenser's employment of fairy mythology in *The Faerie Queene* and focuses in particular upon the use of fairy in the representation of Queen Elizabeth I. Spenser's use of fairy can be clearly seen to have stood out in readers' minds in the earliest recorded responses to *The Faerie Queene*. Gabriel Harvey is privy from an early stage to the composition and development of the '*Eluish Queene*' and expresses his evident concern to Spenser that 'the *Faerye Queene* be fairer in your eie than the *Nine Muses*, and *Hobgoblin* runne away with the Garland from *Apollo*'.[1] Spenser's apparent preference for (and delight in) the element of '*Hobgoblin*' in *The Faerie Queene* that Harvey registers here clearly stands out in the poem and marks out the text as being something rather extraordinary. In a similar fashion, included towards the end of Thomas Nashe's *Pierce Penniless* (1592) there is a short vignette describing the eponymous narrator's experience of reading *The Faerie Queene*. He tells of

> Perusing yesternight with idle eyes,
> The Fairy Singers stately tuned verse,
> And viewing after Chap-men's wonted guise,
> What strange contents the title did rehearse;
> I streight leapt ouer to the latter end,
> Where like the queint Comædians of our time,
> That when their Play is doone do fal to ryme,
> I found short lines, to sundry Nobles pend.[2]

His eyes are drawn to the 'strange contents' advertised by the 'Fairy Singer's' choice of appellation.

However, in the expansive body of Spenser criticism that now exists there have been surprisingly few critics who have followed Pierce's lead and directly addressed the matter of the 'strange contents' promised by the poem's title. Fairy in *The Faerie Queene* has previously been all too frequently either explained away or overlooked, the apparent simplicity of explanation forestalling further study and the paucity of detailed critical treatment having the compounding effect of suppressing

---

[1] *Three Proper and wittie, familiar Letters...* (1580) in Edmund Spenser, *Poetical Works*, ed. J. C. Smith and E. De Selincourt (Oxford: Oxford University Press, 1912; repr. 1970), p. 628.
[2] Thomas Nashe, *Works*, ed. R. B. McKerrow, rev. ed. F. P. Wilson. 5 vols. (Oxford: Blackwell, 1958-66), 1: 244.

questions as to the significance or centrality of fairy in the poem. The present study is the first extended treatment of fairy in *The Faerie Queene* since Isabel Rathborne's 1937 *The Meaning of Spenser's Fairyland* and the first to discuss Spenser's identification of Elizabeth as the fairy queen Gloriana in relation to the now vast range of studies on Elizabethan myth-making. This book will reassert the centrality of fairy to Spenser's overall mythopœic project and demonstrate how the poet is engaged in presenting, not simply an uncomplicated, unequivocal portrait of Elizabeth, but a more self-conscious commentary upon the whole process of using fairy to represent and celebrate the queen.

The 'Letter to Raleigh' provides the most direct expression of Spenser's intentions for fairy and tells of how he uses the image of the fairy queen and fairyland to present Elizabeth and her kingdom. But critical study of Spenser's fairy frequently fails to reach beyond the dictates of the Letter, centring instead on decoding the allegorical 'couert vele' in order to unearth some form of meaning located beneath. Building upon the Augustinian principle resonant throughout medieval and early modern literary and exegetical theory that the greatest truth and pleasure is to be gained from a work where one has to labour in uncovering the poet's meaning, the 'continued Allegory' of *The Faerie Queene* is seen as an opaque shell that is best discarded as soon as possible. Deconstruction of the allegory is undoubtedly an important part of the experience of reading *The Faerie Queene*. Spenser himself tempts us with the promise that the most vigilant readers might 'find' fairyland through 'certein signes here sett in sondrie place' (II.proem.4), and indeed it has been argued that the search for meanings is itself a constitutive structuring principle of the poem.[3] But there is an inherent danger that through the necessary reductivism of the meaning-driven approach more detailed criticism of Spenser's use of fairy mythology may be quickly subsumed within the wider critique of the identifications made once the allegorical 'veil' is pierced. The element of fairy mythology itself is rarely considered in its own right. Studies of this kind are further problematized when the line between interpreting the meaning and imposing a particular meaning upon Spenser's fairy is transgressed. Theories attempting to account for the ambiguity and inconsistencies of Spenser's fairy risk turning into a form of story-telling in themselves as the text is used to ventriloquize a chorus of disparate critical agendas.

My focus is not restricted to what Spenser's allegory must denote; rather, I am concerned with how the allegory of fairy operates. The argument that follows is not discordant with treating Spenser's fairy as part of the allegorical scheme, but my interest is in how Spenser's fairy operates as a sign within the text of *The Faerie Queene*: how the poet draws attention to the employment of fairy as an allegorical and rhetorical device; how interpretation is repeatedly invited and forestalled; and the effect that this has upon the relationship of reader and text. Put simply, what is the significance of Spenser's decision to identify Elizabeth with the mythical figure

---

[3] Patricia Parker, *Inescapable Romance: Studies in the Poetics of a Mode* (Princeton: Princeton University Press, 1979), pp. 4, 59; Jonathan Goldberg, *Endlesse Worke: Spenser and the Structures of Discourse* (Baltimore: Johns Hopkins University Press, 1981), p. xii.

of the fairy queen and employ fairy mythology as the governing mythological scheme in his poem?

To date, the most coherent critical attempts to suggest ways in which to understand, rather than merely identify and describe, Spenser's fairies have been advanced in the works of Edwin Greenlaw and Isabel Rathborne. Both critics try to impose a structure upon Spenser's fairy in order to establish some sense of meaning. For Greenlaw, Spenser wrote as an uncompromising panegyricist of Tudor order and orthodoxy; his treatment of Spenser's fairy provides the central expression of this view. Greenlaw sets the mould for later (new) historicists whose similar fascination with the 'aestheticization' of Tudor politics increasingly enmesh *The Faerie Queene* within a network of texts and practices through which Tudor power was enacted and represented. In his 1918 article on fairy mythology Greenlaw picks up on the associations between Arthur and fairyland that were well established by Spenser's day. Greenlaw considers the myth of Arthur as a returning king who, after healing in the land of fairy, will come again and rule Britain, as finds best expression in book eight of John Lydgate's *Fall of Princes*:

> This errour yit abit among Bretouns,
> Which foundid is vpon the prophecie
> Of olde Merlyn, lik ther oppynyouns:
> He as a kyng is crownid in Fairie,
> With sceptre and suerd, & with his regalie
> Shal resorte as lord and souereyne
> Out of Fairye & regne in Breteyne,
>
> And repaire ageyn the Rounde Table.[4]

Greenlaw stresses that it is the fairy aspect of the returning sovereign which Spenser uses, maintaining that 'Spenser conceives the Tudor rule as a return of the old British line; he conceives Elizabeth Tudor as the particular sovereign, coming out of Faerie, whose return fulfils the old prophecy'.[5] Elizabeth is glorified as an individual through identification with the fairy queen and her lineage is glorified through its associations with Arthur. The chronicles in II.x thus pair Elizabeth's British ancestry found in '*Briton moniments*' with the fairy history '*Antiquitee of Faery* lond' which also ultimately refers to the Tudors. By 'fairy', writes Greenlaw, 'Spenser means *Welsh*, or, more accurately, *Tudor*, as distinguished from the general term British'.[6] According to Greenlaw, for the purposes of the poem, Britain is an allegorical representation of England; in essence, the fairy sovereign of the Tudor house has to come from Wales (fairyland) to rule England (Britain).

Greenlaw's model is, however, dogged by inconsistencies: Arthur is born in Britain and taken to the specifically localized Welsh home of the fairy knight

[4] Edwin Greenlaw, 'Spenser's Fairy Mythology', *SP* 15 (1918), p. 116; *Lydgate's Fall of Princes*, ed. Henry Bergen, EETS ES 123 (London: Oxford University Press, 1924), p. 910.
[5] Greenlaw, 'Spenser's Fairy Mythology', p. 116.
[6] Greenlaw, 'Spenser's Fairy Mythology', p. 120.

Timon (I.ix.4). He then rides from the Welsh or marcher locale into fairyland, which Greenlaw also identifies with Wales (or, more abstractly, the home of the Tudors) and thus rides out of the literal and into the allegorical representation of Wales. The neat equation between Tudors and fairies is also problematized, as it is the Britons Artegall and Britomart who are the mythical progenitors of the Tudor line in Merlin's chronicle. The flexible applicability of the historical identifications that Greenlaw draws are vividly illustrated within the article itself in the brief concluding encomium to the then prime minister, David Lloyd-George: 'For from the country of Arthur and Gloriana has come, to fulfil once more the ancient prophecy, a Welshman who wields a power far greater than theirs, but whose task is the same.'[7]

The most elaborate treatment of fairyland is still Rathborne's *The Meaning of Spenser's Fairyland*. Rathborne's thesis is that Spenser's fairyland is the representation of a land of fame akin to the classical Elysium 'where departed heroes, the ancestors of [Spenser's] royal and noble patrons, enjoy an extended, if not an immortal life, closely resembling their heroic lives on earth'.[8] Arthur's visit to fairyland acts as a preparatory mission to the underworld, as a form of ethical training (for Arthur and also, presumably, the reader) comparable, writes Rathborne, to book six of the *Aeneid*, or to the *Divine Comedy*. Arthur's quest for earthly fame - figured in the form of Gloriana and Cleopolis (literally, 'city of fame') - is discussed in relation to the early modern cult of fame, the 'decisive stimulus to moral action both for the individual gentleman and the national State in whose service he finds his fullest self-expression'.[9] According to Rathborne, Spenser's fairies are humans 'under different conditions'; they represent 'famous men who in Arthur's day were either dead or unborn', a race of gods anticipating the fame of Arthur and future worthies.[10] Rathborne argues for the inclusion of both good and bad characters into her conception of fairyland on the basis that this represents both positive and negative kinds of fame: honour and notoriety. But in suggesting that fairyland represents an ideal world, an Elysium or land of the famous dead, Rathborne encounters a number of problems, not least because fairyland remains a land of struggle and conflict. One cannot claim that Spenser's fairies are dead and/ or immortal for as we read in '*Antiquitee* of *Faery* lond' Elferon did 'vntimely dy' (II.x.75); as Richard McCabe writes, 'time stalks the land of Faery too and Guyon chooses his words carefully when he refers to Gloriana's "rare perfection *in mortalitie*"' (II.ii.41).[11] Guyon himself is referred to by Mammon as 'mortall' (II.vii.38). Rathborne simply does not address what actually

---

[7] Greenlaw, 'Spenser's Fairy Mythology', p. 122.

[8] Isabel E. Rathborne, *The Meaning of Spenser's Fairyland* (New York: Columbia University Press, 1937), pp. 142-3.

[9] Rathborne, *Meaning*, p. 157.

[10] Rathborne, *Meaning*, p. 206.

[11] Richard McCabe, *The Pillars of Eternity: Time and Providence in The Faerie Queene* (Blackrock: Irish Academic Press, 1989), p. 96.

goes on in *The Faerie Queene*. Fairyland is more a realm of testing and anxiety than of certainty or sojourn.

Greenlaw's theory that Spenser uses fairy to represent an idealized projection of Tudor politics finds its most enduring advocacy in Stephen Greenblatt's *Renaissance Self-Fashioning: From More to Shakespeare*. Greenblatt's reading of fairyland as an alluring yet hostile otherworld of idleness, a place in which subjectivity is under continual threat of transgression, has largely displaced the 'old' historicism of Greenlaw's search for one-to-one relationships between allegory and actuality. Guyon's victory over the sexual, moral, and political threats of the Bower of Bliss is, argues Greenblatt, a self-constituting act representative of the necessary steps to be taken in the fashioning of Spenser's 'gentleman or noble person'.[12] Greenblatt's interpretation of the Bower of Bliss has become subtly paradigmatic of subsequent attempts to politicize fairyland as a whole. In this way fairyland itself is negated and folds into a catch-all site of confrontation and negotiation for all forms of otherness. More recent critics, for example, interpret Spenser's teasing mention of fairyland in II.proem.1-5 as a reference to the expansion of colonial boundaries; the discovery of fairyland is seen as a model for enlarging Elizabeth's 'owne realmes', the vision of wonder read in terms of economic desire.[13] Similarly, studies on Spenser and Ireland continue to identify fairyland with the 'dragon-slaying' world of colonial Ireland: a place to be mapped, conquered, solved.[14] Greenblatt comes close to adopting Greenlaw's view of Spenser as an unquestioning advocate of Elizabeth and Tudor orthodoxy, as he asserts that *The Faerie Queene* is 'wholly wedded to the autocratic ruler of the English state' and that 'the rich complexities of Spenser's art, its exquisite ethical discriminations in pursuit of the divine in man, are not achieved in spite of what is for us a repellent political ideology - the passionate worship of imperialism - but are inseparably linked to that ideology'.[15] Spenser attempts to ward off a 'radical questioning' of the role of art in the formation of Tudor ideology through drawing attention to the process of producing his art - by keeping his hands above the table in his construction of national mythography.

The present study does not reject the idea that *The Faerie Queene* was ultimately conceived and constructed as a work of celebration and glorification for Elizabeth. I am hesitant, however, to see the self-consciousness that Greenblatt

---

[12] Stephen Greenblatt, *Renaissance Self-Fashioning: From More to Shakespeare* (Chicago: University of Chicago Press, 1980), pp. 179-85.

[13] See Maureen Quilligan, *Milton's Spenser: The Politics of Reading* (Ithaca: Cornell University Press, 1983), p. 68; Elizabeth Jane Bellamy, 'Spenser's Faeryland and "The Curious Genealogy of India"', in Patrick Cheney and Lauren Silberman, eds, *Worldmaking Spenser: Explorations in the Early Modern Age* (Lexington: University Press of Kentucky, 2000), pp. 177-92; David Read, *Temperate Conquests: Spenser and the Spanish New World* (Detroit: Wayne State University Press, 2000).

[14] See, for example, Willy Maley. *Salvaging Spenser: Colonialism, Culture and Identity* (London: Macmillan, 1997), pp. 78-98; Christopher Highley, *Shakespeare, Spenser, and the Crisis in Ireland* (Cambridge: Cambridge University Press, 1997), p. 13-39.

[15] Greenblatt, *Renaissance Self-Fashioning*, p. 174.

identifies purely as a means of drawing readers' attention back to the circumstances of the text's production as an affirmation of the authority of the royal ideology in whose service the poet loyally writes.[16] More persuasive is Louis Adrian Montrose's argument that Spenser is engaged in 'an interplay between submission and resistance to the project of royal celebration' and that the 'resistance' manifests, not as a 'concerted program of sedition, of political opposition or subversion', but as a result of the conscious foregrounding of Spenser's own role as author within the mythopœic project.[17] The construction of mythopœic images and identities for and/ or of Elizabeth simultaneously saw artists, courtiers, and poets (Spenser included) engaged in a process of 'making' themselves through royal favour and patronage, and the granting of patents and offices. Montrose provides the most enduring statement of this reciprocal model of fashioning as it applies to Spenser and describes the vital role that *The Shepheardes Calender* plays in establishing Spenser's authorial persona at the same time as celebrating Elizabeth. Montrose locates *The Shepheardes Calender* in relation to the multifarious constructions of Elizabeth as a text or fiction perpetuated and manipulated by both the queen and her subjects, and demonstrates how Spenser attempts to signal the initiation of his own participation within this overall myth-making process. Writing primarily of 'Aprill', Montrose identifies how Spenser, through foregrounding his assumed persona of Colin Clout, explicitly demonstrates the potential function and qualifications of the poet-as-mythographer and panegyricist (and specifically his own particular function and qualifications) and advertises his ability to make 'the cultural forms in which royal power is not only celebrated but may actually be effected'.[18] In Spenser's text, continues Montrose, 'the refashioning of an Elizabethan subject as a laureate poet is dialectically related to the refashioning of the queen as the author's subject'.[19] Montrose establishes a compelling framework for understanding how the project of royal celebration may also function simultaneously as a means of establishing and commenting upon Spenser's role as author.

This book does not argue for an overtly subversive reading of the fairy queen, but it does submit that Spenser is engaged both in writing about Elizabeth, and in writing about the process of representing Elizabeth. As I shall demonstrate, Spenser persistently draws attention to his own role as poet and myth-maker throughout *The Faerie Queene*; this authorial self-fashioning is an integral part of his programme of 'elf-fashioning' - of representing Elizabeth as the fairy queen.

My study begins by establishing a framework for understanding the representation of fairy in the early modern period and addresses - for the first time - some of the principal difficulties encountered in the academic treatment of fairy.

---

[16] Greenblatt, *Renaissance Self-Fashioning*, pp. 191, 222-3.

[17] Louis Adrian Montrose, 'The Elizabethan Subject and the Spenserian Text', in Patricia Parker and David Quint, eds, *Literary Theory/ Renaissance Texts* (Baltimore: Johns Hopkins University Press, 1986), p. 323.

[18] Montrose, 'Elizabethan Subject', p. 322.

[19] Montrose, 'Elizabethan Subject', p. 323.

The first chapter proposes a methodology for studying fairy that is influenced by more recent research on representations of early modern witchcraft in which attention is placed on the textual ontology of witches: how they are presented and used within stories and narratives, how they 'exist' within texts. Careful attention to the means through which texts and stories of fairy are transmitted and the way in which those stories are received is a cornerstone of the approach to reading fairy advocated here. The focus of my study overall is on the specifically textual ontology of fairy: on how fairies 'exist' and function within texts. I concentrate on the examination of local, text-based effects rather than on the reconstruction of extra-textual, essentialist meaning. Attention here is on the presentation and effect of fairy mythology as it is used within texts and does not seek to engage with the more nebulous issue of early modern belief in fairies. Accordingly, the question of Spenser's belief in fairies is not a concern of this book. In restricting analysis to how fairy stories are constructed and read, and ignoring the subjective issue of what fairies 'were' or 'are', I have sought to demonstrate the importance of considering how individual texts used and interpreted the concept designated as 'fairy'. Likewise, I have not set out here to establish a global interpretative structure with which to construct or recover the meaning of fairy in Spenser; the focus instead is on the textual ontology of Spenser's fairy. Drawing upon two of the most important sixteenth-century works of Protestant demonology - Reginald Scot's *Discoverie of Witchcraft* and James VI's *Daemonologie* - chapter one also introduces a number of motifs and themes from fairy mythology that Spenser incorporates within *The Faerie Queene*.

Chapter two locates Spenser's poem within the wider context of Elizabethan myth-making and outlines some of the literary and political sources for the use of fairy as a panegyric device, including the entertainments held at Kenilworth and Woodstock during the 1570s. Of particular significance for *The Faerie Queene* is how, in both literary and mythopœic sources, fairies have been incorporated within medieval and early modern political discourse as figures either associated with, or actually representing and embodying, sovereign and political power. In the course of the chapter, I also address the question of why Spenser chooses to employ fairy mythology in particular; why he locates his poem in fairyland rather than in, say, Arcadia or Carolingian Europe.

The method of analysis set out in this book centres on close readings of the episodes within *The Faerie Queene* where fairy actively becomes Spenser's immediate subject in the narrative - as opposed to each occasion where individual characters are simply referred to as fairies or elves - and where an aspect of fairy mythology becomes the focus of Spenser's attention in the narrative. Having closely examined the presence and function of fairy in *The Faerie Queene*, it is evident that the points at which Spenser uses and refers to his use of fairy are all located within stories that are rehearsed or read by characters in the poem and that these then in turn are placed within the 'famous antique history' professedly set forth by Spenser's narrator persona. Spenser's fairies are all constituted as stories within a story, texts within a text. I have chosen to concentrate on a number of these Spenserian fairy stories, treating them not as definitive statements of what fairy

8 *Fairy in* The Faerie Queene

means or signifies throughout the poem as a whole, but as sites of potential interpretative struggle over how to read fairy. The initiation of interpretative engagement or 'play' with the reader is an integral part of Spenser's conception of how he employs fairy within his text. In chapter three I reassert the importance of the framing narrative to the whole discussion of Spenser's use of fairy by tracing how the poet continues to present this first story of fairy right the way through his text. The framing narrative also provides a commentary on the whole process of telling stories of fairy. The doubts, anxieties, and interpretative problems voiced through Spenser's narrator character mirror those presented within the fairy stories found within the 'famous antique history' that the narrator sets forth. It is in the framing narrative that Spenser also draws attention to his own role as poet and myth-maker through continuing to foreground the story of the narrator setting forth his fairy story to his ultimate implied reader, Elizabeth.

The next three chapters each focus upon a different aspect of Spenser's use of fairy mythology, and centre on a close examination of three Spenserian fairy stories in *The Faerie Queene*: the revelation to the Redcrosse knight of his true identity at Mount Contemplation; Arthur's vision of the fairy queen narrated in I.ix.9-16; and Guyon's reading of '*Antiquitee* of *Faery* lond' at the House of Alma. Chapter four discusses the effects of the initial identification between Elizabeth and Gloriana on the way in which fairyland and individual fairy knights are presented in the poem. Chapter five concentrates on the figure of the fairy queen herself and argues that the interpretative ambiguity surrounding Spenser's presentation of Gloriana ultimately serves as a commentary upon the textual ontology of Elizabeth herself and further draws attention back to Spenser's own particular role in representing and mythologizing the queen. Chapter six examines how Spenser adapts the panegyric topos of the mythical genealogy and self-consciously applies it to his dominant mythological scheme to produce the fairy chronicle, '*Antiquitee* of *Faery* lond'.

Reference will be made throughout this study to Spenserian 'fairy stories', though I do not intend to discuss *The Faerie Queene* in relation to those forms of narrative commonly termed fairy tales or 'wonder' tales, many of which do not, in the event, feature characters identified as fairies.[20] Despite perceived distinctions between what may be denoted by 'fairy' and 'elf', for purposes of this study the two terms (with their many different variant spellings) are conflated unless specified otherwise.

---

[20] Several critics have attempted to link *The Faerie Queene* with motifs from fairy- or folktales: Linda Woodbridge, 'Amoret and Belphoebe: Fairy Tale and Myth', *N&Q* 231 (1986), pp. 340-42; Elizabeth Porges Watson, 'Mr Fox's Mottoes in the House of Busirane', *SSt* 13 (1999), pp. 285-90; Mary Ellen Lamb, 'Gloriana, Acrasia, and the House of Busirane: Gendered Fictions in *The Faerie Queene* as Fairy Tale', in Cheney and Silberman, eds, *Worldmaking Spenser*, pp. 97-8.

Chapter 1

Reading Fairies in Early Modern Texts

The Textual Life of Fairies

This chapter establishes a framework both for better understanding the representation of fairy in the early modern period and for locating Spenser's work within the context of contemporary conceptions of fairy. In many ways this study is complicit in what Diane Purkiss identifies as a secularization of supernatural discourses: a transformation of supernatural and, in the immediate case, fairy beliefs into something else in order that they might be discussed with any degree of historical and analytical objectivity.[1] As with witchcraft and witch beliefs, fairies have to be transferred into other discourses - political, social, religious, medical - in order to be studied or written upon, even though, for unquantifiable numbers of people both before and after the sixteenth century, fairies were actually believed to exist.

The common approach in studies of fairy in the early modern period is to reconstruct fairies as a subjective reality and then piece together an over-arching tradition of how that social reality is represented in narrative and dramatic texts. Such an approach denies the rhetorical or formal role of fairy within this process of representation, and consequently there is little critical treatment of the rhetorical function of fairy within texts. The approach that I have taken in this study concentrates not on the essentialist attributes of fairies themselves, nor directly on fairy belief, but on the textual level, at the ways in which fairies are represented, described, depicted, or staged within texts. From Latin *texere* 'to weave', 'text' here denotes the specifically contrived or woven-together nature of a narrative, be it written or oral. My approach treats the ontology or 'existence' of fairies only in so far as they appear within contextualized, shaped narratives. It would be misleading to reconstruct a monolithic fairy tradition or a grand narrative of what fairy belief was in the early modern period, as indeed many nineteenth- and twentieth-century writers and folklorists have attempted in their work. To do so is to reconstruct a conceptual whole that never existed in this form. At best we can talk about a textual tradition of how different forms of narrative represent and use the image of fairy, though even to take this path implies the necessary reconstruction of an invisible network of transmission, imitation, and cross-reference between texts and sources that is beyond the remit of this book, and which is, by nature, inherently both

---

[1] Diane Purkiss, *The Witch in History: Early Modern and Twentieth-Century Representations* (London: Routledge, 1996), pp. 77-9.

contingent and conjectural. I do not intend to identify different classes of fairy, nor even to construct different traditions of representing fairies and simply read off where Spenser falls within such a taxonomy. Equally, I am not concerned with the question of the existence of or belief in fairies, but - within this chapter - in how fairy is used in belief and representational systems, and the use and effect of the image of fairy within individual texts. Analysis is far better suited to the individual example, and to contextualization of the use of fairy within the conditions of textual production and reception.

The approach that I have taken in this study corresponds to ideas and techniques found in studies of early modern witchcraft, and in discussions of how witches 'exist' textually in terms of narratives created within or as part of social, religious, and psychological discourses. Early modern witchcraft has received critical treatment at a much higher level of sophistication than that received by the cognate field of studies on fairy mythology. One of the most fruitful contributions to the study of fairy to come out of witchcraft studies is the social anthropologist approach of Keith Thomas, who has considered the social and domestic function of narratives on fairy in popular belief.[2] In his brief section on fairy, Thomas's attention is less on the texture of the sources on fairy that he cites, than on what they actually do. He considers how, within the sixteenth and seventeenth centuries, direct engagement with fairies is frequently discussed in terms of displacement onto rituals of appeasement, such as leaving out bread and milk and pails of water for fairy baths, sweeping the hearth, and keeping a clean home. These kinds of rituals retain traces of rites performed to appease the classical domestic or fertility deities, with whom fairies were often identified, both in literary and demonological texts. Fairy beliefs 'help to reinforce some of the standards upon which the effective working of society depended', and form the basis of a social code of good housekeeping.[3] Fairy lore is also seen as providing a cognitionist function in stories told to explain or comprehend physical or mental abnormalities, causal fictions of being 'struck' or possessed by the fairy constructed around a perceived physiological effect. This can be seen, for example, in the lore surrounding changelings, where childhood sickness or deformity is ascribed to the fairies having stolen away the healthy human child and substituted it with a sickly replacement of their own.

There has been a shift in more recent years away from a sociological approach to witchcraft, which attempts to establish paradigms and models for witchcraft phenomena, towards a greater emphasis on the reading of witchcraft as a textual construct. The focus is more on the social context of individual trials and localized interpretation of the means by which witchcraft is represented. The different kinds of narratological approach used in a number of recent studies call for more attention to be placed on *who* is constructing witchcraft narratives, and the method and medium of transmission. There is now greater stress placed upon locating the

---

[2] Keith Thomas, *Religion and the Decline of Magic* (Harmondsworth: Penguin, 1973), pp. 724-34.
[3] Thomas, *Religion*, pp. 731-2.

'fiction' of witchcraft within the signifying system of individual early modern community networks, and the means by which the figure or sign of the witch is constructed both at the popular level through accusations of and ascriptions to witchcraft, and by the judicial and discursive practices of elites. The myth of the perfect witch, asserts Robin Briggs, is very much a pieced-together construct born out of a negotiation between accuser and accused.[4] Attention is drawn increasingly to how the objective reality of witchcraft and demonology is *made* by language; witchcraft is studied as a sign or series of signs that operate and circulate within a language community.[5] Equally significant for historians of the supernatural is the importance of viewing popular texts as stories, of considering the element of emplotment and personal projection or fantasy in their construction, as 'strategic' utterances rather than simply 'transparent' documents.[6]

The study of witchcraft within the modern academy is founded therefore not upon the recovery of an objective reality, but upon the critical treatment of a system of subjective representations. It is the study of a site of textual controversy, of a struggle between the propagation of rival readings, ascriptions, and interpretations of events. The study of fairy can be approached in a similar fashion; critical attention must be given to the context and form of the texts in which fairies are represented. This is especially important where representations of fairies can appear very realistic and seem to speak for themselves unmediated, as with the photographs of the Cottingley fairies. As with reading 'witchcraft', sensitivity to the representation of the fairy within a text as a whole, and to the circumstances of that text's production and reception, is required to avoid a merely descriptive and anecdotal methodology. Early modern texts on witchcraft and fairy lore certainly demonstrate an understanding of how they operate dialogically within a reading system. Reginald Scot in *The Discoverie of Witchcraft* (1584), for example, is aware of the context of his writing and the circumstances of its reception, and that he argues against the prevailing opinion of what was understood by the word 'witch' within his language community. Scot expresses a resigned awareness that he 'should no more prevaile herein, than if a hundred yeares since I should have intreated your predecessors to beleeve, that Robin goodfellowe, that ancient bulbeggar, had beene but a cousening merchant, and no divell indeed'.[7] Scot writes of the inexorable link between the number of 'witchmongers' - those who are willing to read and interpret events as witchcraft - and the number of witches that are reported and tried; of the fundamental relationship between the 'producers' and 'products' of witchcraft.

---

[4] Robin Briggs, *Witches and Neighbours: The Social and Cultural Context of European Witchcraft* (London: HarperCollins, 1996), p. 17.
[5] Stuart Clark, *Thinking with Demons: The Idea of Witchcraft in Early Modern Europe* (Oxford: Clarendon Press, 1997), p. 6. See also Armando Maggi, *Satan's Rhetoric: A Study of Renaissance Demonology* (Chicago: University of Chicago Press, 2001).
[6] Purkiss, *Witch in History*, p. 74.
[7] Reginald Scot, *The Discoverie of Witchcraft*, ed. Brinsley Nicholson (London, 1886), p. xx.

The level of sophisticated analysis found in modern witchcraft studies is in stark contrast to the ways in which fairy mythology has been studied to date. The ontological ambiguity and inconsistency in sixteenth- and seventeenth-century representations of fairy has largely been replicated by writers and scholars in their approach to the field. The image of the fairy appears to be infinitely malleable and resistant to any attempt to establish a definitive ascription of physical dimensions, appearance, moral alignment, or associated practices and attributes. Dictionary definitions for 'fairy' (both contemporary and modern) only scratch the surface of what was actually understood by the term 'fairy' in the period. Employed in poetry, drama, and masque; evoked in popular curses, charms, and rituals; and included within contemporary discussions of witchcraft and demonology, representations of the fairy have traditionally required, and acquired, a complex system of nomenclature and categorization.

The study of early modern fairy is founded largely upon a process of taxonomy and description. It is when one begins the inevitable process of distinguishing and defining different traditions of fairy and fairy narratives that difficulties develop. Generations of scholars have attempted to classify the many different ways in which fairies are presented, using an equally diverse number of systems. Nineteenth-century studies of fairy lore commonly identified and classified different kinds of fairy beings according to racial geography,[8] or posited the idea of a universal fairy belief or 'fairy creed' prevalent amongst 'all of the Aryan-speaking people of Europe', in a manner analogous to concurrent interests in philology and the Indo-European language.[9]

In the twentieth century, Minor White Latham, Katharine Briggs, and C. S. Lewis have, variously, constructed different classes of fairy grouped according to common physical traits and features, or theories on origins.[10] Each adopts a different taxonomic system, and identifies different classes of fairy: trooping and solitary fairies; fairies of romance, popular lore, or theological and demonological traditions. Latham's and Briggs's studies are invaluable tools for studying sixteenth- and seventeenth-century representations of fairy. However, both studies take an overwhelmingly descriptive approach and the primary aim and organizational principle is one of delineation and description. There is little attention to, or analysis of, the context or form in which narratives on fairy are produced and transmitted or to the social, religious, and political functions of such

---

[8] See, for example, Thomas Keightley, *The Fairy Mythology; Illustrative of the Romance and Superstition of Various Countries* (London, 1828).

[9] Alfred Nutt, 'The Fairy Mythology of English Literature: Its Origins and Nature', *Folklore* 8 (1897), p. 45.

[10] Minor White Latham, *The Elizabethan Fairies: The Fairies of Folklore and the Fairies of Shakespeare* (New York: Columbia University Press, 1930), pp. 41-6; Katharine Briggs, *The Anatomy of Puck: An Examination of Fairy Beliefs among Shakespeare's Contemporaries and Successors* (London: Routledge, 1959), pp. 13-16; C. S. Lewis, *The Discarded Image: An Introduction to Medieval and Renaissance Literature* (Cambridge: Cambridge University Press, 1964), pp. 123-34.

narratives. An attendant problem is that all three writers - Latham, Briggs, and Lewis - are frequently guilty of intersplicing between works from several centuries apart produced within entirely different contexts to illustrate an individual point. Equally problematic are attempts to sub-divide different classes of fairy into a kind of encyclopedic framework that distinguishes, for example, the difference in nature between an elf and a fairy, or between a fairy and a puck or a brownie.[11]

Perhaps the most frequently made (and most problematic) ramification is between the fairy found in literary texts and the 'real' fairy of popular tradition or belief. In numerous studies born out of an obsession with the fairies of Shakespeare, the nineteenth-century writers and folklorists were keen both to stress the extent to which the 'genius' of Shakespeare had ameliorated the more sinister, often horrific image of fairy found in popular belief, and to take care to illustrate the kind of sources from which his fairies were constructed. At the same time, there is the repeated sentiment that Shakespeare has provided us with the most accurate realization of fairy belief. In the folklorist treatises and dissertations there is certainly a consensus that Shakespeare constructed the most enduring representation of fairy to come out of the sixteenth century; as Alfred Nutt writes 'Shakespeare's vision stood by itself, and was accepted as the ideal presentment of fairydom, which, for two centuries at least, has signified to the average Englishman of culture the world depicted in the *Midsummer Night's Dream.*'[12]

It is difficult to deny the overall conclusions typified here by Nutt. What remains problematic about the methodology applied by the many nineteenth-century writers on fairy, and their twentieth-century heirs and successors, is the phonocentric hierarchy that the folklorist tradition, so inextricably at the heart of fairy studies to date, implicitly predicates. Such a hierarchy foregrounds the presence of fairy as it exists in popular belief and is perpetuated in oral narrative, and affords the most authority to the representations of fairy that are judged to come closest to the nebulous core of fairy belief. Accordingly, Shakespeare's fairies attract the most critical attention, whilst the more 'literary' conception of fairy found in medieval romance, to which Spenser is heavily indebted, receives summarily scant treatment. The 'bookish' fairies of romance (and of Spenser) are commonly mentioned only in the process of excluding them from treatments of Shakespeare's fairies, as is exemplified by Sir Walter Scott's comments:

> Of Spenser we must say nothing, because in his Faery Queen, the title is the only circumstance which connects his splendid allegory with the popular superstition, and as he uses it, means nothing more than an Utopia, or nameless country.[13]

---

[11] See, for example, Katharine Briggs, *A Dictionary of Fairies* (Harmondsworth: Penguin, 1977). The entry for *The Faerie Queene* scarcely mentions Spenser's use of fairy at all (pp. 130-31).

[12] Nutt, 'Fairy Mythology', p. 31.

[13] Sir Walter Scott, *Letters on Demonology and Witchcraft* (London, 1830), p. 184. Floris DeLattre, *English Fairy Poetry: From the Origins to the Seventeenth Century* (London: Froude, 1912), pp. 80-91, is similarly dismissive of fairy in *The Faerie Queene*.

Spenser's use of fairy is seen as little more than a decorative anomaly.

Difficulties arise, however, in the more descriptive approaches adopted to the study of fairy as the boundaries of different taxonomical groups that are established in each attempt at classification are by no means impermeable, and there is frequent overlap between the different traditions of fairy identified. They fail to account, for example, for literary influences on demonological treatises and books of conjuration; for the pervasive interest in popular lore found in sections of *prodigia* or *mirabilia* in Anglo-Norman chronicles and miscellanies - texts that are frequently cited as sources for some of the earliest references to fairies; or for the fact that many authors, including Spenser and Shakespeare, use a confection of both popular and romance tradition.[14] It must be recognized that Shakespeare's fairies - no less than those of Spenser - are drawn from a wide and eclectic range of sources and texts. In *A Midsummer Night's Dream*, for example, Shakespeare appears to go out of his way to bring together as many different motifs and images from fairy mythology as he possibly can within the play: changelings; fairy hunts or 'rades' (II.i. lines 24-25); a sexualized fairy queen; associations with nature, fertility, and generation; fairies' invisibility; and the mischievous and potentially malicious puck.[15] Shakespeare combines elements of fairy mythology found in the romance *Huon of Burdeux* with popular lore relating to fairy rituals and Robin good-fellow; he follows the lead of those court dramas by John Lyly that evoke the fairies of aristocratic entertainments; and, after *The Faerie Queene*, Shakespeare takes up fairies as an artificial, celebratory device, that are employed - whether or not the play was intended to celebrate the occasion of an actual wedding - to bless a ducal marriage.[16] Shakespeare's is just as much an artificial, textual conception of fairy as that which we find in *The Faerie Queene*. The presentation of stories and plays and the limits of credibility are a central concern in the play, a literary self-consciousness underscored by the fact that *A Midsummer Night's Dream* is itself an entertainment about producing entertainments.

---

[14] For the Anglo-Norman sources on fairy lore, see Gervase of Tilbury, *Des Gervasius von Tilbury Otia Imperialia*, ed. Felix Liebrecht (Hannover, 1856), pp. 29-30; Giraldus Cambrensis, *Itinerarium Kambriae* in *Giraldus Cambrensis Opera*, ed. J. S. Brewer, J. F. Dimock and G. F. Warner. RS 21. 8 vols. (London, 1861-91), 6: 75-8; Radulphi de Coggeshall, *Chronicon Anglicanum*, ed. J. Stevenson. RS 66 (London, 1875), pp. 120-21; William of Newburgh, *Historia Rerum Anglicarum*, ed. Richard Howlett. RS 82a (London, 1884), pp. 85-6; Walter Map, *De Nugis Curialium (Courtier's Trifles)*, ed. and tr. M. R. James, rev. ed. C. N. L. Brooke and R. A. B. Mynors (Oxford: Clarendon Press, 1983), pp. 27-31, 155-9, 161-3.
[15] All references from Shakespeare, unless otherwise stated, are from *The Norton Shakespeare*, gen. ed. Stephen Greenblatt (New York: Norton, 1997).
[16] Frank Sidgwick, *The Sources and Analogues of A Midsummer Night's Dream* (London: Chatto, 1908), p. 39; William Shakespeare, *A Midsummer Night's Dream*, ed. Harold Brooks (London: Methuen, 1979), p. lxxxiii, note that many of Shakespeare's references to Puck or Robin good-fellow and his pranks are actually taken from Scot's *Discoverie*, further compounding the inherently textual picture of fairy lore that Shakespeare ultimately sets forth.

The difficulties inherent in the folklorist methodology stem from the fact that the ontology of fairy is studied in terms of fairies' essential properties. The representations of fairy in literary texts, analogous pneumatological and demonological discussions, and later collections of stories by antiquarians and folklorists are used as a refractive means of recovering the sixteenth-century understanding of, and belief in fairy as an extra-textual objective reality. The 'essentialist' mode of studying fairy, as it might be styled, treats the texts (both written and oral) that are used to represent fairies as shadows of objectively real, extra-textual entities.

Problems of methodology arise in that there exists no text from the sixteenth century that solely or directly addresses either popular fairy belief or intellectual and theological positions on fairy, in the same manner as is found for contemporary interactions with witchcraft or ghosts. The nearest text approximating a direct account, Robert Kirk's *Secret Common-Wealth of Elves, Fauns and Fairies*, was completed in 1691, and its usefulness and relevance are obscured by authorial and editorial idiosyncrasies.[17] We are left to rely instead on the tangential, largely dismissive discussions of fairies found in sixteenth-century witchcraft and demonology treatises. Latham's response to the issue of textual evidence is to turn to the 'words' of the Elizabethans and their 'immediate successors' in the seventeenth century to illustrate 'to what race of beings or spirits the fairies were believed to belong'. Latham's methodology is founded upon an attempt to 'reproduce' fairy belief:

> It has seemed necessary, in order to reproduce the everyday belief of the Elizabethans concerning the fairies, to treat the fairies not as mythical personages or as fanciful creations of the literary imagination or of popular superstition, but to regard them, as did their human contemporaries of the 16th century, as credible entities and as actual and existing beings.[18]

---

[17] Briggs, *Anatomy*, pp. 27-32, sees Kirk's researches in the Scottish Highlands during the later seventeenth century as the work of a proto-folklorist, offering an account of local fairy beliefs 'unaffected by the literary fashions of the south', although the image of fairy presented is heavily tempered by neoplatonic pneumatology. Kirk's text was only published in 1815, and reprinted in 1893 edited by Andrew Lang; see Robert Kirk, *The Secret Commonwealth of Elves, Fauns and Fairies*, intr. R. B. Cunninghame Graham, commentary Andrew Lang (Stirling: Mackay, 1933). By the time of Lang's edition the manuscript had been misplaced, leaving some question as to the extent of Lang's editorial emendations, particularly as Lang's commentary seems to apply Kirk's text to illustrate his own work with the Psychical Research Society. Lang's preoccupations with establishing a scientific approach to the supernatural led him to treat Kirk as something of a forerunner and, through the 1893 edition (and 1933 reprint), as an appropriate model and mouthpiece for Lang's own ideas on the supernatural. The most reliable modern edition is Robert Kirk, *The Secret Common-wealth*, ed. Stewart Sanderson (Cambridge: Brewer, 1976).

[18] Latham, *Elizabethan Fairies*, pp. 12-13.

Latham's study thus takes 'credible entities' and essential 'beings' as its object, and uses a cut-and-paste approach to the 'words' taken from sixteenth- and seventeenth-century texts referring to fairies in an attempt to replicate fairy belief. Such a methodology professes to recreate belief by letting the 'words' speak largely for themselves, but fails to take account of the context of the words, or of any level of authorial or rhetorical mediation. The attempt to bring together a piecemeal, fragmented collection of evidence with which to illustrate fairy belief is therefore more a process of reconstruction than reproduction, as such evidence is implicitly assembled around the essentialist, extra-textual core.

This is largely the kind of methodology adopted in subsequent studies of fairy, with the primary variation in approach being the taxonomic principles and classification systems into which material is assembled. Briggs, for example, still assumes a similar essentialism in her studies in her frequent recourse to folktales and tale-types taken from nineteenth- and twentieth-century collections to illustrate particular motifs found in sixteenth- and seventeenth-century texts.[19] Oral narrative and folktale are wielded as an atemporal source of authority, though again - as is characteristic of the folklorist approach - there is little consideration of an individual narrative's context of production and reception, of the function that such might play, or of the effect of constructing and rehearsing that narrative. In relation to the construction of narratives on or about fairies, we need to consider the element of what Hayden White has called 'emplotment', and to treat the narratives within which fairies are represented (both written and oral) as mediated, shaped texts.[20] With regards to contexts of reception, the role of the folklorist collecting (and 'reproducing') narratives on fairies also needs to be taken into account, alongside the (re)construction that occurs in the reception and reproduction of such narratives. Studies of fairy mythology need to pay greater attention to the ways in which fairies are represented within a text, to the elements from which individual examples of fairies are constructed or fashioned, and to the rhetorical effects that may be created through the employment of fairy mythology. The present examination is the first attempt to apply this overall methodology to early modern representations of fairy and, more particularly, to *The Faerie Queene*.

Fairy Stories and Protestant Demonology

From the outset of his major writings Spenser presents and discusses fairy in terms of its acknowledged artifice and inherent fictionality. Spenser's fairies are a construction - an inherently artificial, literary entity put together from many different texts. The question of his belief in fairies is not an issue; as McCabe

---

[19] Briggs, *Anatomy*, pp. 12-13.
[20] See Hayden White, *Metahistory: The Historical Imagination in Nineteenth-Century Europe* (Baltimore: Johns Hopkins University Press, 1973), pp. 1-11; White, 'The Historical Text as Literary Artefact', in *Tropics of Discourse: Essays in Cultural Criticism* (Baltimore: Johns Hopkins University Press, 1978), pp. 81-100.

rightly states: 'With Spenser it is not a question of existence or non-existence - a point much disputed by his contemporaries - but of aesthetic utility.'[21] The aesthetic utility of fairy can clearly be seen in the exposure or 'discovery' of literary and rhetorical devices that takes place in the text and glosses to *The Shepheardes Calender*. Spenser's treatment of fairy mythology in the *Calender* closely relates to some of the most commonly found ways in which fairies are presented in early modern texts. Like the characters and fixtures of classical mythology, fairy was a consciously artificial device to be used within the construction of a text. Fifteenth- and sixteenth-century dictionaries almost always define fairies and elves in terms of classical mythology as *lamiae*, *nymphae*, *strygia*, or *laruae*, terms carrying frequent overlapping associations with witches and enchantresses.[22] Similarly, sixteenth-century translators of classical works, such as Gavin Douglas and Arthur Golding, translate nymphs, fauns, satyrs, dryads, and hamadryads into fairies and elves.[23] E.K. - either Spenser alone or in collaboration with Harvey - offers a comparable translation in his gloss of the 'Aprill' eclogue:

> Ladyes of the lake) be Nymphes. For it was an olde opinion amongste the Auncient Heathen, that of euery spring and fountaine was a goddesse the Soueraigne. Whiche opinion stucke in the myndes of men not manye years sithence, by meanes of certain fine fablers and lowd lyers, such as were the Authors of King Arthure the great and such like, who tell many an vnlawfull leasing of the Ladyes of the Lake, that is, the Nymphes. (*Shorter Poems*, p. 69)[24]

Spenser's translation of the nymphs of the Virgilian *Culex* ('naidum coitu') into 'many Fairies' in line 179 of *Virgils Gnat* was thus a practice that was typical of his day.[25] There are also a number of points in Spenser's works where fairies are simply collocated with nymphs in a synthesis of classical and native mythologies.[26] Collocation with classical domestic deities becomes one of the most common means by which fairies appear within pastoral poetry until well into the seventeenth century.

It is also possible to locate Spenser's early treatment of fairy in relation to the scepticism towards fairies and spirits found within works of Protestant demonology

---

[21] McCabe, *Pillars*, p. 91.

[22] Latham, *Elizabethan Fairies*, pp. 52-5; DeWitt T. Starnes and Ernest W. Talbert, *Classical Myth and Legend in Renaissance Dictionaries* (Westport, CT: Greenwood, 1955), pp. 102-6.

[23] Latham, *Elizabethan Fairies*, pp. 48-52.

[24] Jean Wilson, *Entertainments for Elizabeth I* (Woodbridge: Brewer, 1980), pp. 25-6, uses this passage to make a compelling argument for a wider understanding of how Elizabeth may be addressed as a fairy or fay, and suggests that when Elizabeth is referred to as a 'Nymph' 'the image is of a Lady of the Lake, and not necessarily of a classical Nymph'.

[25] Oliver Farrar Emerson, 'Spenser's Virgils Gnat', *JEGP* 17 (1918), p. 102.

[26] Fairies and nymphs are collocated in lines 32-3 of 'Maye' (*Shorter Poems*, p. 73); *The Faerie Queene* VI.x.7 and 17; and in *The Teares of the Muses*, line 31 (*Shorter Poems*, p. 192).

produced both before and after *The Shepheardes Calender.* By the end of the sixteenth century demonology had become a major field of discourse through which points of Protestant and Catholic controversy were registered. Protestant demonology was particularly concerned with dismantling popular belief in the efficacy of nebulous magical and counter-magical practices, and was related to the wider reformist campaign to eradicate popular religiosity.[27] A common feature of Protestant demonological texts, therefore, was the fashioning of the Catholic past as a time of ignorant superstition. For example, in one of the most comprehensive sixteenth-century studies of belief in ghosts, the Calvinist minister and theologian Ludwig Lavater writes that

> There were farre many more of these kindes of apparitions and miracles seene amongest vs, at suche tyme as we were giuen vnto blindnesse and superstition, than since that the Gospell was purely preached amongest vs.[28]

E.K. draws at length upon the very same section of Lavater's treatise (quoting the translation) during his discussion of 'Great pan' and the cease of miracles in the gloss to 'Maye' (*Shorter Poems*, p. 82). Lavater's sentiments are reiterated in Samuel Harsnet's 1603 *A Declaration of Egregious Popish Impostures*: 'What a world of hel-worke, deuil-worke, and Elue worke had we walking amongst vs heere in England, what time that popish mist had befogged the eyes of our poore people.'[29] Fairy beliefs were dismissed as part of the reformers' wholesale rejection of popular festivities and the more pagan aspects of the old faith. Fairies are included within the Catholic Palinode's enthusiastic evocation of rural pastimes and the popular May festivities set out within the 'Maye' eclogue:

> Tho to the greene Wood they speeden hem all,
> To fetchen home May with their musicall:
> And home they bringen in a royall throne,
> Crowned as king: and his Queene attone

---

[27] Stuart Clark, 'Protestant Demonology: Sin, Superstition, and Society (c.1520-c.1630)', in Bengt Ankarloo and Gustav Henningsen, eds, *Early Modern European Witchcraft: Centres and Peripheries* (Oxford: Clarendon Press, 1993), p. 48. See also John T. Teall, 'Witchcraft and Calvinism in Elizabethan England: Divine Power and Human Agency', *Journal of the History of Ideas* 23 (1962), pp. 21-36; Kathleen R. Sands, 'The Doctrine of Transubstantiation and the English Protestant Dispossession of Demons', *History* 85 (2000), pp. 446-62.

[28] Lewes Lavater, *Of Ghostes and Spirits Walking by Nyght*, tr. R[obert] H[arrison] (1572), ed. J. Dover Wilson (Oxford: Oxford University Press, 1929), p. 89. Lavater evokes the analogy drawn in Protestant demonology between the cease of miracles and oracles that occurred at the coming of Christ, and the professed silencing of popish false prophecies achieved by the establishment of the Gospel through the Reformation; see Lawrence Normand and Gareth Roberts, *Witchcraft in Early Modern Scotland: James VI's Demonology and the North Berwick Witches* (Exeter: Exeter University Press, 2000), pp. 346-7.

[29] Samuel Harsnet, *A Declaration of Egregious Popish Impostures* (London, 1603), sig. S3ᵛ.

Was Lady Flora, on whom did attend
A fayre flocke of Faeries, and a fresh bend
Of louely Nymphs. (*Shorter Poems*, p. 73)

Such sports are curtly dismissed as 'lustihede and wanton meryment' by Palinode's interlocutor Piers, the shepherd representing the figure of a Protestant minister.

The most obvious example of associations between Spenser's work and the sentiments found in Protestant demonological texts is E.K.'s note to 'Frendly faeries' in the gloss to 'June':

> the opinion of Faeries and elfes is very old, and yet sticketh very religiously in the myndes of some. But to roote that rancke opinion of Elfes oute of mens hearts, the truth is, that there be no such thinges, nor yet the shadowes of the things, but onely by a sort of bald Friers and knauish shauelings so feigned; which as in all other things, so in that, soughte to nousell the comen people in ignorounce, least being once acquainted with the truth of things, they woulde in tyme smell out the vntruth of theyr packed pelfe and Massepenie religion. (*Shorter Poems*, p. 92)

The point to stress here is not simply that fairies and elves are a fiction - that 'there be no such thinges' - but that the fiction, and its subsequent reiterations in the form of 'rancke opinion', are a conscious construct, they are the work of human artifice. Something that had been made out to have a tangible, supernatural presence in the world is reduced to the level of a papist fiction. E.K. introduces the issue of ontology by stating that fairies do not exist except through the feigning of 'bald Friers and knauish shauelings'. Crucially, the fiction of fairy is presented as a functional device, used to beguile, to obfuscate, and to extort, as is suggested by fiscal references to 'packed pelfe and Massepenie religion'.[30] Tongue-in-cheek, E.K. then goes on to construct an alternative fiction through professing to assert the 'sooth' concerning the etymological derivation of 'elf' and 'goblin' from 'Guelfe' and 'Gibeline'.[31]

> But the sooth is, that when all Italy was distraicte into the Factions of the Guelfes and the Gibelins, being two famous houses in Florence, the name began through their great mischiefes and many outrages, to be so odious or rather dreadfull in the peoples eares, that if theyr children at any time were frowarde and wanton, they would say to them that the Guelfe or the Gibeline came. Which words nowe from them (as many thinge els) be come into our vsage, and for Guelfes and Gibelines, we say Elfes and Goblins. (*Shorter Poems*, p. 92)

---

[30] Similarly, in *Epithalamion* the 'Pouke' and 'hob Goblin' are among a list of 'dreadfull' entities dismissed as 'things that be not'; their existence is solely as imagined 'hidden feares' that threaten to disturb the newly-weds' sleep (lines 341-4; *Shorter Poems*, p. 446).

[31] James Royster, 'E.K.'s *Elf<Guelph, Goblin<Ghibelline*', *MLN* 43 (1928), pp. 249-52, finds no record of any prior usage of this etymological contrivance, though it was taken up by a number of later writers; see Latham, *Elizabethan Fairies*, p. 48.

Again the (entirely spurious) fiction highlights the function: to scare one's audience. The ontology of fairy shifts from centring on the belief in some form of essential being, to a linguistic level. The academic play with the words 'elf' and 'goblin' sees E.K. actively marking out himself and his readers from those possessed of 'comen' ignorance.

E.K.'s gloss goes beyond making an intuitive association between popular mythology and the superstitious cozenage of the Catholic past, as is found, for example, in the description of practices connected with the oak tree in 'Februarie'. There the oak is 'often crost with the priestes crewe,/ And often halowed with holy water dewe', though both the text and E.K. simply dismiss this as popish foolery (*Shorter Poems*, pp. 46, 50). E.K.'s 'June' gloss, however, engages far more with the rhetorical level and provides a demonstration of the function that fairies play within texts. E.K.'s linguistic play on 'elf' and 'goblin', together with the wider attention to the use of the fiction of fairy within a basic circuit of producer and receiver (the 'bald Friers and knauish shauelings' and the 'comen people'), illustrates that E.K. is very much aware of the rhetorical potential of fairy. It is this attention to the rhetorical and textual utility of fairy that connects Spenser's writings to the representations of fairy discussed in some of the most important works of sixteenth-century demonology, Scot's *Discoverie* and James VI's *Daemonologie*. Although the opinions of the two writers are often diametrically opposed - indeed James's text is written in part to address and refute the arguments of Scot's *Discoverie* - the treatment of fairy found within each text is remarkably similar on a fundamental point: that the discussion of fairy can only really take the form of a discussion about the existence of fairy within different forms of story or text. Both Scot and James provide a pertinent illustration of how fairy narratives are constructed and used, as well as a demonstration of some of the factors that make Spenser's decision to employ fairy mythology potentially problematic, or at least ambiguous.

Reginald Scot

Scot's treatment of fairy is closely related to his 'discovery' of how the actions and powers ascribed to witches are a narrative construction perpetuated largely by persecutors and fraudsters. Scot's stated purpose is not to say whether or not there are witches - they 'exist' if only because people are punished as witches - but 'whether they can doo such miraculous works as are imputed unto them'.[32] Scot draws attention to the inherent subjectivity and narrative reconstruction present in any interpretation or reading of witchcraft, i.e. the difference between reading witchcraft and reading *as* witchcraft. Witchcraft, as Scot ultimately defines it, is a 'cousening art' - a manipulation of language and definition, akin to a form of

---

[32] Scot, *Discoverie*, p. xviii.

'coney-catching' - which particularly lends itself to those who use it for exploitative purposes, be they financial or political.[33]

Through detailed textual and exegetical analysis, Scot deconstructs the rhetorical means by which the idea of witchcraft is constructed and perpetuated. Much of the *Discoverie* is structured around analysis of the language and terms used to discuss witchcraft in the Bible - the central authority cited by witchmongers for the existence of witches and demons. Following the earlier example of the Dutch physician, Johann Weyer, Scot challenges the interpretations of the actual Hebrew, Greek, and Latin words used in Scripture to describe magical practices and the reductive tendency of witchmongers and demonologists to translate all such terms as poisoner, ventriloquist, prophet, or enchanter as 'witch'.[34] The construction of etymologies for words used to describe various forms of magical practitioner was a frequent starting point in many works of Renaissance demonology.[35] E.K. may well be parodying the linguistic and philological obsessions of the demonologists when he posits his own spurious etymology of 'elf' and 'goblin' in the 'June' gloss.

The construction and ascription of the supernatural as a whole becomes a question of reading correctly, and of taking up positions in an interpretative contest. Lavater's *De Spectris, lemuribus et magnis atque insolitis fragoribus* (1570), and the Catholic response, Pierre Le Loyer's *IIII Livres des Spectres ou Apparitions et Visions d'Espirits, Anges et Demons se monstrans sensiblement aux hommes* (1586), are characteristic, for example, of the opposing theological positions taken up in the interpretative struggle over how to 'read' ghosts in the sixteenth century.[36] The latter places ghosts in a distinct genus as the spirits of the departed, the former reads ghosts simply as devils. Spenser acknowledges both theories on ghosts when Redcrosse attributes the moaning voice of Fradubio to either a 'damned Ghost from *Limbo* lake' or a 'guilefull spright wandring in empty aire' (I.ii.32). Similarly in II.xi.39, Arthur offers varying interpretations of Maleger: as 'wandring ghost, that wanted funerall,/ Or aery spirite vnder false pretence,/ Or hellish feend raysd vp through diuelish science'.

Scot's treatment of fairy is also part of an interpretative struggle. Scot incorporates fairies into the process of telling stories about the fantastic powers of witches, and translates a passage based on the tenth-century penitential known as the *Canon Episcopi*:

---

[33] Scot, *Discoverie*, p. 397.
[34] Sydney Anglo, 'Reginald Scot's *Discoverie of Witchcraft*: Scepticism and Sadduceeism', in Anglo, ed., *The Damned Art: Essays in the Literature of Witchcraft* (London: Routledge, 1977), pp. 112-13.
[35] Normand and Roberts, *Witchcraft*, pp. 337-8.
[36] Both texts appear in contemporary translations: Lavater, *Of Ghostes and Spirits Walking by Nyght* (cited above); Pierre Le Loyer, *A Treatise of Specters or straunge Sights, Visions and Apparitions appearing sensibly vnto men*, tr. Zachary Jones (London, 1605).

It may not be omitted, that certaine wicked women following sathans provocations, being seduced by the illusion of divels, beleeve and professe, that in the night times they ride abroad with *Diana*, the goddesse of *Pagans*, or else with *Herodias*, with an innumerable multitude, upon certaine beasts, and passe over manie countries and nations, in the silence of the night, and doo whatsoever those fairies or ladies command, &c... Therefore, whosoever beleeveth that any creature may be either created by them, or else changed into better or worsse or be any way transformed into any other kind or likenes of any, but of the creator himself, is assuredlie an infidell, and woorsse than a *Pagan.*[37]

Such sentiments are clearly sympathetic towards the underlying principle of Scot's text, that those who believe in the powers ascribed to witches are ultimately blasphemers. The confutation of these kind of arguments formed one of the central aims of the fifteenth-century inquisitorial treatise, the *Malleus Maleficarum.*[38] The original passage in the *Canon Episcopi*, of which this is a part, attracted a great deal of commentary and glossing in medieval discussions on heresy and folk-beliefs.[39] Again, as subsequent commentators approach and read the text, various different standpoints are taken up, providing a number of distinct interpretations of both the power of demons and the existence of witch-beliefs.[40] Scot's rehearsal of this passage from the *Canon Episcopi* and incorporation of the reference to 'fairies' into his citation here continues and develops the interpretative struggle over how to read this passage. In the immediate case fairies are incorporated into the wider body of 'fantasticall confessions of witches' that are to be dismissed as fictional or 'imaginations in dreames'.

On a number of occasions Scot uses the obvious fictionality and artificiality of narratives concerning fairies or Robin good-fellow to present a model for his own conceptions of witchcraft. Foremost, Scot insists that witchcraft should be read or interpreted on a textual level; to observe methods and reasons for construction. By, and for whom is witchcraft represented? The attention to reading and interpreting witchcraft as a textual construct - as a sign with a negotiated meaning - sheds important light on the way in which fairies are conceived. Towards the close of book seven, we find the often-quoted passage in which fairies are listed amongst a number of fearful images or 'vaine apparitions' used within other texts (those of 'our mothers' maids') to generate an effect upon the listener or reader.

But in our childhood our mothers maids have so terrified us with an oughlie divell having hornes on his head, fier in his mouth, and a taile in his breech, eies like a bason,

---

[37] Scot, *Discoverie*, p. 51.

[38] [Jacobus Sprenger and Heinrich Kramer], *Malleus Maleficarum*, tr. and intr. Montague Summers (London: Rodker, 1928), pp. 1-12.

[39] Henry Charles Lea, *Materials Toward a History of Witchcraft*, ed. A. C. Howland. 3 vols. (Philadelphia: University of Pennsylvania Press, 1939), 1: 178-80, provides a translation of the passage from the *Canon Episcopi*. Latin text is in Jacques-Paul Migne, *Patrologiae Cursus Completus: Series Latina*, 221 vols. (Paris, 1841-64), 132: 352-3.

[40] See Lea, *Materials*, 1: 180-98.

fanges like a dog, clawes like a beare, a skin like a Niger, and voice roring like a lion, whereby we start and are afraid when we heare one crie Bough: and they have so fraied us with bull beggers, spirits, witches, urchens, elves, hags, fairies, satyrs, pans, faunes, sylens, kit with the cansticke, tritons, centaurs, dwarfes, giants, imps, calcars, conjurors, nymphes, changlings, *Incubus*, Robin good-fellowe, the spoorne, the mare, the man in the oke, the hell waine, the fierdrake, the puckle, Tom thombe, hob-gobblin, Tom tumbler boneles, and such other bugs, that we are afraid of our owne shadowes.[41]

Fairies here are part of a story, a textual entity, something of the past that has to be recreated verbally. Along with a host of creatures that Scot assembles from classical mythology and popular lore and practices, fairies are presented as a rhetorical, textual device *used* to produce an effect as part of a system of producer and receiver. They are part of a textual strategy used to generate fear amongst a certain group; here, the young. Scot takes care to stress the importance of both the context of reception, and disposition of the potential recipient of stories featuring such 'bugs' as fairies and the like. Such stories are more readily embraced when told to certain audiences, such as 'sicke folke, children, women, and cowards, [who] through weaknesse of mind and bodie, are shaken with vaine dreames and continuall feare'.[42] The 'meaning' of fairy, and what is understood by the term 'fairy', thus changes depending on the recipient of a narrative.

There are a number of examples where fairy is used as a veil for fraudsters in deliberate acts of cozenage of the kind that Scot exposes. Commonly the victim pays large amounts of money for the promise of meeting with the queen of the fairies, or for receiving limitless amounts of fairy gold. The victims are summarily duped and, as is described in a 1595 pamphlet *The Brideling, Sadling and Ryding, of a Rich Churle in Hampshire, by the subtill practise of one Judeth Philips, a professed cunning woman or Fortune teller*, also ritually shamed.[43] Such frauds at the hands of those 'playing' fairy queens are evoked in the taunting of Falstaff in *The Merry Wives of Windsor*, in Jonson's *The Alchemist* where Dapper is gulled and pinched by Dol Common dressed up as the fairy queen, and in a similar episode in a play attributed to Robert Armin, *The Valiant Welshman* (1615).[44]

Fairies also appear in the derisory survey of summoning rituals used to conjure devils and spirits included by Scot to illustrate the folly and credulity of witchmongers. Drawing from a book of conjurations 'devised more latelie' Scot details how to conjure a dead spirit by first summoning the 'fairie Sibylia' as

[41] Scot, *Discoverie*, p. 122.
[42] Scot, *Discoverie*, p. 122.
[43] Reproduced in Barbara Rosen, ed., *Witchcraft* (London: Arnold, 1969), pp. 213-18. See also *The Several Notorious and Lewd Cozenages of John West and Alice West, falsely called the king and queen of fairies* (London, 1613).
[44] Jonson and Armin may have drawn upon the same court case; see C. J. Sisson, 'A Topical Reference in *The Alchemist*', in J. G. McManaway, ed., *Joseph Quincy Adams Memorial Studies* (Washington: Folger Shakespeare Library, 1948), pp. 739-41; Joseph T. McCullen, Jr., 'Conference with the Queen of Fairies: A Study of Jonson's Workmanship in *The Alchemist*', *Studia Neophilologica* 23 (1951), pp. 87-95.

intermediary.[45] Sibylia is summoned by rehearsing her name and by calling also upon the spirits of Jupiter and Venus, and the king and queen of fairies.[46] Fairies are thus brought forth through verbal formulae - they are literally constructed through words. Scot's anti-Catholicism is evident here in his dismissal of the reificatory powers of these words to 'make flesh', for fairies to exist in anything more than the ceremonies and formulae that he details.[47]

The consistent feature of Scot's representation of the fairy is that they are always constructed and used within a text or narrative, always part of a story or wider discourse. In each example cited from Scot physical properties of the fairy are never discussed. Like E.K., whilst Scot denies the existence of fairies and Robin good-fellow as essential beings he does not deny their existence within stories and narratives, and he is very much aware of the expedience of constructing such stories. He is particularly attuned to the linguistic and rhetorical operation of words like 'fairy' and 'witch' and the flexibility with which they may be applied as signifiers within a textual and interpretative system:

> heretofore Robin goodfellow, and Hob gobblin were as terrible, and also as credible to the people, as hags and witches be now: and in time to come, a witch will be as much derided and contemned, and as plainlie perceived, as the illusion and knaverie of Robin goodfellow. And in truth, they that mainteine walking spirits, with their transformations, &c: have no reason to denie Robin goodfellow, upon whom there hath gone as manie and as credible tales, as upon witches; saving that it hath not pleased the translators of the Bible, to call spirits by the name of Robin goodfellow, as they have termed divinors, soothsaiers, poisonners, and couseners by the name of witches.[48]

King James VI

Written during the 1590s and published in 1597, James VI's *Daemonologie* presents fairies in a far more sinister light than Scot's *Discoverie. Daemonologie* takes the form of a dialogue between Epistemon, the authority on witches, and Philomanthes, who raises a number of the sceptics' arguments, and the text builds on the work of continental demonologists such as Jean Bodin and Nicholas Rémy, to argue that witchcraft presents a very real threat to both the kingdom and the royal person. Fairies are discussed in book three of *Daemonologie* as part of 'all these kindes of Spirites that troubles men or women'. Epistemon lists the 'Fayrie' as one of four ways or forms through which the Devil 'conuerses' (or interacts

---

[45] Scot, *Discoverie*, p. 327.

[46] Scot, *Discoverie*, pp. 338-9, 341-2.

[47] There are several extant examples of summoning rituals for fairies in conjuration books of the kind derided here; see for example London, British Library, MS Sloane 3851, fol. 129; Oxford, Bodleian MS e Mus. 173, fol. 72ᵛ. In the examination of John Walsh at Exeter in 1566, accusations of witchcraft centred upon a 'book of circles' detailing the raising of familiar spirits and communication with the fairies; see *The Examinacioun of John Walsh*, in Rosen, ed., *Witchcraft*, pp. 68-9.

[48] Scot, *Discoverie*, p. 105.

with) and troubles the bodies of mortals.[49] For James, fairies 'exist' in so far as they are a narrative played upon the human senses by the Devil, whose existence and powers are in no doubt. Again fairy is a tool, a device created to be used. On this occasion, however, construction is by the Devil rather than any human agency. James makes clear that the kinds of stories or 'vaine trattles' popularly told about fairies are to be read reductively as the illusions of the Devil, and dismissed by all true Christians (and loyal subjects).

> That fourth kinde of spirites, which by the Gentiles was called *Diana*, and her wandring court, and amongst vs was called the *Phairie* (as I tould you) or our good neighboures, was one of the sortes of illusiones that was rifest in the time of *Papistrie*: for although it was holden odious to Prophesie by the deuill, yet whome these kinde of Spirites carried awaie, and informed, they were thought to be sonsiest and of best life. To speake of the many vaine trattles founded vpon that illusion: How there was a King and Queene of *Phairie*, of such a iolly court & train as they had, how they had a teynd, & dutie, as it were of all goods: how they naturallie rode and went, eate and drank, and did all other actiones like naturall men and women: I thinke it liker VIRGILS *Campi Elysii*, nor anie thing that ought to be beleeued by Christians, except in generall, that as I spake sundrie times before, the deuil illuded the senses of sundry simple creatures, in making them beleeue that they saw and harde such thinges as were nothing so indeed.[50]

Here again stories of fairy are portrayed as things of obvious fiction. For James, fairy exists as part of the Devil's illusionary arsenal. He explicitly states that fairy is a fiction or outward form that is fashioned by the Devil and used to deceive the senses. The passage again exemplifies the widely made claim that fairies were something of the past, and specifically part of the beliefs and 'illusiones' current in the 'unenlightened' days of Catholicism. Associations between fairies and Catholicism are made both by those arguing for the existence of witchcraft and by the sceptics.

Many writers of the period were in agreement that the Devil had a power to affect what appeared to the senses, causing spiritual entities to appear to the imagination as corporeal. The *Malleus Maleficarum* stated that the Devil works upon the human body by inducing natural disease attributable to a demonic cause, and that he has the power to draw an image gained from the senses in memory and move it through the imagination to one's faculty of reason so that we perceive it as 'real'.[51] The appearance of fairy and demons to the imagination was constructed simultaneously as a religious and medical discourse. The effect upon the imagination is ascribed to the Devil's powers to move the humours of the body, to raise the blood to the sensible faculties and thus deceive the eyes and other senses. Weyer carefully outlines the psycho-pathological means by which the Devil operates; for example, by insinuating himself into the black and melancholic

---

[49] James VI and I, *Daemonologie* (with *Newes from Scotland*), ed. G. B. Harrison (London: Bodley Head Quartos, 1924; repr. Edinburgh: Edinburgh University Press, 1966), pp. 56-7.
[50] James, *Daemonologie*, pp. 73-4.
[51] Sprenger and Kramer, *Malleus*, pp. 124-8.

vapours that rise towards the head containing the images seen in dreams, or by causing bodily effects such as spasms by effecting the source of nerves in the brain.[52]

In essence, James argues, all spirits are of one kind, but it is the Devil who provides the infinite variation in the forms through which they appear:

> although in my discourseing of them, I deuyde them in diuers kindes, yee must notwithstanding there of note my Phrase of speaking in that: For doubtleslie they are in effect, but all one kinde of spirites, who for abusing the more of mankinde, takes on these sundrie shapes, and vses diuerse formes of out-ward actiones, as if some were of nature better then other.[53]

The diversity of names used by necromancers (and frequently catalogued by demonologists) for the Devil and his 'angels' or spirits are attributed to a linguistic illusion and evasion produced by the Devil himself.[54] Fairy is just another form by which the Devil can appear. The reductive tradition of identifying classical domestic deities and pagan gods with fallen angels and demons dates back to the pneumatological writings of the early Church Fathers and Schoolmen.[55] Fairies and elves are also frequently incorporated into the lists of classical deities summarily dismissed as demons or idols in early modern discussions of witchcraft and demonology. Lavater, for example, compares the fairies and elves of Northern mythology to the likes of pans, fauns, and satyrs before ultimately reading all such superstitions reductively as delusions of the Devil.[56] Along similar lines, Stephen Orgel cites an example of a copy of the 1611 Spenser Folio in which marginal annotations to book one of *The Faerie Queene* gloss fairies reductively as devils and then consequently question the value of the poem as royal panegyric. The gloss reads (in Orgel's transcription): 'fayeries are [div]ells, & therefore [fa]yerieland must bee [the] divells land. And [w]hat a glorie is this [to] any, to [ca]ll her queene [of] such a place?'[57]

It was the identification of fairies with demons or witches' familiars that led to several witchcraft trials in which the accused are found guilty of communicating or 'repairing' with fairies and are consequently executed.[58] During the course of

---

[52] Johann Weyer, *De praestigiis daemonum* (1563); translated as *Witches, Devils, and Doctors in the Renaissance*, tr. John Shea, intr. George Mora. (Binghampton, NY: Medieval & Renaissance Texts and Studies, 1991), pp. 35-6, 188-9.

[53] James, *Daemonologie*, p. 57.

[54] James, *Daemonologie*, p. 76.

[55] Briggs, *Anatomy*, pp. 166-9.

[56] Lavater, *Of Ghostes and Spirits*, p. 93.

[57] Stephen Orgel, 'Margins of Truth', in Andrew Murphy, ed., *The Renaissance Text: Theory, Editing, Textuality* (Manchester: Manchester University Press, 2000), p. 103. I am grateful to David Lee Miller for this reference.

[58] On associations with fairy made in witch trials, see J. A. MacCulloch, 'The Mingling of Fairy and Witch Beliefs in Sixteenth and Seventeenth Century Scotland', *Folklore* 32 (1921), pp. 227-44; Margaret Murray, *The Witch-Cult in Western Europe* (Oxford:

judicial examination, stories about fairies are very often simply translated or reduced into stories of familiars, demons, or diabolic possession.[59] The tradition of demonology common in continental texts, and taken up by James, characterized witchcraft as a demonic pact and classed all traffic with spirits (ignoring distinctions) as iniquitous and criminal. In England this becomes the statutory definition in the 1604 Witchcraft Act. Fairies, James argues, are a pleasing image (taking the form of domestic service, prophecy, sexual gratification), employed by the Devil as a form of infernal rhetorical device to fool the recipient of the vision into thinking they are gaining a benefit. At one point James uses an example from fairy lore:

> And yet the Deuill for confirming in the heades of ignoraunt Christians, that errour first mainteined among the Gentiles, he whiles among the first kinde of spirits that I speak of, appeared in time of *Papistrie* and blindnesse, and haunted diuers houses, without doing any euill, but doing as it were necessarie turnes vp and down the house: and this spirit they called the *Brownie* in our language.[60]

James represents the fairy as a device used within the intercourse or 'conuersing' of Devil and mortal - a system of producer and receiver. This kind of relationship is especially significant in that delusion of the senses cannot take place, according to James, without the consent of the deluded: 'For the Deuill durst neuer haue borrowed their shaddow or similitude to that turne, if their consent had not bene at it'.[61] Fairy appears as the pleasing face of demonism, used in trial-confessions to reduce the severity of an alleged crime as 'a cullour of safetie for them [witches], that ignorant Magistrates may not punish them for it'.[62] Seeing fairies was interpreted as a dialogic process and a consensual agreement with the Devil, and thus, anticipating the sentiments of the 1604 Witchcraft Act, a sign of criminality.

In examining the representations of fairy within the texts discussed above I am not searching for an unmediated statement of contemporary fairy belief. Far more than for witchcraft studies, a study of fairy is the record of a representational and interpretative struggle, of different authorities, writers, and sources taking up varying perspectives on how they read and interpret something as being 'fairy'. Demonological treatises of learned elites and clergymen provide only one site of a negotiation over meaning in an ongoing discourse, rather than a safe location from

---

Clarendon Press, 1921; repr. 1962), pp. 238-46; Latham, *Elizabethan Fairies*, pp. 168-75; Thomas, *Religion*, pp. 217-20, 727; Purkiss, *Witch in History*, pp. 159-62; and Purkiss, *Troublesome Things: A History of Fairies and Fairy Stories* (Harmondsworth: Penguin, 2000), chapters three and four; Lizanne Henderson and Edward J. Cowan, *Scottish Fairy Belief: A History* (East Linton: Tuckwell, 2001), pp. 118-41, 217.
[59] Purkiss, *Witch in History*, p. 153; Purkiss, *Troublesome Things*, p. 88.
[60] James, *Daemonologie*, p. 65.
[61] James, *Daemonologie*, p. 79.
[62] James, *Daemonologie*, p. 75.

which to assign meaning.[63] Scot tells a number of stories about fairy from one particular perspective and as such offers one aspect of an interpretative struggle concerning how to read and understand fairy in this period. Scot's is not by any means an objective, unprejudiced work, but then neither necessarily are the accounts produced by those who claim to believe in fairies. The distinction between the representation of fairy in Scot and James is in the exact details of who produces and receives the text. For Scot fairies exist as part of the many different narratives told about the nature and powers of witches, constructed by persecutors and fraudsters. James's response is that fairies exist as a pleasing narrative constructed by the Devil, which is then recorded in subsequent texts, such as trial confessions. In both Scot and James fairies are presented as a rhetorical object located within a text or fiction and operating in a dialogic, 'I-you' relationship with the reader. In basic terms, fairies appear in both texts as narratives played out before the senses to create an effect.

Fairies are made and not born; and made within the dyad of object and subject, that is, in terms of, or in relation to, humans. As Nutt writes, narratives in which fairies are represented are always in some way 'about' the relationship of human and fairy, be it in the form of sightings, amorous encounters, abductions, bodily afflictions, or rituals of appeasement.[64] Earlier I observed Scot's insistence that we can only read or interpret witchcraft and fairy on a textual level: to examine the means by which witchcraft and fairy are represented. Likewise, the common action that unites, for example, Spenser's and Shakespeare's uses of fairy, the appearance of fairies in witchcraft trials and demonological treatises, and the presence of fairies in popular belief, is that, in each case, a narrative or fiction about the fairy is constructed; someone tells a story. Fairies are always already part of a text. Fairies need to be read not merely in terms of the *fabula* of a text, but the performative aspect or point of engagement between reader, listener, or spectator and a text must also be considered. The precise appearance and description of fairy in any given text varies according to the context and condition of the narrator, the form in which the narrative is constructed, and the purposes of construction: to explain, entertain, empower, frighten, obfuscate, trivialize, satirize.

Fairy as it is represented in the early modern period can be best understood as a sign with a negotiated referent, an artificial construction that actively invites interpretation to which varying meanings or significations can be assigned. In the chapters that follow it will be seen that Spenser calls attention to how fairy functions as a sign, and that in *The Faerie Queene* he plays upon the level of ambiguity that the image of fairy possesses. Despite the sceptical, Protestant stance taken up in E.K.'s gloss to 'June', there is obviously a clear line drawn between active belief (and perpetuation of belief) in fairies and elves, and the tacit recognition of the practical and aesthetic expedience of constructing a fiction

---

[63] Sarah Beckwith, 'The Power of Devils and the Hearts of Men: Notes Towards a Drama of Witchcraft', in Lesley Aers and Nigel Wheale, eds, *Shakespeare in the Changing Curriculum* (London: Routledge, 1991), p. 145.

[64] Nutt, 'Fairy Mythology', p. 41.

concerning fairies. Put another way, just as one did not need to believe in the powers ascribed to witches to understand the very real and serious implications of the accusation of being a witch, Spenser did not need to believe in fairies to believe in and appreciate the expedience of a fiction about fairies. I shall now turn to the literary and mythopœic sources and contexts for Spenser's use of fairy in the representation of Elizabeth.

Chapter 2

Sources and Contexts

Spenser's sources for his use of fairy in *The Faerie Queene* can be approached in several ways. Rather than attempting to identify and tabulate precise instances of direct borrowings for the major fairy episodes that form the focus of my later chapters, I intend to examine the representational and formal contexts that both provide a stimulus for Spenser's use of fairy and influence the ways in which fairy mythology is used in the poem.

The 'Letter to Raleigh' is the starting point for consideration of the sources of Spenser's use of fairy mythology. Two broad categories of source can be identified within the Letter. The first is suggested by Spenser's initial statement that he has adopted the 'historye of king Arthure' and its attendant associations with fairy mythology as the poem's allegorical surface narrative, as the 'historicall fiction' with which he 'colours' his work. The second kind of source is suggested by Spenser's decoding of his allegorized representation of Elizabeth: 'In that Faery Queene I meane glory in my generall intention, but in my particular I conceiue the most excellent and glorious person of our soueraine the Queene, and her kingdome in Faery land.' Spenser's explicit identification of Elizabeth with the figure of the fairy queen can be located within the much wider context of Elizabethan myth-making and draws upon many similar representational and mythopœic strategies used to celebrate and glorify the queen. A distinction can be ·made therefore between the contextual source of Spenser's identification of Elizabeth with the fairy queen and the sources of the subject matter, details of narrative incident, and overall story or *fabula* that are used to make that identification.

Both kinds of source function in concert within *The Faerie Queene* and there is obviously a high degree of exchange and reciprocity as a whole between these two general types of source. For example, we find echoes of the annual tournaments that were staged from around 1570 onwards to commemorate the accession of Elizabeth in episodes such as the combat between Redcrosse and Sansjoy held at the House of Pride (I.v.1-16), and in the tournaments set out in IV.iii., IV.iv., and V.iii. of *The Faerie Queene*.[1] Similar martial festivities are celebrated in the

---

[1] On the Accession Day tilts (held on 17 November) see Sir William Segar, *Honor Military and Civil* (1602), Facsimile edn. (Delmar, NY: Scholars' Facsimiles and Reprints, 1975), pp. 197-200; Frances Yates, *Astraea: The Imperial Theme in the Sixteenth Century* (London: Routledge, 1975), pp. 88-106; Roy Strong, *The Cult of Elizabeth: Elizabethan Portraiture and Pageantry* (London: Thames and Hudson, 1977), pp. 129-62; Wilson,

description of the Iberian jousts found in book two of Sir Philip Sidney's *New Arcadia*.[2] Conversely, tournaments had long been designed and structured around themes and commonplaces taken from chivalric romances, and early Tudor entertainments increasingly imitated the Burgundian fashion for elaborate disguisings, allegorical settings, and dramatic speeches, turning the tournament itself into a work of art.[3] Jean Wilson provides an example of a possible influence in turn of *The Faerie Queene* on the Accession Day tilts of 1595, where Sir James Skydmore puns on his own name in his device 'Le Scu d'Amour' and alludes to Spenser's character Scudamour.[4] The reappearance of the fairy queen in the entertainments held at Elvetham and Ditchley in the early 1590s suggests a renewed play upon fairy mythology stimulated by the publication of *The Faerie Queene*.

The 'historye of king Arthure' and the Romance Intertext

The first kind of source for Spenser's use of fairy mythology includes all of the principally romance materials that could provide the subject matter, details of narrative incident, and overall story or *fabula* pertaining to fairy in *The Faerie Queene*. In the 'Letter to Raleigh', Spenser wrote of his choosing 'the historye of king Arthure' to provide the narrative 'colour' or texture for his work which would certainly have carried with it a strong element of fairy mythology, particularly concerning the relationship of Arthur and the figure of the fairy queen.[5] Connections between Arthur and the healing powers of fairy are found from the twelfth century onwards in references to Arthur's departure to Avalon, and these are developed and retained, if only residually, in subsequent reiterations of Arthurian mythology in both chronicle and romance.[6] The relationship of Arthur and fairy powers are well established by the time of Layamon's *Brut* (early thirteenth century), seen in the elvish gifts of prowess, longevity, and wealth; in the provision of his magic weapons and armour; and in Arthur's voyage to Avalon and

---

[^Entertainments]: *Entertainments*, pp. 26-38; Richard McCoy, *The Rites of Knighthood: The Literature and Politics of Elizabethan Chivalry* (Berkeley: University of California Press, 1989), pp. 21-4.

[2] Sir Philip Sidney, *The Countess of Pembroke's Arcadia*, ed. Maurice Evans (Harmondsworth: Penguin, 1977), pp. 352-7.

[3] Gordon Kipling, *The Triumph of Honour: Burgundian Origins of the Elizabethan Renaissance* (The Hague: Leiden University Press, 1977), p. 75; Sydney Anglo, *Spectacle, Pageantry and Early Tudor Policy*, 2nd edn. (Oxford: Clarendon Press, 1997), pp. 98-9.

[4] Wilson, *Entertainments*, p. 35; see also Ivan Schulze, 'Reflections of Elizabethan Tournaments in *The Faerie Queene*, 4.4 and 5.3', *ELH* 5 (1938), pp. 278-84; Strong, *Cult of Elizabeth*, pp. 156-8.

[5] Rathborne, *Meaning*, pp. 157-8.

[6] Lucy Allen Paton, *Studies in the Fairy Mythology of Arthurian Romance*, 2nd edn. enlarged by a Survey of Scholarship on the Fairy Mythology since 1903 and a Bibliography by R. S. Loomis (New York: Franklin, 1960), pp. 7-8.

healing at the hands of 'Argante þere quene; aluen swiðe sceone'.[7] The association of Arthur's court with fairy is also suggested in Chaucer's 'Wife of Bath's Tale' and 'Squire's Tale' (III 8557-81; V 94-6).[8] There remains an unmistakable presence of fairy in the *Morte D'Arthur* in the form of Morgan le Fay, the Lady of the Lake, and Nineve, providing an important part of the imaginative terrain taken up by Spenser.[9] The Lady of the Lake features in the Arthurian pageant mythology employed at the Kenilworth entertainment staged for Elizabeth in 1575, and E.K. makes a similar collocation between Arthur and fairy lore in the 'Aprill' eclogue, in his gloss upon 'Ladyes of the lake' (quoted above).

Study of Spenser's use of medieval romance and Arthurian mythology has advanced to the point that it is no longer accurate to suggest, as did C. R. Baskervill, that the selection of the fairy queen figure to symbolize Elizabethan glory is totally 'anomalous'.[10] The often-quoted humanist pronouncements of Roger Ascham abjuring the 'open mans slaughter, and bold bawdrye' of the *Morte D'Arthur* or Harvey's reference to *The Faerie Queene* as '*Hobgoblin* runne away with the Garland from *Apollo*', are now qualified by a greater contextualization of Spenser's use of the romance form from which he could draw his conception of fairy.[11] But the exact nature of the connection between Arthur and fairy mythology, particularly by the time work begins on *The Faerie Queene*, is by no means as obvious or straightforward as has been previously made out. Reception of the marvels associated with Arthur, right the way through until the sixteenth century, continually alternates between the more sceptical attacks on the veracity of the Arthurian mythology, and the defences of those for whom Arthur represented a potent and enduring symbol of national greatness. There was of course a distinction between the identification of Arthur as an historical figure who appeared in

---

[7] *Layamon's Brut*, ed. G. L. Brook and R. F. Leslie. EETS OS 250, 277. 2 vols. (Oxford: Oxford University Press, 1963-78), 2: 750. Similar associations at this time are made by Gervase of Tilbury and Giraldus Cambrensis, and in the Latin *Gesta Regum Britanniae*, c.1234 (Paton, *Fairy Mythology*, pp. 35, 47).

[8] All references from Chaucer cited in text are from *The Riverside Chaucer*, gen. ed. Larry D. Benson (Oxford: Oxford University Press, 1988).

[9] Muriel Whitaker, *Arthur's Kingdom of Adventure: The World of Malory's Morte D'Arthur* (Woodbridge: Brewer, 1984), pp. 57-9.

[10] C. R. Baskervill, 'The Genesis of Spenser's Queen of Faerie', *MP* 18 (1920-21), p. 49. See Charles Bowie Millican, *Spenser and the Table Round: A Study in the Comparaneous Background for Spenser's Use of the Arthurian Legend* (Cambridge, MA: Harvard University Press, 1932); Arthur B. Ferguson, *The Indian Summer of English Chivalry: Studies in the Decline and Transformation of Chivalric Idealism* (Durham, NC: Duke University Press, 1968); Ferguson, *The Chivalric Tradition in Renaissance England* (Washington: Folger Shakespeare Library, 1986); Paul R. Rovang, *Refashioning 'Knights and Ladies Gentle Deeds': The Intertextuality of Spenser's Faerie Queene and Malory's Morte Darthur* (Cranbury, NJ: Associated University Presses, 1996), pp. 50-74; Andrew King, *The Faerie Queene and Middle English Romance: The Matter of Just Memory* (Oxford: Clarendon Press, 2000).

[11] Roger Ascham, *The Scholemaster* (1570) in *English Works*, ed. William Aldis Wright (Cambridge: Cambridge University Press, 1904), p. 231.

chronicles and the more fabulous adventures of Arthur and his knights that included links with fairy. Belief in the political expedience of the myths and pseudo-history associated with Arthur, however, could not be denied. Arthur's status as a 'cultural icon' extant within a body of popular thought that is never entirely book-based problematizes simple source identification, and no single text ever embodies the entire range of meanings and associations that the figure of Arthur carries.[12]

Equally, there is no single particular text to which we might point and categorically assert that it is Spenser's sole model for his conception of fairy. I have explicitly avoided undertaking a specific source study of Spenser's fairies or proposing that *The Faerie Queene* is a tissue of individual direct borrowings.[13] In the overall construction of his text Spenser drew his conception of fairy from a capacious intertext of associations and images, both positive and negative. The intertextual reservoir of sources from which Spenser could have drawn, might include the fairy *lais* of *Sir Launfal* and *Sir Orfeo*, the Melusine romances, the Ogier romances, the ballad tradition concerning Thomas Rymer, *Partonope of Blois*, *Generydes*, *Arthur of Little Britain*, as well as the fairy tradition found in the French *romans d'aventure*. To this list we must add the Italian romance epics of Boiardo, Ariosto, and Tasso, and note in particular the influence of the enchantress figures of Alcina and Armida upon Spenser's fairy queens. But such a list cannot reproduce Spenser's exact conception or fairy, and ultimately cannot fully describe or account for the extent to which he had access to works in manuscript.[14] Nor can it register the extent of Spenser's knowledge of popular fairy lore. Just as nowadays if we were asked to consider from exactly where our own, individual conception of a mythological figure such as Arthur is derived, the chances are that we could identify some formative key texts, but would be hard-pressed to reconstruct the exact series of sources in favour of much more of a composite, intertextual picture; a picture assembled in a piecemeal, often unconscious manner.

Equally speculative are attempts to gauge the level to which Spenser's fairy was influenced by Irish sources, in part due both to the uncertainty regarding the extent of Spenser's knowledge of Gaelic and to the ambiguity of his attitude to the relative cultural status of the language and its literature.[15] In lamenting that Spenser

---

[12] David A. Summers, *Spenser's Arthur: The British Arthurian Tradition and The Faerie Queene* (New York: University Press of America, 1997), pp. 9, 25.

[13] Spenser's evident debt to Chaucer's 'Sir Thopas' for specific details of Arthur's dream of Gloriana will be discussed separately in chapter five.

[14] On Spenser's access to and use of manuscript materials see Carrie A. Harper, *The Sources of The British Chronicle History in Spenser's Faerie Queene* (Philadelphia: Winston, 1910), pp. 24-6 and 24n1; Rosamond Tuve, 'Spenser and Some Pictorial Conventions', in Tuve, *Essays by Rosemond Tuve: Spenser, Herbert, Milton*, ed. Thomas P. Roche, Jr. (Princeton: Princeton University Press, 1970), pp. 112-38; King, *The Faerie Queene and Middle English Romance*, pp. 38-9.

[15] See Clare Carroll, 'Spenser and the Irish Language: The Sons of Milesio in *A View of the Present State of Ireland, The Faerie Queene*, Book V, and the *Leabhar Gabhála*', *IUR* 26 (1996), pp. 281-90; Richard McCabe, *Spenser's Monstrous Regiment: Elizabethan Ireland and the Poetics of Difference* (Oxford: Oxford University Press, 2002), pp. 177-96.

'wrote as an official, and out of thoughts and emotions that had been organized by the State', W. B. Yeats discounts any form of access on Spenser's part to the 'imaginations' of native lore that are more wonderful even than the islands of Phaedria and Acrasia. Had Spenser gone to Ireland 'as a poet merely', writes Yeats,

> he would have found among wandering story-tellers, not indeed his own power of rich sustained description, for that belongs to lettered ease, but certainly all the kingdom of Faery, still unfaded, of which his own poetry was often but a troubled image.[16]

Spenser does not refer to fairy mythology in *A View of the Present State of Ireland*, but his interests in the antiquities, customs, and topography of Ireland, evident within the *View* and by the further 'observations' promised at its close, suggest that he was certainly well-placed, and sufficiently engaged with the indigenous culture in Ireland, to have come into contact with the Gaelic tradition of fairy, even if only indirectly. McCabe cites an example of the employment of fairy mythology by one of Spenser's Gaelic contemporaries, the bard Tadhg Dall Ó hUiginn, to celebrate the castle of Enniskillen in Ulster.[17] In particular, the fairy mistress motif adopted by Spenser in Gloriana's 'entertainment' of Arthur, invites comparison with the Irish *sidhe* and the fairy queen Danu.[18] As Yeats suggests, Phaedria and Acrasia possess many of the characteristics of the amorous, potentially more malignant enchantress figures of Gaelic fairy, and are analogous to some degree with the Lady of the Lake. Greenlaw identifies a number of features in *The Faerie Queene* where Spenser does not actively come out and distinguish characters as fairies but which bear an analogous relationship to similar figures or motifs in Gaelic fairy tradition, most notably, the comparison of Mammon's guarding of his treasure to a leprechaun guarding a fairy hill, and Guyon's visit to Mammon's cave, to the traditional motif of a hero's journey to the underworld.[19] Mammon's temptation of Guyon to eat the apples in the garden of Proserpina (II.vii.54-6) may be compared to similar episodes in Gaelic tradition where a hero is entrapped by the fairy through eating fruit from the underworld, and to the traditional taboo against eating fairy food. Spenser could of course have also encountered associations between fairy and Proserpina in Chaucer's 'Merchant's Tale'. Comparisons to the body of Gaelic fairy tradition made by Greenlaw and others are, in the absence of direct source attribution, largely based on the identification of analogues or motifs, and

---

[16] Quoted in Paul J. Alpers, ed., *Edmund Spenser: A Critical Anthology* (Harmondsworth: Penguin, 1969), p. 175.
[17] Richard A. McCabe, 'Edmund Spenser, Poet of Exile', *PBA* 80 (1991), p. 77. McCabe, *Spenser's Monstrous Regiment*, p. 42, draws attention to the frequency with which the bardic poetry of Spenser's Gaelic contemporaries employed fairy mythology in works of panegyric.
[18] Greenlaw, 'Spenser's Fairy Mythology', pp. 115-16.
[19] Greenlaw, 'Spenser's Fairy Mythology', pp. 110-12.

are ultimately only illustrative of the potential breadth of possible influences upon Spenser.[20]

Fairy and Sovereignty

The link between fairy and the 'historye of king Arthure' that is of most importance within *The Faerie Queene* centres upon one particular concept or motif: how fairy mythology is employed as a means of elevating, celebrating, and distinguishing an individual. This is a recurrent motif within the tradition of fairy romances and is a vital part of the discernible associations made therein between fairy and the concept of sovereignty. Following the taxonomy of Laurence Harf-Lancner, it is possible to divide medieval stories concerning the relationship between fairies and mortals into two main categories: those that deal with the visitation of a figure from fairyland to the mortal hero within the human ('real') world; and those that see the mortal hero in some way visiting, encroaching upon, or being transported to the fairy world.[21] In both kinds of story the bestowal of fairy aid and/ or affection was a common means of glorifying the romance hero and highlighting his exceptional qualities; Cuchulinn, Oisin, Merlin, and Ogier had all been enraptured by a fairy mistress.[22] Nutt writes of how the existence of the Tuatha de Danann was always secondary to the mortal heroes in the ancient Irish sagas; mortals would play the central role in the narrative with fairies as auxiliaries. The use of fairy foregrounds the virtue and prowess of the mortal hero, and often a wooing or union with a fairy lover would highlight this virtuous quality: 'The love of the fairy maiden who comes from her wonderland of eternal joys lured by his fame is the most striking token and the highest guerdon of [the hero's] prowess.'[23]

On a more material level, fairy, and in particular the relationship between mortal and fairy, is also deployed within medieval romance to represent fantasies of social, economic, and political empowerment. The most commonly cited examples of this particular application of fairy mythology are the romances associated with Melusine. Stories concerning men who marry shape-shifting women, the taboos concerning their necessary occlusion, and the implications once such a condition is broken, are found in many twelfth- and thirteenth-century courtly miscellanies.[24]

---

[20] Pauline Henley, *Spenser in Ireland* (Cork: Cork University Press, 1928), pp. 113, 127; M. Pauline Parker, *The Allegory of The Faerie Queene* (Oxford: Oxford University Press, 1960), pp. 279-82; Rosamond Tuve, 'The Red Crosse Knight and Medieval Demon Stories', in Tuve, *Essays*, p. 47, suggest further comparisons with Celtic mythology to which Spenser could have been exposed in Ireland.

[21] Harf-Lancner, *Les Fées*, p. 77. Harf-Lancner's distinction, it should be noted, is based upon stories specifically concerning the appearance of fairy mistresses.

[22] Paton, *Fairy Mythology*, p. 29.

[23] Nutt, 'Fairy Mythology', p. 41. See also Tom Peete Cross, 'The Celtic Element in the Lays of *Lanval* and *Graelent*', *MP* 12 (1914-15), pp. 585-644; J. A. MacCulloch, *Medieval Faith and Fable* (London: Harrap, 1932), pp. 45-57.

[24] Harf-Lancner, *Les Fées*, pp. 119-54.

Far more extensive are the two French versions of the late fourteenth- and early-fifteenth centuries that explicitly associate Melusine with the Lusignan family of Poitou. One version is in prose and was composed by Jean d'Arras between 1387 and 1395, the other is in verse and was written in the first decade of the fifteenth century by the Paris bookseller Coudrette; both were translated into English by the early sixteenth century.[25] Jean makes the connection between the Melusine stories and fairy mythology clear from the outset, and establishes the subsequent narrative within the context of popular fairy lore:

> We haue thenne herd say and telle of our auncyents that in many partes of Poytow haue ben shewed vnto many oon right famylerly many manyeres of thinges/ the whiche somme called Gobelyns/ the other ffayrees, and the other 'bonnes dames' or good ladyes/ and they goo by nyght tyme and entre within the houses without opnyng or brekyng of ony doore/ and take & bere somtyme with them the children out of theire cradelles and somtyme they tourne them out of theyre wit/ and somtyme they brenne & roste them before þe fyre/ and whan they departe fro them, they leue hem as hoole as they were byfore/ and somme gyue grette happe & ffortune in this world.[26]

This is followed by reference to 'somme other fauntasyes' that appear at night 'in lyknes of wymen with old face', but also to how 'the sayd fayrees toke somtyme the fourme & the fygure of fayre & yonge wymen/ of whiche many men haue hadd som doughtirs, and haue take to theire wyues by meanes of som couenauntes or promysses'. If these covenants are broken, the fairy wives are said to be 'conuerted & tourned into serpentes'.[27] Both versions tell of how Melusine undertakes to help Raimondin of Poitou and promises that she will make him a powerful lord if he marries her. They marry and Raimondin has to swear that he is not to see her on a Saturday, when, unbeknownst to him, she is transformed into a serpent from the waist down. Melusine is then shown to facilitate the acquisition and clearance of land and the building of fortified cities and castles, including the castle of Lusignan. Melusine provides Raimondin with the trappings of aristocratic power as well as with a solid foundation for the Lusignan dynasty by bearing a large number of sons; she is the means by which Raimondin acquires land and riches. The fairy Melusine plays an integral role in defining and 'making' the hero (in material terms) through enhancing the status of this figure from the minor aristocracy; she is 'the symbolic and magical incarnation of [Raimondin's] social ambition'.[28] The love of a fairy mistress can be read in relation to the wish-fulfillment and political

---

[25] See *Melusine: Roman du XIVe Siècle par Jean D'Arras*, ed. Louis Stouff (Dijon: Bernigaud et Privat, 1932), and *Le Roman de Mélusine ou Histoire de Lusignan par Coudrette*, ed. Eleanor Roach (Paris: Klincksieck, 1982); translated respectively as *Melusine*, ed. A. K. Donald. EETS ES 68 (London, 1895), and *The Romans of Partenay, or of Lusignen*, ed. W. W. Skeat. EETS OS 22 (London, 1866).

[26] *Melusine*, ed. Donald, p. 4. See also *Melusine*, ed. Stouff, p. 3.

[27] *Melusine*, ed. Donald, pp. 4-5.

[28] Jacques Le Goff, 'Melusina: Mother and Pioneer', in *Time, Work and Culture in the Middle Ages*, tr. Arthur Goldhammer (Chicago: University of Chicago Press, 1980), p. 220.

fantasies of a specific social class, it plays a tangible role in the formation of an individual hero's identity and status within a text. The fairy Dame Tryamour offers the hero of the late fourteenth-century version of *Sir Launfal* a similar means of fabulous empowerment.[29]

If Melusine, according to Jacques Le Goff, is 'the fairy of medieval economic growth', then Oberon in the *Huon of Burdeux* romance cycle might best be considered to be the fairy of political and military empowerment, perhaps even the fairy of sovereign power itself. Spenser twice refers to Oberon within *The Faerie Queene* (II.i.6; II.x.75) and could have known *Huon* through the French prose edition of 1454 or, as is more likely, through the 1534 English translation by Lord Berners and its subsequent reprintings. Several early articles identified and tabulated the more detailed influences of *Huon* upon Spenser, but of greatest significance for the relevance of *Huon* to fairy in *The Faerie Queene* is the way in which the romance text establishes an association between fairy and the idealization of sovereignty, an association taken up in the Elizabethan entertainments and subsequently in *The Faerie Queene*.[30]

The original *Huon of Burdeux* (before continuations) has the hero aided by the fairy king, Oberon, in a punitive quest set by Charlemagne. During the course of Huon's adventures Oberon intervenes on a number of occasions, and in the continuations incorporated into the prose redaction, finally cedes his powers and title to Huon. Fairy plays a vital part in Huon's rise and empowerment. When Huon leaves the European 'known world' we can identify an analogue of the medieval romance motif involving the hero's movement away from the secure, civilized world of court or castle and their riding forth into the unknown, a place of challenge and testing, enchantment and strangeness. The Orient in *Huon* is presented as a place in which the hero can find adventure, and gain wealth and aid in order to consolidate his position on returning to Europe. It is here that fairyland is located. Comparably, the whereabouts of Spenser's fairyland in relation to the identifiable geography of the real world is by no means as explicitly set out. The tale of the outsider at court who finds succour and support through some form of otherworldly aid, has a precedent in works such as Chrétien de Troyes's *Yvain* or in the various different versions of *Sir Launfal*, and it is Oberon who provides the key to Huon's success.[31] Of most significance is Huon's assumption of power over fairyland at Oberon's death. King Arthur is also present and claims the title, though

---

[29] Thomas Chestre, *Sir Launfal*, ed. A. J. Bliss (London: Nelson, 1960), p. 62. See also Carolyne Larrington, 'The Fairy Mistress in Medieval Literary Fantasy', in Ceri Sullivan and Barbara White, eds, *Writing and Fantasy* (London: Longman, 1999), pp. 36-41.

[30] Jefferson Fletcher, '*Huon of Burdeux* and the *Faerie Queene*', *JEGP* 2 (1898-99), pp. 209-11; J. R. MacArthur, 'The Influence of *Huon of Burdeux* upon *The Faerie Queene*', *JEGP* 4 (1902), pp. 215-38.

[31] See Lee C. Ramsey, *Chivalric Romances: Popular Literature in Medieval England* (Bloomington: Indiana University Press, 1983), pp. 142-7.

Oberon is insistent that his 'dignyte and realme' go to Huon.[32] Possession of territory is a principal measure of an individual's power within the *chanson de geste* tradition as a whole, but with the crown of fairyland comes the extraordinary ability to call readily upon fairy powers, as for example when Huon appears with his fairy armies to enforce the marriage of his daughter to the son of the king of Aragon.[33] Fairy in *Huon* provides the means of empowerment that establishes Huon in a position of royal power and authority that finally surpasses that of Charlemagne.

In Spenser's fairyland there is neither the same sense of royal presence nor the direct appearance of order and control that we find in Oberon's realm, but *Huon* does provide a model for Spenser of how fairy can be used as a celebration of monarchic powers subordinate to a Christian God. Within the text, the link between Oberon's fairy powers and his royal command is inseparable: Oberon is not simply a fairy, he is a fairy king. Fairyland is presented as a fabulous rival kingdom, a hyperbolic representation of a royal, territorial power-base. Oberon himself provides a wondrous exemplar of Christian kingship. In *Huon*, magic is repeatedly located within the bounds of a divinely sanctioned order. Oberon is keen to point out that whilst he is possessed of an ability to manipulate time and space, to see into the future, and to 'will' himself to wherever he cares to go, he is no devil: 'I was neuer deuyll nor yll creature/ I am a man as other be/ but I coniure the by the deuyne puisance to speke to me'.[34] Melusine makes similar claims for her powers.[35]

Oberon can be read as the embodiment of an ideal sovereign and his fairy powers offer a vivid idealized representation and celebration of the powers of kingship: he rules over an ordered, fabulously wealthy kingdom; he has the ability to create castles by command; and he can conjure vast armies out of thin air. *Huon* is a wish-fulfillment of supreme sovereign power operative outside the bounds of economic and practical strictures. One can see how this would have appealed to a monarch such as Henry VIII, in whose reign Berners's translation first appears. If Berners had been so bold as to intend any form of identification between Henry and Oberon (or Oberon's power), it was a connection that would be made again in *The Faerie Queene* in the allegorical presentation of the Tudor dynasty that concludes '*Antiquitee* of *Faery* lond' (II.x.75-6). Interestingly however, fairy empowerment in *Huon* is also shown to have an inherently subversive aspect to it, offering as it does an alternative, somewhat radical means by which an individual is able to assume the status of a king. Fairy powers and the figure of the fairy king hold a certain ambiguity depending on whether one reads him as a celebratory identification of what the king *is*; or as a potential rival or idealized 'other' in the form of a representation of what the king *ought* to be. Both readings are by no means exclusive, and can equally be applied to Elizabeth's reading of the fairy queen seen

---

[32] *The Boke of Huon of Burdeux, done into English by Lord Berners*, ed. S. L. Lee. EETS ES 40, 41, 43, 50. 4 vols in 1. (London, 1882-87), p. 599.

[33] *Huon*, pp. 676-8.

[34] *Huon*, p. 69.

[35] *Melusine*, ed. Donald, p. 31; *The Romans of Partenay*, pp. 22-3.

at Woodstock and, later, within Spenser's poem. What is important to emphasize here is that we can identify a tradition within Spenser's potential romance sources of using fairy as a means of representing and celebrating concepts of sovereignty and political power. This tradition was subsequently drawn upon and developed within the political drama of the Elizabethan entertainments as the link between fairy power and royal power was taken up by Sir Henry Lee, and is suggested in the Woodstock and Ditchley entertainments.

Fashioning Elizabeth

In the 'Aprill' eclogue of *The Shepheardes Calender* Spenser had already offered an inaugural taste of the mythographic richness to come as he celebrated Elizabeth as 'fayre *Elisa*, Queene of shepheardes all'. Within the 'Letter to Raleigh' Spenser explicitly identifies Elizabeth with the fairy queen: 'In that Faery Queene I meane glory in my generall intention, but in my particular I conceiue the most excellent and glorious person of our soueraine the Queene, and her kingdome in Faery land.' This is the first of a number of such identifications made within *The Faerie Queene* and is significant in that it immediately places Spenser's poem within the context of the widespread mythologization of Elizabeth found in numerous and wide-ranging forms - pageants and progresses, panegyrics and portraiture, tournaments and entertainments - and in particular, the incorporation of fairy mythology into the personal mythology constructed around the queen herself.

The construction and manipulation of political iconography and idealized representations of sovereign power were a key part of Elizabeth's strategy for asserting the legitimacy and integrity of her own identity as queen. Elizabeth's sex required a form of negotiation achieved through the construction of a series of mythological identities and artificial bodies. With the accession of a female monarch, the disparity between the queen's body natural and the body politic, the physiological fiction used to describe the office and rights of kingship, was inexorably stressed. As Susan Frye has shown, the disparity between the female body natural and the masculinist legal fiction of the body politic affords Elizabeth a flexibility to shift between the gender roles of women, men, or an androgynous play between the two, and in doing so provides her with a very powerful representational position. What actually takes place is that Elizabeth is able to move the issue of her gender directly into the political sphere and speak of a female body politic through her frequent equation of prince and queen, effectively giving herself two bodies politic.[36] The effect is that the queen's body natural becomes an inherently artificial construction, subsumed within the image or sign of the queen's political body or body politic. As in the speech reportedly given at Tilbury docks in 1588 where Elizabeth claimed 'I know I have the body but of a weak and feeble woman, but I have the heart and stomach of a king, and of a king of England too',

---

[36] Susan Frye, *Elizabeth I: The Competition for Representation* (New York: Oxford University Press, 1993), p. 13.

or in the so-called 'Golden speech' of 1601 in which she refers to herself as 'King', Elizabeth constructs her identity - the public means by which she is represented and with which others interact - as a kind of artificial character or fiction, an androgyne pieced together as a functional and symbolic embodiment of the body politic itself.[37]

There is already a rich literature that explores and examines the forms and techniques through which the mythologization and idealization of Elizabeth takes place.[38] Increasingly, attention has focused upon the many different representational practices and strategies used in the construction, embellishment, and perpetuation of the body politic as it is figured in Elizabeth, and examined the various characters or fictions through which she appeared. These include the transcendental beauty-figure of Petrarchan or neoplatonic discourses; the goddess Astraea; the Virgin Mary, or vestal virgin; and the chaste Diana or Cynthia figure. To study Elizabeth is to study a construct or text: an entity woven together from records of public speeches, from the 'shadows' or 'mirrors' used to represent her in celebratory poems and pageantry, from historical accounts shaped along the teleological trajectory of Elizabeth as Protestant deliverer, and from the symbolic and seemingly ageless images of the queen found in royal portraiture.

Greenblatt confidently claims that Elizabethan fictions of power could never be turned against the queen and that it would be 'enormously difficult' to demystify royal power.[39] However, Frye's revisionist study of representations of Elizabeth begins to challenge the idea that the images used for the perpetuation of a cult of Elizabeth are the product of an homogenous myth-making enterprise and are in any way as fixed and unproblematic as the works of Yates and Strong might suggest, or that the queen's image was necessarily always controlled by the queen and serving her interests. Rather than assuming that Elizabeth and her government were the sole producers of a monolithic and unified public iconography for the queen, Frye argues that the images constructed to represent Elizabeth are seen as sites of potential conflict between different factions and individuals, including the queen herself.[40] The extent to which Elizabeth's power was propagated and exercised through various different forms of her image opened up possibilities for the

---

[37] Elizabeth I, *Collected Works*, ed. Leah S. Marcus, Janel Mueller, and Mary Beth Rose (Chicago: University of Chicago Press, 2000), pp. 326, 346-54.
[38] John Nichols, ed., *The Progresses and Public Processions of Queen Elizabeth*, 3 vols. (London, 1823); E. C. Wilson, *England's Eliza* (Cambridge, MA: Harvard University Press, 1939); David Bergeron, *English Civic Pageantry 1558-1642* (London: Arnold, 1971); Yates, *Astraea*, pp. 29-87; Strong, *Cult of Elizabeth*; Robin Headlam Wells, *Spenser's Faerie Queene and the Cult of Elizabeth* (London: Croom Helm, 1983); Strong, *Gloriana: The Portraits of Queen Elizabeth I* (London: Thames and Hudson, 1987); Philippa Berry, *Of Chastity and Power: Elizabethan Literature and the Unmarried Queen* (London: Routledge, 1989); John King, 'Queen Elizabeth I: Representations of the Virgin Queen', *RenQ* 43 (1990), pp. 30-74; Helen Hackett, *Virgin Mother, Maiden Queen: Elizabeth I and the Cult of the Virgin Mary* (London: Macmillan, 1995).
[39] Greenblatt, *Renaissance Self-Fashioning*, p. 166.
[40] Frye, *Elizabeth*, p. 8.

manipulation of the terms and signification of those images. As Frye states, 'to believe that the queen was in complete control of her representations even at court is to fail to recognize the ongoing struggle for control of the queen's image so central to its production'.[41] The basis of Frye's analysis centres upon the difficulties in controlling how the visual and verbal images of the queen are read, how through the construction of the queen's image as an allegorical abstraction or a sign, the figure of Elizabeth becomes an object for interpretation. The images used in Elizabethan myth-making, including the fairy queen, provide the terms of representation, but with a set of potentially very different significations. There is thus 'a competition for representation' of the figure of Elizabeth:

> By investing familiar icons with political ideas supporting Elizabeth, the Crown maintained that allegory was its own. But the meanings encoded in allegory were continually altered in the competition for their authority - that is, for control of those meanings.[42]

The image of the queen becomes a sign with a negotiated signification or referent.

Frye focuses upon particular 'representational crises' that use the image of the virgin queen, but it is certainly possible to recognize the potential doubleness of many of the images and iconographical figures used to celebrate or represent the queen, and to identify a number of other sites of contested signification or 'competition for representation'. There are also examples of where figures used in panegyrics for Elizabeth can be reappropriated and, in particular, how Elizabeth's place in mythographic schemes can be reassigned for subversive ends. The apochryphal Old Testament figure Judith appears in a number of pageants celebrating the queen, as part of the imagery setting out models and exemplars of the kind of attributes and virtues for the queen to emulate. The Judith figure appears in many early panegyrics for Elizabeth as an example of God's use of weak instruments as part of the establishment of a new Protestant iconography for the female ruler, and as an idealized image of the power of female militancy combined with chastity for the overthrow of tyranny.[43] In August of 1578, for example, as part of the royal progress through Suffolk and Norfolk, the queen visited Norwich and was entertained by a pageant devised and scripted principally by Thomas Churchyard.[44] During the entry celebrations for the queen's arrival on 16 August, Elizabeth encounters a pageant bearing figures representing Deborah, Judith, Esther, Martia ('sometime Queene of England'), and the city of Norwich itself. Judith heroically addresses the queen:

---

[41] Frye, *Elizabeth*, p. 10.

[42] Frye, *Elizabeth*, p. 17.

[43] Yates, *Astraea*, p. 37; Berry, *Of Chastity*, p. 87.

[44] Nichols, *Progresses*, 2: 134-213, reprints records of the queen's reception at Norwich. See also Zillah Dovey, *An Elizabethan Progress: The Queen's Journey Through into East Anglia* (Stroud: Sutton, 1996).

Oh floure of grace, oh prime of Gods elect,
Oh mighty Queene and finger of the Lord,
Did God sometime by me poore wight correct,
The Champion stoute, that him and his abhord:
Then be thou sure thou art his mighty hand,
To conquere those which him and thee withstand.

The rage of foes Bethulia did besiege,
The people faint were ready for to yeeld:
God ayded me poore widow nerethelesse,
To enter into Holofernus field,
And with this sword, by his directing hand,
To slay his foe, and quiet so the land.

If this his grace were given to me poore wight,
If Widowes hand could vanquish such a Foe:
Then to a Prince of thy surpassing might,
What Tirant lives but thou mayest overthrow?
Persever then his servant as thou art,
And hold for aye a noble victors part. [45]

But it was also possible to reassign Elizabeth's place within the story of Judith. In 1584 the printer William Carter was tried and executed for printing Gregory Martin's treatise *De Schismate* or *A Treatise of Schism*, a work, written in 1578, in which Martin discussed the issue of Catholic responses to church attendance and the 'heresy' of the English church.[46] Martin praises the example of Judith's outward conformity to the tyrant Holofernes: 'Judith foloweth, whose godlye and constant wisedome if our Catholike gentlewomen would folowe, they might destroye Holofernes, the master heretike, and amase al his retinew, and never defile their religion by communicating with them in anye smal poynt.'[47] According to the defence of Carter made in William Allen's 1584 *A True, Sincere and Modest Defence of English Catholiques*, Judith's murder of Holofernes is deliberately read by the authorities as an incitement for women at court to murder the queen. Elizabeth can be assigned the role of Holofernes just as easily as she can be associated with the widow Judith. The case of Carter illustrates the potential doubleness, and propensity for reappropriation, of representational schemes used in celebration of Elizabeth.[48] Through the abstraction or 'textualization' of the queen's body, the image of the queen becomes a site for both glorification and subversion

---

[45] Nichols, *Progresses*, 2: 147.

[46] Cyndia Susan Clegg, *Press Censorship in Elizabethan England* (Cambridge: Cambridge University Press, 1997), pp. 93-5.

[47] Gregory Martin, *A Treatise of Schism* (London, 1578), quoted in Clegg, *Press Censorship*, p. 93.

[48] On the role of the Judith figure in ideological and interpretative struggles between Protestants and Catholics, see Margarita Stocker, *Judith, Sexual Warrior: Women and Power in Western Culture* (New Haven: Yale University Press, 1998), pp. 54-66, 70-106.

depending upon the contexts and motives of representation, interpretation, and signification. Figures and mythological schemes used to represent Elizabeth can be seen as sites of interpretative ambiguity, as sites inviting further critical engagement and decoding.

Fairy in the Elizabethan Entertainments

The use of the fairy queen as a figure for Elizabeth in Spenser's poem finds its origins, as was suggested long ago, in the appearance of the fairy queen in a number of entertainments and pageants staged for Elizabeth in the 1570s.[49] The image of the fairy queen is related to many of the representational strategies used in the mythologization of Elizabeth. The frequent appearances of fairy queens or fairy mistresses in Arthurian romance provided a central point of entry for fairy mythology into the overall culture of Elizabethan festivities and into the chivalric discourse with which Elizabeth patterned her interactions with her subjects, and consciously fashioned her own position as monarch. The use of the fairy queen also develops out of the contemporary associations made between fairy and classical deities that was discussed in chapter one, and in particular from the identification of the fairy queen with the goddess Diana. The elision between elements taken from native medieval sources and classical mythology is a characteristic feature of Elizabethan and Jacobean masques and entertainments. Such a blending of medievalism and classicism can be seen throughout the consciously literary worlds of Spenser's fairyland and Sidney's Arcadia.

An analysis of Spenser's use of fairy requires that one goes further than simply identifying the presence of the fairy queen in the Elizabethan entertainments and *The Faerie Queene*, and equating the employment of the fairy figure with earlier Diana/Cynthia imagery. The figure of the fairy queen needs to be located within the system of techniques and gestures through which Elizabeth's subjects addressed and communicated with the queen. The entertainments of the 1570s reveal that the fairy queen plays a significant role in speaking to the queen and ventriloquizing a contrasting set of political messages. In the political dramas played out at Kenilworth and Woodstock, the fairy queen is not, even at this stage, an unproblematic or uncontested representation of Elizabeth, but a means of modelling the queen's response to the question of marriage.[50]

In July 1575 as part of the royal summer progress the queen was entertained by the Earl of Leicester at Kenilworth castle in Warwickshire.[51] Kenilworth was

---

[49] Baskervill, 'Genesis', pp. 49-54.

[50] For a more detailed examination of fairy mythology in the royal entertainments, see Woodcock, 'The Fairy Queen Figure in Elizabethan Entertainments', in Carole Levin, Debra Barrett-Graves, and Jo Eldridge Carney, eds, *Elizabeth I: Always Her Own Free Woman*, pp. 97-115.

[51] See Nichols, *Progresses*, 1: 420-523; Robert Langham, *A Letter*, ed. R. J. P. Kuin (Leiden: Brill, 1983).

Leicester's most extravagant attempt to assert his own powers and authority as an equal to the queen, and as the queen's most suitable marriage partner. As part of the entertainments staged at Kenilworth that were loosely based on an Arthurian theme the queen is welcomed to the castle by 'the Lady of the Lake (famous in king Arthurz book) with too Nymphes wayting upon her' floating upon a movable island in a pool.[52] Later in the festivities Elizabeth learns that Sir Bruse, a villainous character taken from Malory's *Morte D'Arthur*, held the Lady of the Lake captive, requiring the 'prezens' of the queen to put him to flight and deliver the Lady.[53] As Merlin was said to have prophesied, 'she could never be delivered but by the presence of a better maide than herself', and indeed it is through 'sovereigne maiden's might' that Elizabeth's (otherwise passive) presence is sufficiently powerful to overcome Sir Bruse.[54] The episode is used to display and affirm the 'magical' powers of sovereignty, and replaced an alternate version of the rescue of the Lady of the Lake, scripted by George Gascoigne, in which Leicester is cast in the role of rescuer. Leicester was to have clashed with Sir Bruse in a military skirmish, defeated his foe, and then rescued the Lady of the Lake, and in so doing the Earl would prove his worthiness as protector of the queen and the queen's interests overseas.[55] As in several entertainments of this kind in the 1560s, Gascoigne's intended Leicester-centred masque refused to equate Elizabeth with Diana and chastity, and sought instead to dwell upon the queen's marriageability.[56] The narrative of Leicester-as-rescuer demanded that Elizabeth identify with the Lady of the Lake. But the queen refused to play the part of the fairy queen that was assigned to her at Kenilworth, preferring instead a narrative that allowed her to unequivocally assert and display her sovereign authority. The figure of the Lady of the Lake provided a site whereby the performance of authority and prowess could be enacted, but where direct identification with the Lady of the Lake within the rescue narrative was actually a means of disempowerment.

In the autumn of the same year Elizabeth stayed with Sir Henry Lee at Woodstock manor in Oxfordshire. We do not have as complete an account of the entertainments at Woodstock as those existing for the Kenilworth festivities, but the centre-piece was clearly the dramatized presentation of the tale of Hemetes the Hermit and its sequel. At the climax of the elaborate narrative Hemetes leads the queen to an elaborate banqueting house that was built around the trunk of a great oak and decorated with pictures and couplets written by nobles and 'men of great credite'. It is here, during the banqueting, that a figure dressed as the fairy queen makes an appearance: 'Her Maiesty thus in the middest of this mirth might espy the

---

[52] Nichols, *Progresses*, 1: 431.

[53] Nichols, *Progresses*, 1: 457.

[54] Nichols, *Progresses*, 1: 498-500.

[55] Frye, *Elizabeth*, pp. 78-86.

[56] Marie Axton, *The Queen's Two Bodies: Drama and the Elizabethan Succession* (London: Historical Society, 1977), pp. 49-53; Susan Doran, 'Juno Versus Diana: The Treatment of Elizabeth's Marriage in Plays and Entertainments, 1561-81', *Historical Journal* 38 (1995), pp. 257-74.

Queen of the Fayry drawn with 6. children in a waggon of state: the Boies brauely attired, & her selfe very costly apparrelled, whose present shew might wel argue her immortality'.[57] The fairy queen figure offers gifts and exhibits a much greater degree of engagement with Elizabeth than we find in the Kenilworth entertainments. The fairy queen clearly suggests a level of familiarity and intimacy as she states: 'This loue hath caused me transforme my face,/ and in your hue to come before your eyne,/ now white, then blacke, your frende the fayery Queene.'[58] The fairy queen continues her praise:

> Which marking all, as all to me is knowen,
> your face, your grace, your gouerment of state,
> your passing sprite whereby your fame is blowen:
> doe knowe by certain skill you haue no mate:
> and that no man throughout the worlde hath seene
> a prince that may compare with th' English Queene.[59]

Whereas the spectacles at Kenilworth functioned as an elaborate attempt at asserting Leicester's masculinist, martial prowess and his worthiness as an equal to the queen, Lee's contrivance of the fairy queen's appearance at Woodstock centres far more upon Elizabeth's singularity. The fairy queen's reference to how Elizabeth has no 'mate' could refer to the queen being without an 'equal' but also to her being unmarried, and in reading the final couplet of the passage quoted above one cannot help but think of Leicester's attempted suit.

In a second day of entertainments the characters from Hemetes's tale appear once more, though here the narrative pointedly addresses the theme of public duty. The story centres on two lovers, Caudina and Contarenus, and their flight from the mythical kingdom of Cambia. Caudina's father, the ruler of Cambia, has come to seek his daughter at Elizabeth's court and in his opening speech frames Caudina's flight as a breach of duty: 'She set her loue where she her selfe likt best,/ I much mislikt because her choise did light,/ Beneath her birth, though I might like the rest.'[60] The entertainment raises the same kind of issues that we find in Sidney's *Arcadia* concerning the duty of a prince to their country, and the need for individuals with public duties to subordinate their private desires to the country's good. The fairy queen, now named in the text as Eambia, plays a key role in the drama of Caudina's rapprochement with her father, in part through offering counsel (with the aid of the 'English Queene') regarding how Caudina might best make her return. In her speech to Occanon about the pervasive power of love, we witness the fairy queen addressing a 'Prince of high degree' on the levelling effect that love has: 'loue doth alwaies fight on equal ground,/ And where he mindeth match, he

---

[57] J. W. Cunliffe, 'The Queenes Majesties Entertainment at Woodstocke', *PMLA* 26 (1911), p. 98.

[58] Cunliffe, 'Queenes Majesties Entertainment', p. 98.

[59] Cunliffe, 'Queenes Majesties Entertainment', p. 99.

[60] Cunliffe, 'Queenes Majesties Entertainment', p. 104.

makes them peeres:/ if mynds agree the ground of states is found.'[61] Whilst admitting the undeniable power of love, especially upon those of noble state, the fairy queen is made to vocalize the central theme of the entertainment: that Caudina's duties to her father and her kingdom outweigh her private desires. The fairy queen advocates public duty and honour, and the narrative closes with Contarenus subordinating his love for Caudina to his country's good:

> Good Madam though I loue as no man more,
> yeeld yet to him [Occanon], withstand him not so sore.
>
> You shal obteine such one by his foresight,
> as he shal like, and countries weale shal craue,
> You must regard the common weales good plight,
> and seeke the whole not onely one to saue.[62]

Lee's conclusion here further suggests that the Woodstock entertainments functioned as a response or riposte to the Kenilworth entertainment with its insistence on the advantages of matrimony.

Elizabeth was particularly taken with this image of a bountiful, clearly powerful, female sovereign that had been presented before her and she leaves the banquet 'with good cheere', and she registers her delight in the day's entertainment by commanding that a copy of the narrative be brought to her. The popularity of the iconography and entertainment employed at Woodstock evidently provided Gascoigne with the perfect means for reaffirming his fealty to the queen following the censorship of his entertainments at Kenilworth. Gascoigne's transcription of the *Tale of Hemetes the Heremyte* presented to Elizabeth in 1576 is an attempt to locate himself within the gestural system of compliment and gift-exchange so successfully initiated at Woodstock.[63] At this point the fairy queen is not identified as a figure for Elizabeth, but rather, as in the Norwich entertainment where the figure of Judith was employed to suggest some of the ideal qualities and characteristics that Elizabeth might strive to espouse, she provides a fabulous image with which to address the queen; a means of speaking to Elizabeth.

The image of the fairy queen that Lee initiates at Woodstock forms an enduring part of Elizabeth's representational vocabulary, not only in those texts and presentations where she is used as a direct avatar of the queen, but also as a means of establishing a figurative engagement with the queen. It appears that the particular use of fairy seen at Woodstock continues to be played out in the ongoing romance of the devices employed in the Accession Day tilts. In the collection of Lee's tournament devices known as the Ditchley manuscript one finds a speech presented by the hermit of Woodstock as well as a 'Message of the Damsel of the Queen of

---

[61] Cunliffe, 'Queenes Majesties Entertainment', p. 110.

[62] Cunliffe, 'Queenes Majesties Entertainment', p. 121.

[63] Wendy Wall, *The Imprint of Gender: Authorship and Publication in the English Renaissance* (Ithaca: Cornell University Press, 1993), pp. 127-9.

the Fairies' delivered on behalf of an 'inchanted knight', that tells of the great renown of the tilts.[64] The piece is undated but it does suggest that fairy played a significant and recurrent part in one of the central dramatic vehicles for Elizabethan myth-making.

Lee's success at entertaining Elizabeth led to further use of fairy mythology in the years prior to the publication of *The Faerie Queene*. On the final day of the queen's visit to Norwich in the summer progress of 1578, Churchyard prepared a show for Elizabeth to be presented by boys dressed as water nymphs, in which there is reference to the more popular conceptions of fairy lore:

> The Phayries are another kind of elfes that daunce in darke,
> Yet can light candles in the night, and vanish like a sparke;
> And make a noyse and rumbling great among the dishes oft,
> And wake the sleepie sluggish maydes that lyes in kitchen loft.
> And when in field they treade the grasse, from water we repayre,
> And hoppe and skippe with them sometime as weather waxeth fayre.[65]

Rained off on the previous day, Churchyard now set his boys, dressed as they were as nymphs, 'to play by a device and degrees the Phayries, and to daunce (as neare as could be ymagined) like the Phayries'.[66] Churchyard's appropriation of fairy mythology is markedly different from Lee's and his conception of fairy associates itself both with native folklore and with classical demigods, if only from expedience. On the journey from Norwich, Elizabeth was entertained by Sir Thomas Kidson at Hengrave Hall in Suffolk with 'a shew representing the Phayries (as well as might be)... in the whiche shew, a rich jewell was presented to the Queenes Highnesse'.[67] Fairy is once again used as a mechanism of courtly compliment and gesture.

Though there is a paucity of extant narrative devices from the Accession Day festivities of the 1570s and 80s that actually feature the fairy queen, the publication of a description of the Woodstock devices in 1585 attests to the continued interest in the iconography and mythology employed in the 1575 entertainment, and provides a renewed advocacy of the priority of public duty over private interests and desires in a period momentarily starved of extended public progresses and entertainments.[68] In Thomas Blenerhasset's *A Revelation of the True Minerva* (1582), the classical gods' search to find a new mortal worthy of replacing Minerva quickly leads them to Elizabeth. The inclusion of the fairy queen into the host of classical deities that prepare Elizabeth for her 'ascension' to the position of new

[64] Nichols, *Progresses*, 3: 198-9. See also Yates, *Astraea*, pp. 98-101.
[65] Nichols, *Progresses*, 2: 210.
[66] Nichols, *Progresses*, 2: 211.
[67] Nichols, *Progresses*, 2: 215.
[68] Mary Hill Cole, *The Portable Queen: Elizabeth I and the Politics of Ceremony* (Amherst: University of Massachusetts Press, 1999), p. 158, notes that due to fears regarding the queen's safety, between 1580 and 1590 Elizabeth limited her progresses to the London area and Thames palaces.

Minerva, and who attend the queen at her court, illustrates that the fairy queen's place in Elizabeth's representational vocabulary was, by this time, well-established.[69] As in the entertainments at Kenilworth and Woodstock, the fairy queen and the ladies of the lake appear alongside the many classical deities employed in celebration and mythologization of the queen.

The Faerie Queene may well have functioned, and been received, in concert with the particular mythological schemes evoked in the ongoing romance of the Accession Day tilts and, at the very least, publication of the 1590 edition stimulated renewed interest in the use of fairy mythology in celebration of Elizabeth. On the fourth day of entertainments held by the Earl of Hertford at Elvetham in 1591, for example, Elizabeth is again cast as the favourite of the fairy queen (here named Aureola), a Proserpine-like figure who dwells underground and who nightly evokes Elizabeth's name in a form of Dianic prayer.[70] Lee used the figure of the fairy queen again in 1592 on the occasion of Elizabeth's visit to Quarrendon, Lee's ancestral home at Ditchley in Oxfordshire.[71] At Ditchley Lee consciously evokes the use of fairy mythology that he had employed in celebration of Elizabeth seventeen years earlier. Entering the mythical terrain of the entertainment, Elizabeth finds a grove peopled by despairing knights and ladies enchanted into the form of trees, and a hall hung with allegorical 'charmed pictures', alluding to the same devices seen at the Woodstock banquet of 1575. Here she finds a knight cast into an enchanted sleep for offending the fairy queen. There is an appeal to the queen's powers of interpretation and her willingness to play the figurative games presented to her by her subjects - useful skills for the implied ultimate reader of *The Faerie Queene* - as the knight would be freed if Elizabeth could interpret the pictures around the hall. The queen successful, the knight wakes and his subsequent speech hearkens back to the events of 1575 where 'Not far from hence, nor verie long agoe/ The fayrie Queene the fayrest Queen saluted'. The knight tells of the reactions and response of those who first witnessed the fairy queen at the Woodstock entertainment and received her gifts of posies and allegorical pictures or 'tables'. In order to protect the pictures from those who were over-curious of their meaning, 'the Tables were conveied hither,/ Such power she had by infernall Arte;/ And I enjoyned to keepe them altogether'.[72] The knight was commanded by the fairy queen to abjure the affections of any of the 'divers Ladies' who would come to untie the pictures' charms, and it was for his falling under 'a stranger ladies thrall' that the knight was put to sleep by the 'just revengefull Fayrie Queene'.

---

[69] Thomas Blenerhasset, *A Revelation of the True Minerva*, intr. J. W. Bennett (New York: Scholars' Facsimiles and Reprints, 1941), sig. E4.

[70] Wilson, *Entertainments*, pp. 115-16.

[71] On the Ditchley entertainment (also called the Quarrendon entertainment), see Chambers, *Sir Henry Lee*, pp. 145-9; Yates, *Astraea*, pp. 104-06. Wilson, *Entertainments*, pp. 119-42, reproduces the entertainment text.

[72] Wilson, *Entertainments*, p. 130.

The role of the fairy queen at Ditchley is more problematic than in any other dramatized representation of the figure used in royal celebrations. The fairy queen as she is presented at Ditchley is reconstructed as a figure who resembles Spenser's Acrasia as much as she does Gloriana and plays upon more negative associations of fairy. The entertainment celebrates Elizabeth but obscures one of her most distinctive avatars. Elizabeth's redress of the 'punishment' meeted out upon the knight sets her in direct opposition to the fairy queen but does not fully eliminate associations between the two. The figure of the fairy queen never actually appears at Ditchley; Elizabeth only hears reports of her powers and of the control that she exercises over her subjects. Ditchley evokes Spenser's poem through the way in which the presence of the fairy queen is only registered through what is said about her, and through the visible manifestations of her power over her subjects. The fairy queen's acute interest and involvement in the affections of others had been seen in the second day's entertainment at Woodstock. In her attempts to exert control over the marriages and sexual relations of her nobles and ladies-in-waiting, Elizabeth would have found her image in the fairy queen. As problematic as they appear, and indeed there is reference to her 'infernall Arte', the fairy queen's powers are clearly seen as analogous to Elizabeth's royal powers. The fairy queen is used as the vehicle with which to represent or anatomize - not explicitly to judge or criticize - the kind of power that Elizabeth wields. At Ditchley, fairy power is to be read as royal power. Lee's reappropriation and adaptation of the fairy queen figure in 1592 to speak to and about Elizabeth further illustrates the interpretative ambiguity of fairy and emphasizes that a definitive identification of what the fairy queen represents or means is continually open to renegotiation.

It is important to locate *The Faerie Queene* within the context of the myth-making enterprises employed in the representation of the queen as it is Elizabeth's identification with the fairy queen that is the central point of Spenser's appropriation of fairy mythology. From the first mention of Spenser's poem in the correspondence with Harvey nearly ten years prior to publication, repeated references to *The Faerie Queene* demonstrate that Spenser intended to focus upon the figure of the fairy queen from the very earliest stages of production.[73] It is fair to argue that the work's title denotes the relative importance of the fairy queen character and her role in the text, and by implication that it was through this figure that Spenser sought to represent Elizabeth from the outset. The identification of Elizabeth with the fairy queen made both in the text of *The Faerie Queene* and the 'Letter to Raleigh' certainly bear this out. As will be shown, the centrality of the fairy queen's role in the text is marked out by the over-arching structure of Arthur's search for Gloriana, during the course of which Arthur assists the quests of the individual knights of *The Faerie Queene*. The fairy queen played an important part in the figurative interactions and courtly gestural system of the 1570s, the era in which Spenser first formulated *The Faerie Queene*. The fairy queen's role in the

---

[73] *Three Proper and wittie, familiar Letters*, pp. 612, 628.

political drama of the entertainments, and her shifting identification with Elizabeth, or with attributes and characteristics that Elizabeth should possess, together with the conjectured centrality of fairy in the Accession Day tilts, provides the context for Spenser's explicit identification of Elizabeth with the fairy queen. *The Faerie Queene* is the final stage of the incorporation of fairy mythology into the personal mythology of Elizabeth. Combined with existing associations between Arthur and fairy lore, the entertainments of the 1570s offer the most persuasive explanation for Spenser's overall decision to employ fairy mythology. As is established in the next chapter, it is the figuration of Elizabeth that forms the central 'invention' and focal stimulus for Spenser's use of fairy in *The Faerie Queene* - everything else is generated from this initial identification: fairyland, individual fairy knights, and the fairy chronicle. But our understanding of how the entertainments of the 1570s can be said to have influenced Spenser needs a certain amount of reconsideration. My concern is to demonstrate that the wider context of Elizabethan myth-making examined here is not simply suggestive of the fairy theme, but that Spenser is consciously reacting to the techniques, images, and structures used in the representation of Elizabeth, and indeed that Spenser's own fashioning of mythical identities and figures for the queen is one of the central themes of *The Faerie Queene* itself.

Chapter 3

Spenserian Fairy Stories

The previous chapter identified how we can locate the figure of the fairy queen within the system of representational strategies by means of which Elizabeth constructed herself and was reconstructed by others, and through which she interacted with her subjects. The historical context of Spenser's identification of Elizabeth with the fairy queen in relation to Elizabethan myth-making as a whole provides the basis for developing a greater understanding of exactly how fairy mythology is used in *The Faerie Queene*. From the first comments in the 'Letter to Raleigh' about how his poem is constructed and how it should be read, Spenser stresses the textual ontology of fairy in *The Faerie Queene* through drawing attention to how fairy functions within the framework of the poem's allegory. From the outset of the poem, fairy is established as a sign for something else - a transparent surface inviting continued decoding and interpretation. As will be argued in the following chapters, based upon analysis of those episodes in *The Faerie Queene* where fairy receives the most extended treatment, the transparency and patent artificiality of the particular mythopœic scheme that Spenser employs to represent Elizabeth and her sovereign powers consciously and repeatedly draws attention back to the myth-making process itself, and Spenser's own role in this process. Spenser is engaged, not simply in the representation and celebration of the queen, but in writing about the process of writing about the queen, and constructing and consolidating his role as author. In this chapter I discuss how he self-consciously foregrounds his role as author and mythographer through the first of the fairy stories that we encounter in *The Faerie Queene*: the story of Spenser's narrator persona setting forth a story of fairy to Elizabeth that forms the principal framing narrative of the poem as a whole.

Fairy and the 'Letter to Raleigh'

The evident fictionality of fairy is clearly stated in the 'Letter to Raleigh' as Spenser explains how he intends to use the figure of the fairy queen within the allegorical schema of his great poem. He begins the Letter by setting out how he establishes the poem's narrative in relation to the 'historye of king Arthure'. The 'historicall fiction' of Arthur, it is observed, is employed as a means of presenting Spenser's 'generall end': 'to fashion a gentleman or noble person in vertuous and gentle discipline'. The initial focus is on the rhetorical effect that the history of Arthur might have upon Spenser's reader. The reasons given for the specific evocation of Arthur are closely bound up with the authority and legitimacy that the 'historye' is professed to possess: 'it is made famous by many mens former workes, and also furthest from the daunger of enuy, and suspition of present time'. Use of the history of Arthur is given credibility on the basis of precedent and on its perceived authority as a legitimate subject for his poem in the 'present time'. Our understanding of Spenser's apparent confidence that Arthur is suitably distanced from 'enuy' and 'suspition', if we do not read it simply as irony, requires some qualification. Confidence is generated by the enduring political and symbolic authority that the history of Arthur had long possessed through its formulation as an established mythopœic scheme used to celebrate the Tudors. There has been much written on the formation and propagation of Tudor propaganda, and the representational practices latterly known as the 'Tudor myth', that actively constructed and demonstrated the Tudor right to rule through tracing the genealogy of the royal house back through the line of British kings to Arthur, Cadwallader, and ultimately the mythical founder of the Britons, the Trojan Brutus.[1] The myth of British succession enabled Henry VII to construct an extended and ennobling lineage with which to negotiate the relative innovation of the house of Tudor. Henry VII's accession was constructed as the return to the throne of the British line. The title of Arthur Kelton's 1547 *A Chronycle with a Genealogie declaryng that the Brittons and Welshemen are lineallye dyscended from Brute* succinctly encapsulates the thesis argued in many works of Tudor 'apology'. Spenser's use of Welsh in '*Briton moniments*' in reference to Brutus Greenshield is a further allusion to the tradition of identifying and valorizing the Tudor's Welsh heritage (II.x.24.8-9).

Equally well-documented is the controversy largely initiated by Polydore Vergil's *Anglica Historia* (first published 1534), in which, as part of his commitment to establishing the authority of the Tudor title through the construction of a new history of England, Vergil voiced scepticism concerning the British history and the mythical tales of Brutus and Arthur recounted or invented by Geoffrey of Monmouth and adapted in subsequent chronicles.[2] The use of the British history was an object of controversy throughout the sixteenth century as historians, poets, and scholars took up polarized, though by no means static, positions concerning the use and relative veracity of the Brutus and Arthur materials. At the heart of the controversy was the ideological value that the British history had in serving, not only to authorize and glorify the Tudor title, but to

---

[1] Millican, *Spenser and the Table Round*, pp. 7-105; Edwin Greenlaw, *Studies in Spenser's Historical Allegory* (Baltimore: Johns Hopkins University Press, 1932), pp. 1-58, esp. pp. 7-20; Josephine Waters Bennett, *The Evolution of The Faerie Queene* (Chicago: University of Chicago Press, 1942), pp. 61-79; T. D. Kendrick, *British Antiquity* (London: Methuen, 1950), pp. 34-44; Sydney Anglo, *Images of Tudor Kingship* (London: Seaby, 1992), pp. 40-60; Anglo, *Spectacle*, pp. 44-5, 55-6.

[2] F. J. Levy, *Tudor Historical Thought* (San Marino: Huntingdon Library, 1967), pp. 64-7, 130-33. Accounts of Tudor myth-making in Millican, Greenlaw, Bennett, and Kendrick overlap greatly with discussion of controversy regarding Arthur and the British history.

provide a proleptic forebear and precedent for future Tudor greatness.[3] It is this ideological currency that stands behind both the vehemence with which Vergil was attacked and refuted by John Leland, John Bale, Richard Harvey, Sir John Price, and many others, and the vigour with which Vergil's critics sought to further furnish documentary and physical evidence supporting the pro-British or Arthurian argument. As Arthur Ferguson writes, Spenser's proven skill as an antiquary meant that he would not have taken the Arthurian legends at face value, and whereas belief in the veracity of the Arthur myths remained a site of contestation throughout the sixteenth century, the political expediency of Arthur was not in question.[4] Earlier, in the 'Aprill' gloss, E.K. refers to the 'fine fablers and lowd lyers, such as were the Authors of King Arthure the great and such like', but again - as is maintained in the 'Letter to Raleigh' - the political, mythographic expedience of constructing an Arthurian 'fable' cannot be denied (*Shorter Poems*, p. 69).

Spenser's reference to the 'historye' of Arthur should not be interpreted as a statement of any form of belief that the Arthur materials constituted objective facts, as the modern use of 'history' might suggest. Spenser uses the word 'historye' in the Letter to denote a 'narrative sequence of events' (*OED*). Later in the Letter Spenser refers to *The Faerie Queene* itself as his 'history'. Spenser claims from the outset that he draws upon the history of Arthur so far as it constituted a 'historicall fiction', a narrative texture for his 'continued Allegory', and we are told how Arthur is to be read and interpreted in the text. Arthur is to be used as a surface on which to portray the perfection of the twelve private moral virtues. In professing to choose the history of Arthur to 'colour' his narrative, Spenser locates his poem in relation to an established mythopœic scheme used in celebration of the Tudors. He creates the effect of continuing to acknowledge the political expediency of the Arthur legend by setting out to recast within his great poem what had become a familiar component in the symbolic vocabulary of Tudor myth-making.

As we continue to read down the Letter, however, Spenser signals his deviation from the received, well-known pattern of Arthur's history and declares that the poem presents Arthur *before* he becomes king. Spenser contrives the basic details (expanded upon in I.ix.3-5) concerning Arthur's upbringing and education under the auspices of Timon and Merlin, evoking names familiar from Arthurian romance (Merlin and Igrayne) but now also asserting his own space within the existing mythology. Spenser then refers to Arthur's dream of the fairy queen, the initiation of the quest to 'seeke her forth in Faerye land', and makes the identification between Elizabeth and the as-yet-unnamed Gloriana. The link between Arthur and the fairy queen evokes what was by this time (as has been shown) a consistent, recognizable feature of the mythology associated with Arthur. But we see Spenser going much further in elevating the relative importance that the fairy queen has in

---

[3] Levy, *Tudor Historical Thought*, p. 66.
[4] Arthur B. Ferguson, *Clio Unbound: Perception of the Social and Cultural Past in Renaissance England* (Durham, NC: Duke University Press, 1979), p. 36; Ferguson, *Utter Antiquity: Perceptions of Prehistory in Renaissance England* (Durham, NC: Duke University Press, 1993), p. 124.

that history and foregrounding the role that a powerful female sovereign will play in his poem in order to facilitate the representation of an appropriate figure for Elizabeth. Spenser then locates the fairy queen at (and *as*) the centre of the history that he professes to present. He establishes that three of the quests presented and pursued in the first three books of the poem are initiated at the fairy queen's annual feast and goes on to propose that this feast is to form the subject of the final book of *The Faerie Queene*. Spenser constructs the fairy queen's feast as one of the central structural and organizational principles of the poem by framing the 'historye' that he says he will set forth between what is *said* to have taken place at the feast and what will be *shown* to have taken place at the feast in the final book of the poem.

Spenser authorizes his text by locating *The Faerie Queene* in relation to an existing mythological scheme used to celebrate Elizabeth and the Tudors - that of Arthur and the British history - but he also personalizes his text by marking out and highlighting the distinct mythological scheme with which he proceeds to represent Elizabeth. The Letter is a demonstration of how Spenser's construction of a new mythological representation of Elizabeth involves the 'overgoing' of the known history of Arthur. The Order of Maidenhead, for example, is the fairyland equivalent of the Arthurian Round Table and its professed distillate, the Order of the Garter.[5] The Letter simultaneously signals a connection to the world of Arthur evoked both in medieval romance and Tudor myth-making, but at the same time registers how his text establishes a completely new and distinct mythical environment within which to represent and celebrate the queen.[6] Within the poem itself, the events of the narrative are temporally located relative to the known history of King Arthur: Britomart leaves in search of Artegall whilst Arthur's father Uther still reigns and currently battles against the Saxons (III.iii.52); and at the end of book six the actions of Calidore are located a 'long time' before more familiar figures from Arthurian romance, Sir Pelleas and Sir Lamorak (VI.xii.39). Similarly, fairyland is spatially contiguous with the world of the events presented in Malory, as knights ride in from Britain and Lionesse without obstruction.

The Letter also indicates how Spenser has implicitly appropriated the figure of the fairy queen from the Elizabethan representational vocabulary of the 1570s entertainments and incorporated her into the very heart of his own myth-making strategy to form his central mythopœic representation of the queen. The explicit identification between Elizabeth and the fairy queen made in the Letter goes further than any suggestion of parity made in the entertainments staged before or after 1590.

The identification made here is an important part of the profession of intimacy constructed throughout the Letter whereby Spenser offers to help his implied reader

---

[5] Michael Leslie, *Spenser's 'Fierce Warres and Faithfull Loves': Martial and Chivalric Symbolism in The Faerie Queene* (Cambridge: Brewer, 1983), pp. 138-46, discusses associations made between the Orders.

[6] In chapter six I examine how Spenser uses the British history as a model for the form and content of '*Antiquitee* of *Faery* lond'.

through the text. We are able to observe how Raleigh ought to read *The Faerie Queene*, seeing Raleigh's intended reading as a paradigm for the reader of the printed text, as the allegorical schema and 'general intention and meaning' are set out on the broad scale. There are repeated references to ways in which Spenser crafts his text with the reader in mind: in Spenser's preference for ornamentation ('shows') and narrative amplification of his theme above 'good discipline deliuered plainly'; and in the crucial interface with the reader at the heart of the poet's 'generall end'. The allegorical form is noted by Spenser as having rich potential for engaging the reader and for offering something new, which, by 'the most part of men', can be enjoyed for its delightful effects alone, rather than for any specific ethical or moral lesson. The reader of the Letter is spared any exposition of the 'particular purposes or by-accidents' of *The Faerie Queene* but is armed both with a strategy for reading the text in the form of the elementary observation that it should be read as a 'continued Allegory', and with background information about the origins or 'wel-head' of the quests played out within the main text, imparting information concerning events leading up to the initial 'A gentle knight was pricking on the playne. &c'. Spenser thus explicitly states that he chose the 'historye of king Arthure' (and, by extension, the fairy queen) as a means of talking about other things, highlighting the presence of deeper 'meaning' to stimulate the reader's interest.

In announcing his decision to 'conceiue' Elizabeth using the image of the fairy queen, Spenser draws attention to his allegory and provides an inaugural, albeit partial decoding for the reader. Subsequent readers of *The Faerie Queene* have attempted to augment the level of historical identification in the Letter by reading the fairy queen's twelve-day 'Annuall feaste' as an allusion to the Accession Day celebrations.[7] Spenser affects that he is imparting privy information through taking apart his central continued metaphor and revealing from the outset that fairy in his text operates principally as a sign for something else. This is an important statement in revealing that fairy is a means of 'speaking the other', drawing attention to the function of fairy as a veil, and in the first instance as a means of representing Elizabeth and her sovereign glory. Similar suggestions of identification are made in the dedicatory sonnet to Sir Henry Carey, Lord Hunsdon, in a line referring to his 'nearnes to that Faerie Queene', Spenser here alluding to the fact that Carey was Elizabeth's first cousin. Within the text of *The Faerie Queene* proper, Elizabeth is expressly exhorted to identify herself with the fairy queen:

> In this fayre mirrhour maist behold thy face,
> And thine owne realmes in lond of Faery,
> And in this antique ymage thy great auncestry. (II.proem.4)

---

[7] Ivan Schulze, 'Elizabethan Chivalry and the Faery Queene's Annual Feast', *MLN* 50 (1935), pp. 158-61; Alastair Fowler, *Spenser and the Numbers of Time* (London: Routledge, 1964), p. 170n1.

The identification is repeated in *Amoretti* XXXIII in reference to the 'Queene of faëry,/ that mote enlarge her [Elizabeth] liuing prayses dead' (*Shorter Poems*, p. 404). Harvey's persona Hobynoll continues the scheme of identification in his commendatory poem:

> So mought thy *Redcrosse knight* with happy hand
> victorious be in that faire Ilands right:
> Which thou doest vaile in Type of Faery land
> Elyzas blessed field, that *Albion* hight. (CV3 'To the learned Shepheard')

Following on from his own implicit statement of his role in the myth-making of Elizabeth, Spenser proceeds to locate *The Faerie Queene* in relation to Raleigh's use of the 'excellent conceipt' of Cynthia as a figure for the queen in early drafts of his *Book of the Ocean to Cynthia*. Spenser's use of the fairy queen as a figure for Elizabeth, in addition to the means whereby he 'doe otherwise shadow her', is thus associated with another one of the many different representational strategies, detailed above, that were used in the construction of an idealized image of the queen. In the proem to book three, Spenser subordinates his own representation of idealized chastity to that found in Raleigh's poem but implores that the implied reader Elizabeth

> In mirrours more then one her selfe to see,
> [But] either *Gloriana* let her chuse,
> Or in *Belphoebe* fashioned to bee: (III.proem.5)

In the figuration of Elizabeth as Gloriana, Spenser professes to represent 'her rule'; and in the figure of Belphoebe 'her rare chastitee'. But the 'mirrours more then one' might easily be extended to allude to the mirrors provided by more than one author: by the different configurations of a Cynthia figure in the works of Spenser and Raleigh, and also by the myriad forms through which writers, poets, artists, and historians throughout the reign of Elizabeth constructed mirrors within which the queen might see an idealized image of herself. Spenser sets his use of the fairy queen alongside other figures from Elizabeth's representational vocabulary.

The 'Letter to Raleigh' is an important opening statement of Spenser's intentions concerning his use of fairy in *The Faerie Queene*. He invites his reader to read through or deconstruct fairy to find some form of deeper meaning and immediately complicates how his reader is to engage with the literal, surface narrative of the poem. The dual identification of what the fairy queen represents - glory in Spenser's 'generall intention', Elizabeth in his 'particular' intention - provides an inaugural guide to reading and decoding fairy in the poem. As we shall see, Spenser continues to provide such guides within *The Faerie Queene* itself and repeatedly deconstructs those characters that he presents as fairies, further drawing attention to the use of fairy as part of the allegory of his poem. It is in the Letter that we can also identify the first suggestions of an association between the use of fairy and Spenser's assertion of his authorial role, as we are introduced to two further conceits upon which the whole of the poem is structured. The first is that of Arthur's quest for Gloriana, the ur-quest upon which Arthur is ostensibly employed in each book of the poem. The second conceit might best be described as the story of telling the story of Arthur and Gloriana. Throughout the Letter Spenser engages in this kind of metanarration - commenting to the reader on how the narrative will be presented and on how the text should be read - but this is also something that is seen throughout *The Faerie Queene* proper, where it is presented in the form of a sustained, self-conscious commentary upon the process of 'setting forth' the poem provided by Spenser's narrator persona. Whilst I do not wish to suggest a conflation between this first-person voice within *The Faerie Queene* and the more authorial 'I' of the Letter, the initial demonstration in the Letter of Spenser's preoccupation with writing about how he is going to write about Elizabeth and the role that fairy plays within that process, is consistent with Spenser's treatment of fairy within the poem itself.

The Story of Tanaquill and the Briton Prince

I now want to turn to the very beginning of *The Faerie Queene* in order to identify the presence and nature of fairy within the poem itself for it is here that we encounter the first, and most enduring, Spenserian fairy story.

> Lo I the man, whose Muse whylome did maske,
> As time her taught, in lowly Shephards weeds,
> Am now enforst a farre vnfitter taske,
> For trumpets sterne to chaunge mine Oaten reeds,
> And sing of Knights and Ladies gentle deeds;
> Whose prayses hauing slept in silence long,
> Me, all too meane, the sacred Muse areeds
> To blazon broade emongst her learned throng:
> Fierce warres and faithfull loues shall moralize my song. (I.proem.1)

No fairies so far. But it is in the first two stanzas taken together that Spenser establishes the scenario dramatizing the narrator's presentation of the text that we have before us. This model is maintained throughout *The Faerie Queene*. Whereas the other five proems each introduce their own respective books and the themes contained therein, the proem to book one serves as introduction to the work as a whole. From the very outset of the poem, the act of rehearsing a text or story is a central concern. As is argued below, it is within this overall story, the framing narrative of *The Faerie Queene*, that we can identify Spenser's first treatment of fairy. The subtle, often latent presence of Spenser's first fairy story underlies *The Faerie Queene* in its entirety but until now has been silently passed over in criticism of the poem.

In order to fully appreciate how Spenser presents his story of fairy it is necessary to pay particularly close attention to what Paul Alpers terms the 'rhetorical mode' of Spenser's narrative. As Alpers writes,

In turning narrative materials into stanzas of poetry, Spenser's attention is focused on the reader's mind and feelings and not on what is happening within his fiction. His poetic motive in any given stanza is to elicit a response - to evoke, modify, or complicate feelings and attitudes. His stanzas, then, are modes of address by the poet to the reader.[8]

It is perhaps unnecessary to labour the point that the 'I' of 'Lo I the man, whose Muse whylome did maske' is a rhetorical construct operative within a consciously poetic tradition. The 'speaker' of the addresses to the implied reader found in the proems and narratorial apostrophes within the body of *The Faerie Queene*, should not simply be taken to represent the unmediated 'voice of the author'. From the opening stanza of *The Faerie Queene* and invocation of the consciously literary *rota Virgilii*, the apostrophic call for attention, 'Lo, I the man', adopts the pose of the vocal presence and performance of the poet. The persona adopted echoes the dramatized, 'at once personally allusive and fictive' narrator of *The Canterbury Tales*, and is also very much in the tradition of the self-conscious narrators of Italian mock-epic or romance-epic.[9] With Ariosto's *Orlando Furioso* we find a shift from this suggestion of an idea of presence to more of a general dynamic of textual presentation. The effect created in *Orlando Furioso* is of the narrator constructing his text in the presence of the reader. Narratorial interruptions help to restate the artifice of the text, serving to 'expose the poem as a fictional construct manipulated at the author's will'.[10] Another narrative device for intervening in the action is the canto, giving Ariosto's narrator occasion for breaking off the action to generate suspense and to comment upon the text in hand. The effect of authorially stepping out of the world of the poem, establishing contact with the reader, and commenting on the relevance of the subject to his own or the reader's situation, draws the reader's attention back to the 'performance' of the text. The narrator functions to stress the aspect of human craftsmanship in the poem, eschewing the idea of the divinely inspired poet in favour of the poet's god-like powers of creation.[11]

It is clear from the overall similarity of their presentation that Spenser drew heavily upon both the manner and matter of Ariosto's narratorial interventions. The scenario that Spenser models in *The Faerie Queene* is that of a narrator setting out and reflecting upon the project of writing with which he is engaged. We witness the narrator of *The Faerie Queene* 'setting forth' his text in the presence of the reader.

---

[8] Paul J. Alpers, *The Poetry of The Faerie Queene* (Princeton: Princeton University Press, 1967), p. 5.
[9] Judith Anderson, 'Narrative Reflections: Re-envisaging the Poet in *The Canterbury Tales* and *The Faerie Queene*', in Theresa M. Krier, ed., *Refiguring Chaucer in the Renaissance* (Gainesville: University Press of Florida, 1998), p. 88.
[10] Daniel Javitch, *Proclaiming a Classic: The Canonization of Orlando Furioso* (Princeton: Princeton University Press, 1991), p. 155.
[11] Robert M. Durling, *The Figure of the Poet in Renaissance Epic* (Cambridge, MA: Harvard University Press, 1965), pp. 130-31.

Helpe then, O holy virgin chiefe of nyne,
Thy weaker Nouice to performe thy will,
Lay forth out of thine euerlasting scryne
The antique rolles, which there lye hidden still,
Of Faerie knights and fayrest *Tanaquill*,
Whom that most noble Briton Prince so long
Sought through the world, and suffered so much ill,
That I must rue his vndeserued wrong:
O helpe thou my weake wit, and sharpen my dull tong. (I.proem.2)

The conceit is one of the narrator accessing and reading a text (the 'antique rolles'), 'translating' it, and then presenting a selected rendition to the reader in the form of *The Faerie Queene*. He professes to draw upon a textual reserve or 'scryne' comparable to that found in the House of Alma, from which Guyon similarly reads a fairy history. The commendatory verse by H. B. alludes to this role as intermediary in referring (with obvious homonymy) to Spenser as the 'rare dispenser' of the muses' grace. Though he begins by calling upon his muse to reveal the source of his 'history', the narrator's role is not simply that of a vatic medium for supernaturally inspired poetry. The muse lays out the antique rolls which the narrator is then impelled to read and re-present to his reader.[12]

The fundamental importance of the element of fairy here should be identified and stressed. When the narrator gives us a brief, allusive indication of the overall content of the 'antique rolles' in I.proem.2., it is to fairy knights and to Arthur's search for the fairy queen, Tanaquill, that attention is drawn. The presence of fairy knights within the surface narrative of the poem is, at least notionally, maintained throughout; four of the six main books of the poem each focus upon a central, titular character who is referred to both in narratorial report and by other characters (whether he actually is or not) as a fairy or elf. It is Arthur's love for Gloriana that generates the suffering referred to in line seven of I.proem.2. There is a deliberate evocation here of the first lines of the *Aeneid* and the sweeping introduction to Aeneas's enduring struggle and ultimate fate. Comparison is invited between the opening statements of the overall theme of each author's work with the implication that Arthur's struggle in his search for the fairy queen forms the underlying subject of Spenser's overall 'song'. Arthur's presence in each book is a reminder of the centrality of that story; so, paradoxically, are his deviations from his 'first quest', since attention is regularly drawn to them *as* deviations.

The theme of Arthur's love for Gloriana is maintained in the following stanza (I.proem.3) as Cupid is credited with shooting the 'cruell dart' that initiates Arthur's quest. In I.proem.4 the narrator's direct address to Elizabeth (as 'Goddesse') calls for aid in raising his humble and vile thoughts 'To thinke of that true glorious type of thine,/ The argument of mine afflicted stile', and in doing so first makes the typological identification between Elizabeth and Gloriana, and then

---

[12] Jerome S. Dees, 'The Narrator of *The Faerie Queene*: Patterns of Response', *TSLL* 12 (1970-71), pp. 537-68.

locates Gloriana, the fairy queen, at the centre of the work as the narrator's notional 'argument' or invention. The love of Arthur and Gloriana is again placed at the centre of *The Faerie Queene* in the proem to book four when Spenser addresses the censure received for his earlier 'looser rimes' that praised love. The final glimpse that we have of Arthur in the poem sees the Briton prince riding off once more upon his 'first quest' (VI.viii.30). Arthur's quest for the fairy queen is mentioned in every book of the poem. It is a story of fairy that provides the central and seminal stimulus for everything that the narrator proceeds to present. The principal framing narrative of *The Faerie Queene* is a story about telling this story.

    Attention is drawn from the outset to a process of textual transmission, a process about which Spenser's narrator maintains a running commentary throughout the poem. In the proem to book two, for example, the narrator refers to his presentation of 'this famous antique history' and its anticipated reception.

> Right well I wote most mighty Soueraine,
> That all this famous antique history,
> Of some th'aboundance of an ydle braine
> Will iudged be, and painted forgery,
> Rather then matter of iust memory,
> Sith none, that breatheth liuing aire, does know,
> Where is that happy land of Faery,
> Which I so much do vaunt, yet no where show,
> But vouch antiquities, which no body can know. (II.proem.1)

The 'history' in line two to which the pronoun 'this' refers requires careful identification. This 'history', i.e. the basic 'story' or *fabula* that the narrator has and continues to relate, should be distinguished from the narrator's purported emplotment of this material into the work we have before us. It is important to identify the separability of the narrator and the history that he professes to narrate as this draws attention to the means by which the narration of *The Faerie Queene* is organized and represented. It is this separability that characterizes the distinction between the *fabula* and the performance or performative level of the text. The *fabula* is the story of fairy taken from the 'antique rolles' that the narrator endeavors to set forth: the 'famous antique history' of Gloriana and Arthur, and both the accidents and 'intendments' of the Order of Maidenhead and the knights of each book. The performative level of the text is the moment of engagement between reader and text - that moment at which the effect of having the *fabula* played out to us is presented in the text, and where Spenser, through the voice of the narrator, plays out or sets forth his text to the reader and simultaneously comments on the task in hand. The narrator's interruptions and interjections in the text are, as Jerome Dees writes, 'a continuing reminder that he is mediator of the significance of a received tale to a group of more or less willing receivers'.[13] In the narratorial interventions in the proems and body of each book, attention is drawn to

---

[13] Dees, 'Narrator', p. 545.

the action of presenting the *fabula* as the narration momentarily comes to a halt. Similarly at the end of each book Spenser creates the effect that it is the telling of the story that comes to an end and not the tale itself. The commentary is part of Spenser's self-conscious technique employed to draw attention to both his and his readers' interface with the text. We are made to witness the narrator's ongoing relationship both with his muse and his source, and this includes moments where he exclaims his unworthiness or inability to reproduce his material, such as at the first sight of an un-wimpled Una:

> To tell, were as to striue against the streame.
> My ragged rimes are all too rude and bace,
> Her heauenly lineaments for to enchace. (I.xii.23)

The narrator of *The Faerie Queene* does not possess the same sense of confidence in his abilities as the self-conscious narrator of *Orlando Furioso*. Instead, the vocal presence of the narrator, at its most pronounced in the proems, records the struggle of an engagement with the material of the text, a struggle further registered in the analogies drawn between his literary project and the ploughing of a furrow (V.iv.40) or the undertaking of a voyage (I.xii.1 and 42; VI.xii.1).[14]

The narrator's engagement with his materials is sustained throughout *The Faerie Queene*. Attention is drawn to the process of setting forth the 'antique rolles' that tell of 'Faerie knights and fayrest *Tanaquill*' through allusions and references to the narrator's recondite textual source, and in narratorial apostrophes calling upon the muses' aid in the presentation of that source (I.proem.2; IV.xi.10). Claims of his ability to access sources 'which no body can know' (II.proem.1) stress the narrator's own role as the lens through which we view the fairy realm. In the proem to book three the narrator resolves that although the ideal of chastity is embodied by his sovereign, his own inability to 'figure plaine' her 'glorious pourtraict' leads him to fit 'antique praises vnto present persons' and perforce 'fetch from *Faery*/ Forreine ensamples' (III.proem.1). At one point the narrator claims to be privy to fairy hearsay as he details the provenance of Florimell's girdle, the prize in the beauty contest following Satyrane's tournament (IV.v.3). The conceit of the hidden text of fairy is taken up in the proem to book six as the narrator once more asserts that he alone is granted access to the 'strange waies' of fairyland 'where neuer foote did vse,/ Ne none can find, but who was taught them by the Muse' (VI.proem.2). Even within the Mutabilitie cantos the narrator promises to set forth the 'antique race and linage ancient' of the Titaness Mutabilitie 'As I haue found it registred of old,/ In *Faery* Land mongst records permanent' (VII.vi.2). As will be shown in subsequent chapters, each of Spenser's more extended treatments of fairy is in turn located within stories or texts that are rehearsed or read by characters within the *fabula* of *The Faerie Queene* - the characters, like the narrator, tell stories about fairy.

---

[14] Dees, 'Narrator', p. 554.

The narrator is cast into the role of reader, and in his professed attempt to mediate the raw materials of his source, as a *compilator*: one who moves around the words of others but adds nothing of his own. In the same manner as many of Spenser's key sources - Geoffrey of Monmouth with the '*vetustissimus liber*', Chaucer in *The Canterbury Tales* and *Troilus and Criseyde* (with the seminal 'Lollius'), Malory's French book, and Ariosto with pseudo-Turpin - the 'euerlasting scryne' is a fictional authority from which Spenser's narrator is made to draw in order to create the effect of the compilator. A. J. Minnis indeed notes how the concept of the 'scrine' or textual treasury became used by medieval compilators in reference to their own texts, to designate them as a place or collection of things of great delight, utility, and wisdom.[15] In *Amoretti* LXXX Spenser uses 'compile' to describe the record of his 'race' through fairyland, the process - now completed - of writing the first six books of *The Faerie Queene* (*Shorter Poems*, p. 427). In *The Canterbury Tales*, Chaucer uses the conventions of *compilatio* by professing to rehearse the tales of his pilgrims as accurately as he can whilst at the same time disclaiming responsibility for what they actually say. In a similar fashion, Spenser's narrator plays down the sense of personal agency or culpability for the history that is presented, and at the same time stresses the fictionality of the composition process in which he is engaged and the ultimate artifice of the product that he sets forth. But Spenser simultaneously draws attention to the very artifice of his project by reference to his 'hidden' source text. Chaucer's Canterbury pilgrimage we can envisage; the narrator's profession of access to fairyland, however, in search of 'antiquities' is much harder to accept.

The story of Spenser's narrator gaining (and allowing) access to a treasury of potential texts enclosed or hidden within the muses' scryne creates the effect that the poem already exists in some form inaccessible to the narrator's audience. The fiction is evoked in the commendatory verse by W. L., where it is said that Spenser's poem is a response to the extant fame 'spredd so large,/ Through Faery land of their renowned Queene'. The pose is one of using a secret, almost occult source to gain access to fairyland that is reminiscent of the demonological treatises and grimoires of the period that feature invocations and rituals offering the means by which one could actually gain contact with fairies: verbal and textual formulae that provide access to hidden powers. Spenser makes the simple statement that *The Faerie Queene* is a text made up from other texts; from, as it were, the very reservoir of literary tradition itself. The text from which the narrator draws, if we read the conceit at face value for a moment, is representative of the whole intertext of literary sources and the many different types of story featuring fairy that Spenser could have accessed in his construction of the poem.[16] The antique rolls represent the 'type' of text that Spenser both draws upon, and himself creates the effect of

---

[15] A. J. Minnis, *Medieval Theory of Authorship: Scholastic Attitudes in the Later Middle Ages* (London: Scolar, 1984), p. 200.
[16] In IV.ii.32 the conceit of reproducing an 'antique story' that is now 'no where to be found' genuinely evokes what actually takes place as Spenser sets out to continue Chaucer's unfinished 'Squire's Tale'.

providing, in his own work. Although some have suggested that the textual metaphor used here serves as a figure for memory itself and indeed that fairyland as a whole is an image of a communal, national and literary memory,[17] the 'euerlasting scryne' represents specifically recorded memory.[18] The narrator draws upon a textual resource. Just as in Eumnestes's library where Guyon reads '*Antiquitee* of *Faery* lond', the book of memory is a figure for the place at which memory is recorded.

In order to further delineate the principal components of Spenser's framing narrative and to reassert the centrality of the narrator's story of fairy, we might again turn to one of Spenser's principal narrative models. Throughout *Orlando Furioso* attention is drawn to the continued presence in the text of the sixteenth-century house of Este. Ariosto's narratorial persona repeatedly steps back from Carolingian France and the 'history' he has set out to present, to draw encomiastic comparison between the heroic exploits of the Estense's mythical ancestors and those of the contemporary Ferrarese. The narrator shifts between two temporal contexts.[19] At the beginning of the final canto Ariosto compares his literary project to a voyage, the closing of his fiction modelled as a friendly reception in a safe harbour.[20] The end of Ariosto's voyage sees his friends and contemporaries awaiting him on the shore, comparable to a kind of dramatized acknowledgments page. Ariosto's narrator once again juxtaposes the presentation of his mythological history with the author's own myth-making for the Estense and his praise for the kind of material conditions that make his writing possible.

Like *Orlando Furioso, The Faerie Queene* is set in two distinct and discrete temporal contexts. The first is fairyland and its bordering realms (including Britain), the 'world' of the *fabula* of the poem in which all of the characters and locations are set. The poem is also set in sixteenth-century England and the second temporal context is that of the narrator-figure expressed in the proems, addresses, exclamations, and narratorial interventions, as he presents the *fabula* to his implied readers and, by extension, to subsequent readers of *The Faerie Queene*. It is in the sixteenth-century setting of *The Faerie Queene* - what I term here as the poem's 'performative' level - that Spenser's narratorial persona sets forth his story of fairy and constructs a dramatized model of the relationship between reader and text. The production and narration of the work is modelled as a dramatic playing out to a reader of the narrator's fairy story. Equally important within this model is therefore the recipient of the narrator's labours, the implied reader. The narrator's audience includes a number of hypothetical readers through whom points of potential

---

[17] Michael Murrin, *The Veil of Allegory: Some Notes Towards a Theory of Allegorical Rhetoric in the English Renaissance* (Chicago: University of Chicago Press, 1969), p. 82.

[18] Judith Anderson, '"Myn auctour": Spenser's Enabling Fiction and Eumnestes' 'immortall scrine', in Logan and Teskey, eds, *Unfolded Tales*, p. 19.

[19] Peter Marinelli, 'Ariosto', in A. C. Hamilton, gen. ed., *The Spenser Encyclopedia* (Toronto: University of Toronto Press, 1990), p. 56.

[20] Ludovico Ariosto, *Orlando Furioso*, tr. Guido Waldman (Oxford: Oxford University Press, 1974), 46.1. References are to canto and stanza.

opposition to the text are voiced and negotiated, such as the 'rugged forhead' of proem four, or the sceptical 'Clarkes' of V.x.1, but the most important implied reader of *The Faerie Queene* is of course the dedicatee, Elizabeth herself. The first line of the second proem, 'Right well I wote most mighty Soueraine', is a bald statement of the kind of dialogue being modelled at the poem's performative level, the completion of the dialogic 'I-you' relationship between narrator and reader in his address to the queen. It is easy to overlook what Spenser establishes in such a simple line, and compounds by similar addresses in the other proems and at incidental points throughout *The Faerie Queene*. It establishes what might be termed a reading 'system'. In the dialogic relationship of narrator and reader - 'I' and 'Soueraine' - we have the contrivance of a speaker and a listener. We are made aware of the narrator addressing a specific addressee placed into the text as an imagined reader. Attention is drawn both to the act of writing, with the Spenser-narrator's act of mediation couched, in accordance with Virgilian and Ariostan convention, in the form of an heroic song ('O pardon, and vouchsafe with patient eare/ The braue aduentures of this faery knight/ The good Sir *Guyon* gratiously to heare' (II.proem.5)); and to *The Faerie Queene*'s actual reception and reading. The presentation of *The Faerie Queene* that Spenser models in his text is not simply an 'offering-up' or 'consecration', with Spenser figuratively sending off his work to Elizabeth and then withdrawing, as the phrasing of the poem's dedications might suggest. The scenario that Spenser constructs predicates much more of an ongoing process of presentation. In the initial dedications and in repeated direct addresses and apostrophes to the queen in the second person using a multitude of different titles, Spenser constructs the model of an interface between his text and the queen. A scenario is contrived of Elizabeth receiving *The Faerie Queene* as it is presented to her by the narrator. The principal framing narrative of the poem as a whole is that of Spenser's narrator setting out a story of fairy to the queen. The presentation modelled in the text is then observed in turn by subsequent readers of *The Faerie Queene*.

The Narrator's Guide to Reading Fairy

In reading *The Faerie Queene* it is hard not to notice the increasing frequency with which the narrator expresses his concern regarding the difficulties involved in his ongoing project, and in the way in which he imagines his text may be read. The tone of great seriousness that the narrator adopts is set against the very real backdrop of increased governmental measures during the 1580s aimed at restricting public dissent.[21] In 1579 Sidney famously received extended censure for attempting to counsel Elizabeth against the marriage to the Duke of Alençon; that same year, John Stubbs and William Page, the writer and publisher (respectively) of *The*

---

[21] On censorship measures of the 1580s, see Robert Lane, *Shepheards Devises: Edmund Spenser's Shepheardes Calender and the Institutions of Elizabethan Society* (Athens, GA: University of Georgia Press, 1993), pp. 14-16; Clegg, *Press Censorship*, pp. 32-5.

Discoverie of a Gaping Gulf, each lost a hand for publicly voicing similar sentiments. The social and visceral realities demonstrated by these related episodes could have only heightened Spenser's awareness of the political implications consequent to a 'bad' reading or a misinterpretation of his work. The proems of *The Faerie Queene* clearly evince Spenser's sensitivity to how his text may be read, and are instrumental in his attempt at negotiating misinterpretation or misreadings within the text, acting as a kind of 'lightning rod' for criticism.[22]

The proem to book two provides the most direct, reflexive consideration of the kinds of uncertainties, anxieties, and interpretative problems attendant upon constructing stories of fairy that are actually encountered in those told within the *fabula* of *The Faerie Queene*. Spenser's argument outlined here provides an introduction to many of the ideas important in questioning how Spenser uses fairy throughout *The Faerie Queene*; in particular those concerning the ambiguities inherent within producing a story of fairy, and the effect that fairy has upon one's reading of the poem. The proem to book two sees the narrator providing a commentary upon his overall myth-making project with a particular focus on the credibility of his recondite (though of course contrived) fairy source. It provides a model of how Spenser imagines that the element of fairy as a whole might be read. The second proem is also of special importance as it presents Spenser's first direct discussion of where he chooses to 'locate' the majority of the poem's narrative: 'the happy land of Faery'. I discuss it here in relation to the rest of the framing narrative before moving on in subsequent chapters to examine the Spenserian fairy stories presented within the *fabula*.

The second proem is of particular interest in that the narrator focuses upon his awareness that the text is being read and 'iudged', and the whole of the proem is based around an imagined reading of the text so far. It provides, in effect, two potential 'first readings' - one positive, one negative. As in the 'Letter to Raleigh' and the concern to avoid 'gealous opinions and misconstructions', awareness of the text's reception quickly extends to the possibilities of a bad reading or misreading. This is the scenario on which the argument of the second proem is based.

> Right well I wote most mighty Soueraine,
> That all this famous antique history,
> Of some th'aboundance of an ydle braine
> Will iudged be, and painted forgery,
> Rather then matter of iust memory. (II.proem.1.1-5)

The second proem does not simply present a rhetorical gesture of humility or *diminutio* as found in the proems of books one and three, nor is there directly a narratorial profession of inadequacy. Rather, Spenser takes issue with the possible ways in which the text might be read using the imagined response 'of some', and

---

[22] Debra Belt, 'Hostile Audiences and the Courteous Reader in *The Faerie Queene,* Book VI', *SSt* 9 (1988), pp. 107-135, discusses Spenser's attempts to forestall criticism of his text and the spectre of bad readers that haunts *The Faerie Queene*.

then works through his argument in defence of telling his story of fairy and setting *The Faerie Queene* in fairyland. Spenser's hypothetical reader is realized in the proem to book four. The fear of misreading has many points of departure. Read literally, 'th'aboundance of an ydle braine' suggests an over-production of a disorderly creative faculty, or of a mind confused and deluded by sickness or foul spirits. As discussed in chapter one, infernal manipulation of human physiology was commonly presented in contemporary demonological treatises as the means by which fairies might be caused to 'appear'. Mercutio's evocation of Queen Mab, 'the fairies' midwife' in *Romeo and Juliet* (I.v. lines 96-8), is ultimately dismissed as 'vain fantasy' and the product of an idle brain. The line also anticipates some of Spenser's seventeenth-century critics and their objections to a seeming lack of structure or unity in *The Faerie Queene*. In his preface to *Gondibert* (1650), Sir William Davenant compared Spenser's allegorical story to 'a continuance of extraordinary Dreames; such as excellent Poets, and Painters, by being overstudious may have in the beginning of Feavers'.[23] The word 'ydle' in the third line of the stanza is a particularly damaging criticism. At the opening of *Mother Hubberds Tale* the nugatory subject matter of the 'pleasant tales (fit for that idle stound)' bears a striking resemblance to the kind of stories forming the basis of *The Faerie Queene*:

> Some tolde of Ladies, and their Paramoures;
> Some of braue Knights, and their renowned Squires;
> Some of the Faeries and their strange attires;
> And some of Giaunts hard to be beleeued,
> That the delight thereof me much releeued. (lines 28-32; *Shorter Poems*, p. 235)

One can identify Spenser's overall argument in II.proem.1-5 as a careful negotiation of the traditional humanist eschewal of idleness as he attempts to distance *The Faerie Queene* from the 'books of fayned cheualrie' condemned by Ascham. Thus the worst way to read *The Faerie Queene* would be to dismiss it as a purely facile work devoid of utilitarian import. There is a need for fairy to be placed within a structure of meaning.

The core objection that Spenser believes can be made to the overall legitimacy and authority of his work so far is centred upon his use of fairy 'Sith none, that breatheth liuing aire, does know,/ Where is that happy land of Faery' (II.proem.1). Of particular importance is how, in this passage, Spenser himself 'reads' the employment of fairy in *The Faerie Queene*. The basis of the imagined argument that Spenser raises here is that the location of the 'antique history' in the 'happy land of Faery' will cause the reader to question the nature of what it is that they are reading. It is fairy that creates the impression that his text is mere 'painted forgery' and not the 'matter of iust memory'. The issue is one of textual authority. Spenser identifies that the use of fairy draws attention to the fact that *The Faerie Queene* is

[23] Sir William Davenant, 'The Author's Preface to His Much Honor'd Friend M. Hobbes', *Gondibert*, ed. David F. Gladish (Oxford: Clarendon Press, 1971), p. 7.

a constructed text, and that the narrator is not simply drawing forth the scrolls from 'iust memory' but is actively engaged in the creative process of constructing the text. The narrator's use of antiquities 'which no body can know' opens the door to the suggestion that he has just 'made it all up'. The agency of any sort of imaginative or creative faculty is deliberately played-down here, as is the narrator's editorial role. The narrator seeks to compare his text with 'old records from auncient times deriud' (II.ix.57) produced through the faculty of memory, rather than drawn from Phantastes's chamber, a props cupboard for the 'books of fayned cheualrie' and romance form as a whole:

> His chamber was dispainted all with in,
> With sondry colours, in the which were writ
> Infinite shapes of thinges dispersed thin;
> Some such as in the world were neuer yit,
> Ne can deuized be of mortall wit;
> Some daily seene, and knowen by their names,
> Such as in idle fantasies doe flit:
> Infernall Hags, *Centaurs*, feendes, *Hippodames*,
> Apes, Lyons, Ægles, Owles, fooles, louers, children, Dames. (II.ix.50)

But the 'history' that the narrator sets forth *is* full of all such things: only outside the House of Alma the 'monstrous rablement' of Maleger's forces that lay in siege includes many creatures found within the list above. The stories of fairy presented in the *fabula* are seen to bear an increasing resemblance to the contents of Phantastes' chamber:

> idle thoughtes and fantasies
> Deuices, dreames, opinions vnsound,
> Shewes, visions, sooth-sayes, and prophesies;
> And all that fained is, as leasings, tales, and lies. (II.ix.51)

The feared 'painted forgery' of *The Faerie Queene* echoes the 'dispainted' obvious artifice of the chamber. The second proem records the narrator's struggle to source himself in the chamber of 'iust memory' rather than that of Phantastes.

Although any form of gloss or scholia is absent from *The Faerie Queene* the presence of the self-concious narrator responding to his text provides a kind of internal commentary, a reading that is always already present for the reader. Whilst the narrator in the second proem adopts the pose that we ought not to question the veracity of what he presents, he actually draws attention to the interpretative challenge that fairy stories raise. The employment of fairy in the text is viewed as a potentially alienating device that makes the reader look at the text in a different way. Spenser realizes that the presence of elements of fairy will affect the way in which a reader engages with the text through breaking up the mimetic surface of the text, and he draws attention to such a breakage here. Our 'guide' to reading fairy provides a similar function to E.K.'s glosses to *The Shepheardes Calender*. As George Puttenham asserted, the self-evident artifice of pastoral - the presentation of philosophical, literary, and political discussion through the mouths of shepherds - made it the most appropriate vehicle for publicly 'speaking the other'.

> The Poet devised the *Eglogue*... not of purpose to counterfait or represent the rusticall manner of loues and communication: but vnder the vaile of homely persons, and in rude speeches to insinuate and glaunce at greater matters, and such as perchance had not bene safe to have beene disclosed in any other sort.[24]

It is an accepted truism of scholarship on pastoral that the inherently un-mimetic nature of the form provided a self-conscious means of saying 'other things'. E.K. is deliberately coy regarding the 'generall dryft and purpose of the Æglogues', the author having laboured to conceal his meaning, but the clear intention to draw attention to the presence of 'secret meaning' in *The Shepheardes Calender* is signalled by E.K.'s glosses and his thematic subdivision of the eclogues in the 'generall argument' (*Shorter Poems*, pp. 32-4). E.K. does not explicitly spell out how to read the text, his glosses are often more suggestive than explicatory. But E.K. plays a vital role in drawing attention to the reader's point of engagement with the text, forcing the reader to consider both the status of what they are reading and the manner in which their reading takes place. As with E.K.'s glosses, a literal reading of Spenser's epic is put into question in order to lead the reader to consider the possibility that fairy is being used to convey 'secret meaning'. The commendatory verse by R. S. explicitly makes this comparison, with the concluding couplet describing how Spenser 'hath taught hye drifts in shepeherdes weedes', and now performs a similar process of veiling and speaking: 'And deepe conceites now singes in *Faeries* deedes'. Spenser's direct reference to his presentation of fairies and fairyland consciously stresses the inherently un-mimetic nature of his surface narrative. The use of beast fable in the 'Maye' eclogue, *Virgils Gnat*, *Mother Hubberds Tale*, and *Muiopotmos* further illustrates a continued preference throughout Spenser's career for forms that deliberately signal their capacity for conveying 'secret meaning'.

The second proem has the effect, therefore, of compromising a straightforward, unproblematic reading of fairy. Instead, the narrator consciously and consistently leads the reader to question the text, drawing attention to the fact that fairy serves as a veil, a means of concealing further layers of meaning, and that fairy may be reduced to the level of a sign that is used to 'speak the other'. If we continue to follow Spenser's argument, the hypothetical character doubting the validity of the text because of not knowing of the location of fairyland - and thus calling into doubt the authority upon which *The Faerie Queene* is ostensibly based - is advised to consider the value of exploring the possibilities offered by similar places and experiences that are not readily accessible or visible. The occurrence of fairy in the text is to be used as a stimulus for contemplating otherness and difference. Spenser sets out how this process of contemplation can function. The imagined reader is

---

[24] George Puttenham, *The Arte of English Poesie*, ed. Gladys Doidge Willcock and Alice Walker (Cambridge: Cambridge University Press, 1936; repr. 1970), pp. 38-9.

called to 'with better sence aduize,/ That of the world least part to vs is red'. 'With better sence aduize' can be read as an admonition simply to take a more sensible perspective, but also, when read literally, calls for the application of a 'better' or enhanced faculty of vision ('aduize'): a better way of reading, or to look at things in a different way. The criticism that no one breathing 'liuing aire' knows the location of fairyland is relativized by the observation that there are many parts of the world of which we have no knowledge. Such locations had great creative potential, as Tasso noted:

> among distant peoples and in unknown countries we can easily feign many things without taking away the authority from the story. Therefore from the land of the Goths and from Norway and Sweden and Iceland or from the East Indies or the countries recently discovered in the vast ocean beyond the pillars of Hercules, the subjects of such poems should be taken.[25]

But like Sir Thomas More in *Utopia*, Spenser identifies the boundaries of the 'known world' and then contemplates the existence of locations beyond these limits. The 'who knows not?' formula used in reference to Colin Clout and Arlo Hill is inverted to establish a common perspective, a common cognitive boundary in order to effectively pose the question 'who knew about "Indian *Peru*", "the *Amazons* huge riuer", "fruitfullest *Virginia*", that were previously unheard of but which are now discovered?' Attention is drawn to the horizon of knowledge relative to the reader, and of the possibilities for a world existing outside the bounds of knowledge, illustrated here by the difference between the verbs 'to be' and 'to know': 'Yet all these were, when no man did them know'. The unknown is always a subjective ascription based upon the perspective of the viewing subject. The logic of the argument here is taken up again in the proem to book four, as the narrator attempts to curtail further criticism of his having written praising love (and 'magnifying louers deare debate'), by effectively maintaining that one cannot deny the existence of something purely on the basis of having not experienced it oneself. Spenser can only speak to those who already know and practice love.[26]

The process of 'discovering' or more rightly, uncovering and revealing, is ongoing: 'And daily how through hardy enterprize,/ Many great Regions are discouered,/ Which to late age were neuer mentioned' (II.proem.2). This is not the degenerative view of time found in the *Complaints* and elsewhere in *The Faerie Queene*. There is a sense of temporal advancement and potentiality here echoed in 'fruitfullest *Virginia*' and compounded by the prophetic promise that 'later times thinges more vnknowne shall show'. The revelation of previously hidden worlds is put forward in Spenser's view as being determined by the nature of the reader, and the way in which they read. Just as the undiscovered 'great Regions' are revealed

---

[25] Torquato Tasso, *Discourses on the Heroic Poem*, tr. Mariella Cavalchini and Irene Samuel (Oxford: Clarendon Press, 1973), p. 50.
[26] A. Leigh DeNeef, *Spenser and the Motives of Metaphor* (Durham, NC: Duke University Press, 1982), p. 118.

through 'hardy enterprize', so the revelation of subsequent new worlds requires a similar proactive effort on the part of the imagined reader. The same referent of 'Indian *Peru*' is used to denote the distance of Britain and fairyland at the point of Britomart's initial vision of Artegall in III.iii.6, and she too vows to reach him though it entails 'infinite endeavour'. This effort, Spenser's argument continues, requires that we realign our valorization of purely sensory phenomena that wrongly maintains that nothing exists except that which is seen: 'Why then should witlesse man so much misweene/ That nothing is, but that which he hath seene?' (II.proem.3). Spenser maintains that should the imagined reader hear report of other worlds in the Moon or other stars 'He wonder would much more'.

As II.proem.3 closes, Spenser continues to instruct how to read fairy in *The Faerie Queene* beginning with an enigmatic statement that access to the kind of hidden worlds mentioned in the first three stanzas *is* possible: 'Yet such to some appeare'. It is possible to reach the happy land of fairy but one has to know the way, or more precisely, to know the way to read fairy correctly.

> Of faery lond yet if he more inquyre,
> By certein signes here sett in sondrie place
> He may it fynd; ne let him then admyre,
> But yield his sence to bee too blunt and bace,
> That no'te without an hound fine footing trace. (II.proem.4.1-5)

Fairyland is to be apprehended through means of reading and decoding 'certein signes' (or 'deepe conceites') in the text. It is through abjuring a limited 'blunt and bace' reading that fairyland can be found. The image of searching with a hound compounds the idea that the reading process is a 'hardy enterprize' to which to apply oneself. Fairy is thus to be used as a means of stimulating a new way of looking by means of the process of signification that the narrator sets out.[27] Indeed, there is encouragement to use fairy as a trigger for speculative enquiry and contemplation, as the basis for wonder and *admiratio*.[28] It has often been noted that the second proem draws upon similar sentiments expressed at the beginning of canto seven of *Orlando Furioso* regarding the location of Alcina's isle:

---

[27] Michael Murrin, 'The Rhetoric of Fairyland', in Thomas O. Sloan and Raymond B. Waddington, eds, *The Rhetoric of Renaissance Poetry: From Wyatt to Milton* (Berkeley: University of California Press, 1974), pp. 73-95, argues that Spenser's entreaty here to seek out fairyland for ourselves functions as part of a complex strategy forcing the reader to reconsider their relationship to the poem. Speculation over the nature of fairyland is a means of modelling the disparity between the eternal world and the temporal world.

[28] On the use of the marvellous to stimulate critical enquiry in this period, see T. G. Bishop, *Shakespeare and the Theatre of Wonder* (Cambridge: Cambridge University Press, 1996), pp. 17-41; Peter G. Platt, *Reason Diminished: Shakespeare and the Marvelous* (Lincoln: University of Nebraska Press, 1997), pp. 1-18. Platt briefly discusses the second proem but does not refer to the element of fairy specifically (pp. 68-9).

He who travels far afield beholds things which lie beyond the bounds of belief; and when he returns to tell of them, he is not believed, but is dismissed as a liar, for the ignorant throng will refuse to accept his word, but needs must see with their own eyes, touch with their own hands. This being so, I realise that my words will gain scant credence where they outstrip the experience of my hearers.[29]

Both Spenser's and Ariosto's texts have echoes of Plato's myth of the cave and the general dismissal that Socrates says that one would face should a person return to the cave after having been released and had experience of the reality outside.[30] Plato's myth, together with its numerous echoes in medieval and early modern mirror lore, had a particular fascination for sixteenth-century writers, and provided an enduring model for the interrogative potential of constructing refracted representations of reality ('second worlds' or 'heterocosmic spaces'), such as those found in the *Praise of Folly* or *Utopia*.[31] Allegorization of the fantastic - reading fairies and the like as signs for other things - played a central role in affirming the legitimacy and authority of the romance form in the ongoing debate on genre in the sixteenth century. There is a precedent in medieval and early modern theories concerning the 'monstrous' that the representation of creatures such as fairies could function as a sign, a means of showing (from Latin *monstrare* - 'to show') the extent of God's powers.[32] Witness Sir John Harington's rationalization of the fantastic in his 1591 translation of *Orlando Furioso*, and the elaborate interpretative apparatus set out in order that the readers might discriminate between the marvellous and the miraculous.[33] Tasso in his *Discourses on the Heroic Poem* wrote that 'The poet ought to attribute actions that far exceed human power to God, to his angels, to demons, or to those granted power by God or by demons, for example, saints, wizards, and fairies.'[34] This is certainly the reading of fairy found in *Huon* and *Melusine*, though there is not the same explicit stimulus or encouragement to deconstruct that we find in *The Faerie Queene*. Throughout the second proem Spenser pays particular attention to the potential for gaining an

---

[29] Ariosto, *Orlando Furioso*, tr. Waldman, 7.1.

[30] Plato, *Republic*, tr. F. M. Cornford. (New York: Oxford University Press, 1945), pp. 230-31.

[31] Dominic Baker-Smith, 'Uses of Plato by Erasmus and More', in Anna Baldwin and Sarah Hutton, eds, *Platonism and the English Imagination* (Cambridge: Cambridge University Press, 1994), pp. 86-99. See also Lily B. Campbell, *Shakespeare's History Plays: Mirrors of Elizabethan Policy* (San Marino: University of California Press, 1947), pp. 106-16.

[32] On the symbolic function of the monstrous, see Claude Kappler, *Monstres, Démons et Merveilles à la fin du Moyen Age* (Paris: Payot, 1980), chapter seven; John Block Friedman, *The Monstrous Races in Medieval Art and Thought* (Cambridge, MA: Harvard University Press, 1981); David Williams, *Deformed Discourse: The Function of the Monster in Medieval Thought and Literature* (Exeter: Exeter University Press, 1996).

[33] Ludovico Ariosto, *Ludovico Ariosto's Orlando Furioso*, tr. Sir John Harington (1591), ed. Robert McNulty (Oxford: Clarendon Press, 1972), pp. 16-17. Judith Lee, 'The English Ariosto: The Elizabethan Poet and the Marvelous', *SP* 80 (1983), p. 298, notes that Harington dismisses fairies as being 'meerely fabulous'.

[34] Tasso, *Discourses*, p. 38.

alienated, though enlightening perspective through a 'correct' reading of his text. We are told to read more into fairy and not to make do with the seemingly idle surface phenomena of the text, to critically engage and question what is read.

For the first five lines of II.proem.4 the narrator urges his hypothetical male reader to read allegorically, to find additional 'meanings' within the text; fairy is to be read *through* as a sign. But there is little or no indication here of exactly how individual fairy characters in the poem are to be interpreted within the context of Spenser's overall allegory. Spenser encourages us to pay close attention to how his fairies function as signs within the allegorical system of the text, though he is far less explicit on the issue of exactly what they must signify. Attention is drawn instead to the imagined reception of fairy within *The Faerie Queene* and the effect that this has upon the relationship between reader and text. There is a marked shift in the sixth line as the narrator again directly addresses the queen. Having made an obvious point of stressing that his story of fairy is not merely an idle tale, and introduced us to the potential doubleness of the image of fairy as it is employed at the text's literal level, Spenser's narrator proceeds to direct the interpretation of fairy in the poem. In the remainder of stanza four the queen is urged to read through fairy in order to identify veiled allusions to herself and her realm, though always with the feeling that this identification is somehow partial or contingent, as suggested by the subjunctive 'maist' in line seven.

> And thou, O fayrest Princesse vnder sky,
> In this fayre mirrhour maist behold thy face,
> And thine owne realmes in lond of Faery,
> And in this antique ymage thy great auncestry. (II.proem.4.6-9)

Hamilton in his gloss to this stanza draws parallels between episodes in book two and particular historical identifications: Belphoebe is the 'fayre mirrhour' for the 'fayrest Princesse'; the 'history' of England ('thine own realmes') is found in '*Briton moniments*' (II.x); and 'this antique ymage', rather awkwardly, is said to represent '*Antiquitee* of *Faery* lond' (II.proem.6-9n). But these three lines point towards a more unified model of identification and present the whole of *The Faerie Queene* as the 'mirrhour', offering a means of looking at things in a different way. Spenser uses the same basic formula in three different ways here, with only slight syntactic variation, urging the queen to look '*in* this fayre mirrhour', to find her own realm '*in* lond of Faery', and to see '*in* this antique ymage [her] great auncestry' (emphasis mine). The narrator makes sense of fairy by explaining its use as a means of representing Elizabeth and her England. The role of fairy in the mythologization of the queen is made explicit. The final stanza of the proem constitutes a direct apology for Spenser's encouragement of such a reading practice through his 'enfolding' and 'wrapping' Elizabeth's glory in 'shadowes light'. The seeming oxymoron of 'shadowes light' here perhaps echoes the association of fairy with triviality or matters of 'light' importance.

A subtle, but important distinction can be made between the rhetorical effect produced by the presence of fairy in the text, and the definitive meaning that fairy is supposed to have. Both of these aspects are encountered in the II.proem.4: the first by the suggestion in the first five lines that fairy may be read allegorically as a sign, the second (in lines six to nine) by the attempt to control the way in which that sign is interpreted. Criticism of Spenser's fairy has traditionally leapt straight in and sought to confront the question of what fairy *means* in the text. Such an approach quickly discards the aspect of fairy in the text as a mere 'veil' or integument; for fairyland read the New World or Ireland, for example. The crucial first stage of reading fairy, and the reading strategy presented in the second proem, considers the *effect* that it has upon our reading of the text. The first question to ask here should address what the text is doing rather than what it means. As Theresa Kelley remarks, the word 'veil' is deeply unsatisfactory in describing the process of reading allegory, but rather 'allegorical texts and commentaries are oddly porous linguistic skins, figurally bound to each other and, by such means, doubly bound to their absent referents'.[35] The play of signification between sign and signified that allegory stimulates requires both constituent elements. The most sensitive treatments of how Spenser's allegory works in *The Faerie Queene* are those that refuse to simply dismiss fairy as an allegorical veil, and consider sign and signified as equal components that initiate and perpetuate an ongoing loop of interpretative play between reader and text. Such an approach is proposed by Gordon Teskey as he argues that Spenser's self-conscious identification of *The Faerie Queene* as a 'continued Allegory' in the 'Letter to Raleigh' should not be taken as an objective description of the poem, but rather as an indication of how the poet would like us to respond.[36] Spenser initiates a 'game' of interpretative play between reader and text by sensitizing the reader to the gap between sign and signified, but never establishes a global structure of meaning in advance with which to valorize every interpretation.[37]

The second proem initiates a similar form of interpretative play by using the imagined reading of the poem to draw attention to how Spenser uses fairy as an allegory. Whilst the narrator in II.proem.4 suggests how fairyland may be located outside of the 'famous antique history' by reading the 'signes' within the text, what we are actually offered is most ambiguous and defers signification onto other things: 'mirrors' and 'images', surfaces requiring further explication and interpretation. Even if we argue that 'this fayre mirrhour' and 'this antique ymage' do indeed refer to *The Faerie Queene* itself then the emphasis is upon what the poem and poet are doing rather than on exactly how the queen is to locate herself and realm within the text. The second proem adds little information to that presented in the 'Letter to Raleigh' or Hobynoll's commendatory poem, and reads simply as a restatement of the overall mythopœic framework that Spenser employs

---

[35] Theresa M. Kelley, *Reinventing Allegory* (Cambridge: Cambridge University Press, 1997), p. 26.

[36] Gordon Teskey, 'allegory', in *Spenser Encyclopedia*, pp. 16-17. Quilligan, *Milton's Spenser*, p. 30, similarly argues that allegory plays a crucial part in the complicated rhetorical procedure for engaging the reader in the production of the text.

[37] Teskey, 'allegory', pp. 17-18.

in his poem. Whilst not a key to unlocking each individual instance of fairy in the poem, the second proem does offer guidance for what to do when reading fairy in the poem as it suggests that the implied reader might make sense of Spenser's use of fairy by referring back to the seminal identification of Elizabeth with the fairy queen. We are thus led back to the central preoccupation of the framing narrative: the issue of how Spenser, via the narrator, constructs and presents the poem. The focus once more is upon Spenser's ongoing myth-making project, as the proem reiterates that it is through the fairy story that the narrator professedly labours to set forth that the queen and her realm are represented. In each of the main fairy episodes discussed below attention is similarly drawn back to this overall story and to how Spenser uses fairy in the allegory.

There is a persistent critical tendency to view the narrator figure and the overall performative dimension of *The Faerie Queene* as marginal to the poem as a whole, oftentimes by incorporating the narrator's voice into a general conception of what Spenser is 'saying' without first considering the consistent distinction and management of voices in the text. As such the constituent importance of fairy is often downplayed. But *The Faerie Queene* possesses a narrative structure that, in the words of Seymour Chatman, 'communicates meaning in its own right, over and above the paraphrasable contents of the story'.[38] Identification of the subtle presence of fairy within the framing narrative leads us to reconsider the relative importance that fairy has within the poem as a whole. We cannot ignore the fundamental conceit around which *The Faerie Queene* is structured: *not* simply that of Arthur's search for the fairy queen, but rather the narrator's setting forth of a story about that search. The first fairy story that we encounter in *The Faerie Queene* is all about the process of representing the queen and her kingdom using fairy mythology, and of constructing the seminal identification between Elizabeth and Gloriana. The narrator figure is obviously a powerful means by which Spenser can foreground the vital role that he as poet plays in the mythologization of Elizabeth. It was shown above how Spenser's narrator consistently asserts that it is only through his powers of retrieval and representation that we are permitted access to the 'famous antique history' that forms the medium of his representation and celebration of Elizabeth. Spenser authorizes his own function and that of the mythographer as a whole (official or otherwise) through constructing Elizabeth as a fiction, an object of discourse, a story to be told, and then deliberately vaunting and asserting his own unique power and ability to tell or not to tell that story.[39] In the proem to book two, for example, the narrator's appeal to antiquities 'which no body

---

[38] Quoted in Clare Regan Kinney, *Strategies of Poetic Narrative: Chaucer, Spenser, Milton, Eliot* (Cambridge: Cambridge University Press, 1992), p. 3.

[39] Richard Rambuss, *Spenser's Secret Career* (Cambridge: Cambridge University Press, 1993), p. 76, asserts that the narrator's claim that he maintains sole access to, and control of, the story of Tanaquill and the Briton prince is an advertisement of Spenser's own abilities as a secretary, a keeper of secrets.

can know' advertises that his over-arching fairy story is a secret that only he can reveal.

I will now continue to discuss the employment of fairy mythology in Spenser's panegyric project in relation to the conterminous fashioning processes that take place within that project, and to relate the way in which fairy is used in *The Faerie Queene* to Spenser's continuing preoccupation with his own authorial identity. In particular it will be shown that in each of the three main fairy episodes of *The Faerie Queene* discussed in the next three chapters, the artificiality of Spenser's fairies is consciously redoubled by an added layer of narratorial self-consciousness. Each of the episodes deals with a story of fairy that is narrated or read by characters within the *fabula* of *The Faerie Queene*: the revelation that Redcrosse is a human and not a fairy is narrated to him by the figure of Contemplation; Arthur's whole encounter with Gloriana is narrated from the doubt-ridden perspective of the Briton prince; and the fairy chronicle '*Antiquitee* of *Faery* lond' is already located within a text that Guyon is shown to be reading in II.x. In each of these stories and in different ways, Spenser deconstructs his fairies, or invites the deconstruction of his fairies, in order both to foreground the rhetorical function that they have within the poem, and to draw attention to his ongoing myth-making project and the constitutive role that he plays therein.

Chapter 4

Setting Forth Fairyland and Fairy Knights

As is repeatedly stressed at the poem's performative level, the seminal story of Arthur's search for Gloriana is used as a means of celebrating Elizabeth both through the provision of a mythical ancestry for the queen (as had Virgil for Augustus, and Boiardo and Ariosto for the Estense), and by identifying her with the mythological figure of the fairy queen. Before examining in more detail how Spenser 'conceives' the queen as Gloriana and represents her 'great auncestry' in the chronicles of fairyland, we must consider how the focal identification of Elizabeth with the fairy queen provides the imaginative basis for the use of fairy throughout Spenser's poem and is the governing image that frames all of the subsequent stories of fairy in *The Faerie Queene*. This identification plays a vital role in determining the way in which both fairyland and its fairy knights are presented in the poem.

Setting Forth the 'happy land of Faery'

Firstly, it is important to locate fairyland within the *fabula* of *The Faerie Queene*. The narrator plays out fairyland to the reader as the poem progresses and in doing so draws attention to the inherently textual ontology of fairyland. This has a great effect upon the way in which fairyland is presented in the poem. Fairyland resembles the indeterminate landscapes of medieval romance far more than it does the specifically localized worlds of Ariosto and Tasso.[1] Earlier generations of commentators were particularly intrigued by the incoherent topography of Spenser's fairyland. Thomas Warton had written of how the reader is transported by Spenser's artistry into 'some. fairy region' that is highly pleasing to the imagination, and that Spenser's fairyland is a fictional world created to engage the imagination.[2] In the notes for his lectures of 1818, Samuel Taylor Coleridge, looking at *The Faerie Queene* I.vii.31-2, famously writes that Spenser's descriptions are in fact not, in the truest sense, picturesque, but might be compared to dreams:

---

[1] Murrin, 'Rhetoric', p. 87.
[2] Thomas Warton, *Observations on the Fairy Queen of Spenser* (1762), Facsimile ed., 2 vols. (New York: Haskell, 1969), 1: 197.

You will take especial note of the marvellous independence and true imaginative absence of all particular space or time in *The Faerie Queene*. It is in the domains neither of history or geography; it is ignorant of all artificial boundary, all material obstacles; it is truly in land of Fairy, that is, of mental space. The poet has placed you in a dream, a charmed sleep, and you neither wish, nor have the power, to inquire where you are, or how you got there.[3]

Coleridge's influential comments on the topography of the poem suggest that fairyland is a totally fictional realm where the absence of time and space display the dominance of the poet's imagination. As David Norbrook observes, Spenser's fairyland is a far 'cloudier' realm than the precisely imagined political landscape of Sidney's *Arcadia*.[4] The reason for this is that, unlike Sidney's Arcadia to which the reader is granted immediate and uncompromised access from the outset, we are permitted a negotiated access to fairyland through the medium of the narrator's reading and composition process that is similar to the manner in which More's island of Utopia is revealed to us through Raphael Hythlodaeus. Spenser himself, via the narrator, tells us specifically that fairyland is 'vaunted' - proclaimed, extolled, perhaps even boasted of - yet is nowhere explicitly 'shown' or located (II.proem.1).

Very few real insights may be gained into the nature of the landscape or geography of fairyland as a whole, the emphasis being far more on the allegorical and functional nature of individual locations and scenes as the characters move between them. Any form of description of Spenser's fairyland only takes place when characters encounter specific locations, and is frequently based on consciously literary topoi such as the romance forest, the underworld, or the *locus amoenus*. Our only description of the fairy capital Cleopolis (aside from brief reference to civic works in '*Antiquitee* of *Faery* lond' (II.x.72-3)) provided by Redcrosse in I.x.58, forms an immediately negated temporal analogy to the New Jerusalem and the visionary tradition from which this image is derived. Equally, the proem to book two shows no interest in the physical details of the 'happy land of Faery'. Spenser's fairyland has a fantastic, animate quality about it that one might intuitively call 'magical', as is seen for example in the Fradubio episode, itself a literary topos found in Virgil, Dante, and Ariosto. But the closest that Spenser ever really gets to the descriptions of the fairy world found in medieval romance is in the Bower of Bliss, where negative connotations of luxuriance, idleness, and

---

[3] Quoted in Alpers, ed., *Edmund Spenser*, p. 144. With the resurgence of 'neo-romantic' criticism on Spenser in the 1960s and 70s, and a fascination with the visual and imaginative texture of the poem, several critics posited theories suggesting that *The Faerie Queene* is constructed as an imaginative world into which one may enter, or that the poem somehow mirrors the imagination itself: Graham Hough, *A Preface to The Faerie Queene* (New York: Norton, 1962), pp. 95-9; Kathleen Williams, *Spenser's Faerie Queene: The World of Glass* (London: Routledge, 1966), p. xviii; Isabel MacCaffrey, *Spenser's Allegory: The Anatomy of Imagination* (Princeton: Princeton University Press, 1976), p. 70.
[4] David Norbrook, *Poetry and Politics in the English Renaissance*, rev. ed. (Oxford: Oxford University Press, 2002), p. 97.

emasculation (such as are often suggested by captivity in the fairy world) elide into the presentation of the 'wicked Fay' Acrasia herself.[5]

Spenser evinces little concern to construct fairyland as the kind of coherent, autonomously operating world that has long been proposed by many critics. Attempts to 'map' fairyland merely hearken back to a perennial feature of Spenser criticism: the quest to find some kind of unity in *The Faerie Queene*, to contain its potential endlessness and assert a framework of unity through the provision of an external structure.[6] As a consequence, the project of finding, fixing, and mapping fairyland has, in many ways, become representative of critical approaches taken to Spenser's fairy as a whole. Wayne Erickson has focused upon distinguishing exactly between what lies 'inside' and 'outside' of fairyland using generic distinctions:

> The distinction Spenser draws between Faeryland and places outside of it - that is, between the respective subject matters and modes of representation characteristic of these locales - is roughly analogous to the Renaissance distinction between, respectively, romance and epic or, alternatively, between romance epic and heroic epic.[7]

In doing so, Spenser attempts to legitimize his use of romance through framing fairyland with the heroic epic form. Erickson's attempts to define fairyland are contingent upon the ability to draw precise lines identifying and distinguishing the discrete characteristic features of each generic mode, though the lines of delineation that he constructs persistently fail to capture and contain all and only the features of each mode.[8] The attempt to identify fairyland is displaced onto the wider difficulty of establishing precise generic definitions for the romance form. It can be seen, nevertheless, that both fairyland and the 'extramural' geography of *The Faerie Queene* are encompassed within the *fabula* that is played out to Spenser's imagined reader. What we encounter in reading *The Faerie Queene* is a far more 'writerly' conception of narrative space. Fairyland is by no means a fixed and stable setting for the actions of the poem. It is not simply to be 'consumed' by the reader and critic, rather, the reader participates in an ongoing process of having

---

[5] Paton, *Fairy Mythology*, p. 40n2, notes the difference between the terrain of struggle that forms Spenser's fairyland as a whole and the sensuous delights of the fairy world of earlier Arthurian romance. See also Howard Rollin Patch, *The Other World: According to Descriptions in Medieval Literature* (New York: Octagon, 1970), pp. 230-319. On emasculation and fairy captivity, see Larrington, 'Fairy Mistress', p. 42.

[6] Terence Clifford-Amos, '"Certaine Signes" of "Faeryland": Spenser's Eden of Thanksgiving on the Defeat of the "Monstrous" "Dragon" of Albion's North', *Viator* 32 (2001), p. 373, for example, argues that 'structure and processes of text in the poem is determined by geographic influences', believing that the landscape and spatial relationships in fairyland are directly based upon the actual geography of Spenser's England.

[7] Wayne Erickson, *Mapping the Faerie Queene: Quest Structures and the World of the Poem* (New York: Garland, 1996), p. 4.

[8] Erickson, *Mapping*, pp. 51-2n6.

fairyland produced as the text progresses. We can only consider fairyland as it is played out to us in the poem, rather than attempting to reify the metaphor of a narrative space with its own internal logic, or a world that exists when we close the book in which the perceived spatial relationships between locations in fairyland are recorded and reproduced within a framework external to the narrative of *The Faerie Queene* itself.[9]

The framing narrative of *The Faerie Queene* can be directly related to the structure of presentation employed in representational strategies engaged in the mythologization of Elizabeth and further demonstrates the extent of Spenser's debt to Elizabethan pageants, masques, and entertainments. Spenser's first fairy story - the scenario of the narrator presenting his text to the queen - operates in the manner of a pageant or masque. The narrator acts as the presenter or expositor of the *fabula* in *The Faerie Queene*, playing out individual episodes of the poem to the implied reader. On one occasion Guyon's quest is referred to as a 'pageant' (II.i.33) and several scenes in *The Faerie Queene* function as pageants or masques: the procession of the seven deadly sins at Lucifera's court; Busirane's mask of Cupid; the wedding of the Thames and Medway; the ring-dance at Mount Acidale; Mutabilitie's pageant of Nature before Jove. But Spenser's debt to these forms embraces structure just as much as theme. Lewis writes that 'just as a pageant or a masque is not completely dramatic, so Spenser's art is not completely narrative. Instead we are meant to look and to see the shows it presents.'[10] In the same way as a pageant, the allegory of *The Faerie Queene* presents a form of symbolic play - a surface spectacle that then encourages the reader to interpret the political or moral significance beneath, or at the very least initiates the reader into a form of interpretative play. A scene is set forth for us which may then be read and interpreted, occasionally with some narratorial commentary, before we are then moved on to the next scene or location. Fairyland is played out to the reader scene by scene, as with the mythical image of Elizabeth's realm in which she encounters the Lady of the Lake at Kenilworth or the fairy queen, Eambia, at Woodstock. Knights and hermits rubbing shoulders with mythical personages, an environment confected from classical and romance mythology, accompanying direct addresses to the audience - all are very much the common stock of Elizabethan tournaments and entertainments. Seeming incongruities or inconsistencies in the topography of *The Faerie Queene* need not therefore require global explanatory structures aimed at construing the specific meaning of Spenser's fairyland. *The Faerie Queene* is

---

[9] See however Waldo F. McNeir and Foster Provost, *Edmund Spenser: An Annotated Bibliography 1937-1972* (Pittsburgh: Duquesne University Press, 1975), in which there is a (rather Tolkienesque) fold-out chart offering an attempt at mapping Spenser's fairyland.

[10] C. S. Lewis, *Spenser's Images of Life*, ed. Alastair Fowler (Cambridge: Cambridge University Press, 1967), p. 3. See also Howard Hintz, 'The Elizabethan Entertainment and *The Faerie Queene*', *PQ* 14 (1935), pp. 83-90; Enid Welsford, *The Court Masque: A Study of the Relationship Between Poetry and the Revels* (New York: Russell and Russell, 1962), pp. 303-07; A. Bartlett Giamatti, *Play of Double Senses: Spenser's Faerie Queene* (Englewood Cliffs, NJ: Prentice-Hall, 1975), pp. 78-85; Kipling, *Triumph*, pp. 152-68.

structured as a series of individual functional units. The spaces in-between - the 'spacious and wyde' ways of fairyland - are little more than an elliptical backdrop against which the mythologization of Elizabeth takes place. The individual units do not appear in clear spatial and temporal relationship to each other, their distribution being more rhetorical than spatial.[11] The fact that *The Faerie Queene* is a 'continued Allegory' necessarily dictates, after all, that individual locations in each book are used to dramatize a segmented aspect of the central character's virtue, thus subordinating the presentation of any form of landscape and topography within the poem to a purely functional role. As Michael Murrin writes 'No one seriously wonders what road Arthur took from Orgoglio's Castle to the area by Mammon's vale or what happened at Medina's after Guyon left.'[12]

Deconstructing the Fairy Race

Just as there have been many attempts both to construct a consistent conception of the meaning of fairyland in *The Faerie Queene* and to map the imagined geography of the poem, so critics have long been concerned with establishing the essential meaning of those characters that Spenser identifies as fairies. Such an approach attempts to maintain that the fairy race constitutes a distinct ontological group throughout the poem. Greenlaw and Rathborne, for example, argue that Spenser's fairies represent, respectively, the Welsh nation (and specifically the Tudor dynasty), and a race of the famous dead. The creation of a separate fairy race is at the heart of the discussion initiated by A. S. P. Woodhouse concerning Spenser's distinction in *The Faerie Queene* between the human order of grace and the elfin order of nature.[13] Yet such rigid dichotomies between grace and nature are difficult to maintain, even within those books of the poem upon which this direction of analysis has commonly focused. When Guyon faints on emerging from Mammon's cave, it is an angel that protects him, and Arthur, acting under providential guidance, who leads him to recovery. Upon their first encounter Guyon refers to the

---

[11] John Bender, *Spenser and Literary Pictorialism* (Princeton: Princeton University Press, 1972), p. 136.

[12] Murrin, 'Rhetoric', pp. 86-7.

[13] The key positions are set out in A. S. P. Woodhouse, 'Nature and Grace in *The Faerie Queene*', *ELH* 16 (1949), pp. 194-228; Robert Hoopes, '"God Guide Thee, Guyon": Nature and Grace Reconciled in *The Faerie Queene*, Book II', *RES* n. s. 5 (1954), pp. 14-24; Woodhouse, 'Nature and Grace in Spenser: A Rejoinder', *RES* n. s. 6 (1955), pp. 284-8. The speculative potential of such a distinction is taken up in Harry Berger, Jr., *The Allegorical Temper: Vision and Reality in Book II of Spenser's Faerie Queene* (New Haven: Yale University Press, 1957), pp. 104-14. Along similar lines, Carol V. Kaske realigns the distinction between humans and elves so as to represent the difference between Christian and classical conceptions of ethics, see 'Spenser's Pluralistic Universe: The View from the Mount of Contemplation (*The Faerie Queene* I.x.)', in Richard C. Frushell and Bernard J. Vondersmith, eds, *Contemporary Thought on Edmund Spenser* (Carbondale, IL: South Illinois University Press, 1975), pp.'127-30.

cross on Redcrosse's shield as the 'sacred badge of my Redeemer's death' (II.i.27), thus including fairies within a Christian soteriological framework.[14]

Spenser shows no concern with establishing the fairies of *The Faerie Queene* as a distinct and rigidly defined ontological category, and global schemes of explanation persistently fail to adequately record and explicate what actually takes place as regards the presentation of individual fairy characters in the text. There is no description of any physical or essential qualities that mark out a fairy from a human. Any physical detail of Guyon, for example, the first 'real' fairy knight that we encounter in the poem, is obscured by the armour that covers him from head to foot (II.i.5.9). With the possible exception of Duessa and Acrasia's powers of enchantment and the nebulous magic 'arts' practised by Elfinor and Agape (II.x.73; IV.ii.44), Spenser's fairy characters do not possess supernatural or magical powers that might distinguish them from humans. Furthermore, as Rathborne notes, the principal magic weapons - Arthur's shield, Britomart's spear, and Artegall's sword Chrysaor - belong to the Britons.[15] Such arms clearly stand out in fairyland as being 'straunge' and 'forraine' (III.iv.51; IV.vi.9). Equally, no consistent distinction is made in the poem between the terms 'fairy' and 'elf', and attempts to suggest a consistent method of distinction have proved difficult to support from the text.[16] The closest that we get to an exception to this is where 'fay' and 'elf' denote, respectively, the female and male progenitors of the fairies in '*Antiquitee* of *Faery* lond'. Throughout the rest of the poem the primary determining factor influencing the decision to use either term may simply be metrical utility. The terms 'fairy' and 'elf' were largely synonymous by the sixteenth century and are certainly used in this way in *The Faerie Queene*.[17] Gloriana, Redcrosse, Guyon, Artegall, and Calidore are all identified using both terms (and both adjectival equivalents: 'Faery' and 'Elfin' or 'Elven'). Fairyland is referred to at one point as 'Elfin land' (III.v.4).

The initial identification made between Elizabeth and Gloriana dictates the parameters for reading the fairy characters presented within the narrator's 'famous antique history'. Spenser's statements both in the 'Letter to Raleigh' and within the poem itself regarding the central identification of Elizabeth with the fairy queen, and her realm with fairyland, determine the narrative texture of the poem. It is

---

[14] McCabe, *Pillars*, p. 94. The difficulties of the grace/ nature dichotomy are discussed further in Anthea Hume, *Edmund Spenser: Protestant Poet* (Cambridge: Cambridge University Press, 1984), pp. 59-71; Darryl Gless, 'nature and grace', in *Spenser Encyclopedia*, pp. 506-07.

[15] Rathborne, *Meaning*, p. 173. See, however, Archimago's 'charmed launce' (I.iii.25) and Scudamore's 'enchaunted shield' (IV.x.19).

[16] For example, Sverre Arestad, 'Spenser's "Faery" and "Fairy"', *MLQ* 8 (1947), pp. 37-42, attempts to suggest that Spenser orthographically marks out his 'faeries' from any potentially negative connotations that the word 'fairies' might hold. This argument breaks down when we consider that the same faeries/ fairies are frequently also referred to in the poem using the similarly ambiguous term 'elf', and that Spenser also uses the spelling 'faerie' in the 'March', 'Maye', and 'June' eclogues of *The Shepheardes Calender*.

[17] Latham, *Elizabethan Fairies*, p. 19.

Arthur's quest for the fairy queen that provides the literal level or the vehicle for the allegory, the scheme of imagery with which the poet constructs his continued metaphor. In turn, Spenser's initial establishment of the fairy texture of the surface narrative determines that the implied location in which the quest takes place is designated as 'fairyland' and that, with the exception of those whom we are explicitly informed are not native to fairyland, the default term used to refer to characters encountered within this location will be 'fairy'. Spenser evokes the identification of Elizabeth and Gloriana through presenting a surprisingly diverse range of concepts and motifs from fairy mythology. Within the *fabula* of *The Faerie Queene* we encounter a wide range of figures and characters that are either identified as fairies and elves or otherwise connected with fairy mythology: fairy knights, the fairy queen, changelings, fays. Even the more popular or folkloric conception of fairies are found dancing at Mount Acidale (VI.x.7 and 17) and at whose appearance Hamilton exclaims excitedly that 'at last the aboriginals of the heavily colonized faery land make their debut' (VI.x.7.6n).[18] The poem also incorporates various creatures or individuals - nymphs and sprites, the Fates, and the goddess Proserpine - that have associations with or are analogous to fairies, although Spenser does not explicitly present them as such within his work. There is a reference to the Lady of the Lake in part of the description of Merlin's cave in III.iii.10, though this is taken from Spenser's source for this passage: canto three, stanza ten of *Orlando Furioso*. 'Elf' and 'fairy' also carry a number of negative associations in the text: as an infant, Redcrosse is exchanged for a fairy's 'base Elfin brood' (I.x.65) and Artegall is similarly stolen away by 'false *Faries*' (III.iii.26). 'Elf' in particular is used on a number of occasions to refer to various forms of malignant or wicked beings: Saturn (III.xi.45), Cupid (III.xii.22), Care (IV.v.34), Grantorto (V.viii.19), and perhaps also Pœna's dwarf (IV.viii.61).

The inchoate nature of the poem as a whole inevitably frustrates attempts to draw hard and fast rules and conclusions regarding Spenser's ultimate intentions for individual fairy characters. In III.vi.4 we learn of Belphoebe's ancestry: 'Her mother was the faire *Chrysogonee*,/ The daughter of *Amphisa*, who by race/ A Faerie was'. Nothing more is made of Belphoebe's fairy lineage here, but would this play a part at a later point in the poem? Does this predicate that Elizabeth would be celebrated using fairy queens more than one? How many other fairy champions in the unwritten books of *The Faerie Queene* might have turned out to be changelings? What of all those other indeterminate characters such as Cambell and Triamond, Florimell, and Sir Sergis (V.xi.37) that are stated as being simply 'of' fairyland or 'from' the fairy court? Such lines of questioning are, perforce, inconclusive. As with corresponding approaches adopted in studying fairyland, the temptation is to take those episodes of the poem where the focus is upon individuals identified as fairies and then fill in the gaps to construct a unitary conception of what Spenser's fairies 'are' and, as a contrived racial group,

---

[18] See also Humphrey Tonkin, *Spenser's Courteous Pastoral: Book Six of the 'Faerie Queene'* (Oxford: Oxford University Press, 1972), pp. 131-6, on the folklore background to the fairy dance at Acidale.

represent. But the explicit signals in the text that fairy is employed as part of the poem's allegory should not be forgotten. Attempts to identify a distinct fairy race risk imposing an uncharacteristic consistency upon the allegorical figures of the poem's surface narrative. The points in the text where Spenser actually draws a distinction between human and fairy are episodes that return attention back to the poem's performative level and stress how fairy functions within the allegory as a signifier or sign. This is how we are directed to read fairy in the proem to book two and in the second Spenserian fairy story that I wish to examine: the tale of Redcrosse.

The Saint who Thought he was a Fairy

Ostensibly, Redcrosse is the first fairy encountered in *The Faerie Queene*. The narrator promised to tell of fairy knights and Redcrosse appears to fulfil our expectations of what to find in a poem signalled as being a fairy romance. As we follow his adventures through book one Redcrosse is repeatedly referred to, both by the narrator and by other characters within the *fabula*, using the terms 'Faerie' and 'Elfe', and he is clearly identified as being a 'Faery' and 'Elfin' knight. Thus, for nearly the first ten cantos, book one is, by all appearances, the story of a fairy knight. The specific fairy story that I wish to concentrate on, however, takes place at the culmination of Redcrosse's spiritual healing and education at the House of Holiness. It takes the form of a story told within the narrator's overall story.

After being taught at Mercy's hospital to frame his mortal life in 'holy righteousnesse', Redcrosse is led to a steep hill, at the top of which dwells the hermit Contemplation. Redcrosse's fairy identity is alluded to at a number of points within the stanzas detailing his schooling at the House of Holiness but as soon as he encounters Contemplation the 'valiant Elfe' is subjected to a process of continued decoding as his true identity is revealed. In I.x.51-2 Contemplation hints enigmatically at what will be revealed in the remaining stanzas of the canto. He alludes to Redcrosse's saintly identity as St. George in addressing him 'man of earth', playing on the association with the Greek *georgos* ('ploughman') that is made directly in I.x.66. There is also the teasing reference to the vision of the New Jerusalem that 'neuer yet was seene of Faries sonne', but which Redcrosse is nevertheless about to attain. It is as Redcrosse gazes upon the New Jerusalem that we are afforded a brief, oblique glimpse of the fairy capital Cleopolis as it is compared deferentially to the glories of the heavenly city:

> Till now, said then the knight, I weened well,
> That great *Cleopolis*, where I haue beene,
> In which that fairest *Fary Queene* doth dwell,
> The fairest Citty was, that might be seene;
> And that bright towre all built of christall clene,
> *Panthea*, seemd the brightest thing, that was:
> But now by proofe all otherwise I weene;

> For this great Citty that does far surpas,
> And this bright Angels towre quite dims that towre of glas. (I.x.58)

Cleopolis is evoked only to be surpassed. Contemplation then makes the connection between Redcrosse and the city before them as he promises that after further pursuit of earthly conquests the knight too can seek the path to the New Jerusalem. In doing so Contemplation deconstructs Redcrosse's identity as a fairy as he addresses the knight: 'And thou faire ymp, sprong out from English race,/ How euer now accompted Elfins sonne', (I.x.60) and in the following stanza names him as '*Saint George* of mery England, the signe of victoree'. There is then a dialogue: Redcrosse professes himself not worthy of such grace. Contemplation replies that the other saints were just as wretched and 'liued in like paine'. The knight cannot believe that he must give up 'deeds of armes' and 'Ladies loue' (I.x.62), but Contemplation replies that there will be eternal peace in his final resting place, and as for loose loves, they are 'vaine, and vanish into nought'. For now, Redcrosse must nevertheless return to the world to fulfil his obligations to Una. The final component of Contemplation's revelation of Redcrosse's 'name and nation' refers back to the appellation used in the first two lines of stanza 60 as the knight enquires 'But now aread, old father, why of late/ Didst thou behight me borne of English blood,/ Whom all a Faeries sonne doen nominate?' (I.x.64). Contemplation then tells a short story of fairy, or rather, a story about not being a fairy:

> For well I wote, thou springst from ancient race
> Of *Saxon* kings, that haue with mightie hand
> And many bloody battailes fought in place
> High reard their royall throne in *Britans* land,
> And vanquisht them, vnable to withstand:
> From thence a Faery thee vnweeting reft,
> There as thou slepst in tender swadling band,
> And her base Elfin brood there for thee left.
> Such men do Chaungelings call, so chaungd by Faeries theft.
>
> Thence she thee brought into this Faery lond,
> And in an heaped furrow did thee hyde,
> Where thee a Ploughman all vnweeting fond,
> As he his toylesome teme that way did guyde,
> And brought thee vp in ploughmans state to byde,
> Whereof *Georgos* he thee gaue to name;
> Till prickt with courage, and thy forces pryde,
> To Fary court thou cam'st to seeke for fame,
> And proue thy puissaunt armes, as seemes thee best became. (I.x.65-6)

The vision of apocalypse - of the revelation of things hidden - to which Redcrosse is granted access is aligned with the changeling motif from fairy mythology. We know from the 'Letter to Raleigh' what took place when Redcrosse came to the fairy court. Spenser also combines the changeling motif with that of the 'fair unknown' found in medieval romance. Fairy is used to explain the background of the 'clownishe younge man' who presents himself before Gloriana at her feast, and his means of conveyance into fairyland. Spenser offers a unique perspective on the changeling story as he focuses on the human child stolen by fairies rather than on the 'base Elfin brood' that are the traditional subject of such stories. Several critics have attempted to further suggest how Spenser uses the changeling motif to distinguish his 'Saint *George* of mery England' from the more commonly known mythical history of the saint's legend and to purge the legend of all the Catholic associations that it naturally carried.[19] More consistent with Spenser's overall use of fairy is the way in which the changeling story momentarily directs our gaze out of fairyland and towards the sixteenth-century temporal context - the world of the poet and the narrator - as it looks ahead to the role of Redcrosse as St. George as a 'signe of victoree' for Protestant England.[20] Hobynoll's commendatory verse printed with *The Faerie Queene* makes a similar allusion to the symbolic function of Redcrosse within Elizabeth's own realm:

> So mought thy *Redcrosse knight* with happy hand
> victorious be in that faire Ilands right:
> Which thou dost vayle in Type of Faery land
> Elyzas blessed field, that *Albion* hight. (CV3 'To the learned Shepheard')

The changeling episode has implications for the rest of the poem concerning the effect that it has upon how to read the fairy characters of *The Faerie Queene*. The particular reference in I.x.64.2 to how Redcrosse is 'named' as a fairy is significant in demonstrating how identification of his fairy identity is founded upon a linguistic, onomastic ascription. Redcrosse has been a fairy by virtue of having been named as such up until this point; he now has his original name '*Georgos*' revealed to him (I.x.66). Contemplation reveals that Redcrosse's identity as a fairy is merely a veil or screen. The fairy story of Redcrosse in book one is a means of talking about other things; he is not intended to be read literally as a fairy. This seems an obvious observation given that Spenser signals from the outset that the poem is an allegory, and the revelation to Redcrosse of his real identity is fully anticipated from the time that he first appears in the poem for he bears the arms of St. George on his shield and breastplate. But Contemplation's decoding of the elfin knight leads us to distrust a literal reading of the fairies, and draws attention to the allegorical nature of the surface narrative. Contemplation - himself an abstract figure - effectively reads through the literal level of Redcrosse. Spenser incorporates a reading and interpretation of his fairy knight within the poem itself. The changeling story is used therefore as an appropriate analogue to how Spenser's fairies function as allegorical figures within the poem and is a reminder that things

---

[19] Hume, *Edmund Spenser*, pp. 154-5; John N. King, *Spenser's Poetry and the Reformation Tradition* (Princeton: Princeton University Press, 1990), p. 190.

[20] Strong, *Cult of Elizabeth*, pp. 167-85, discusses the development of the Tudor cult of St. George and its relation to celebrations for the Order of the Garter. See also *Variorum*, pp. 1: 379-90.

are not always as they may at first seem. It reiterates the intimation in the 'Letter to Raleigh' that fairies are to be read carefully and critically in order that they may reveal further meanings located beyond the surface narrative. Whilst he does reveal Redcrosse's Saxon parentage and the later identification as St. George, Contemplation's decoding of the would-be fairy knight is by no means exhaustive or complete. Indeed we can speak with most certainty about what Redcrosse is not, i.e. a fairy. Redcrosse is revealed to be a 'signe' who is open, in turn, to many further interpretations.[21] The experience of following the adventures of the fairy knight Redcrosse for ten cantos only to have it revealed that he is human puts us on our guard concerning how to read Spenser's subsequent fairy knights. It cannot help but persuade us that all of Spenser's fairies might in some way be taken apart or explained in a similarly straightforward manner, or indeed that they might be decoded in the text itself at a later point.

Our reading of the fairies in *The Faerie Queene* is problematized further by the second changeling episode in the poem: the brief story that Merlin tells to Britomart concerning Artegall's true identity. At the beginning of his prophetic recitation of Britomart's 'fruitfull Ofspring', Merlin identifies the individual ordained by heaven to be the maiden knight's spouse. Before he ever appears in the poem it is revealed that Artegall is not what he seems:

> He wonneth in the land of *Fayeree*,
> Yet is no *Fary* borne, ne sib at all
> To Elfes, but sprong of seed terrestriall,
> And whylome by false *Faries* stolne away,
> Whyles yet in infant cradle he did crall;
> Ne other to himselfe is knowne this day,
> But that he by an Elfe was gotten of a *Fay*. (III.iii.26)

Little more is made of Artegall's background outside of Merlin's prophecy, although throughout book five he is referred to as an elf, and as a fairy and elfin knight, both in narratorial report and by other characters. Presumably at a later point in the poem Artegall, like Redcrosse, would have had his destiny and true identity revealed to him. But in the poem as we have it, the effect of having the fairy knight Artegall 'decoded' to the reader before he ever appears, and yet presented as a fairy throughout his central book, forces us once more to distrust any literal reading of Spenser's fairies. It is a reminder that fairy is a means of veiling. The story of Artegall puts us on our guard again, particularly upon beginning book six where one of the main characters, Calidore, is identified as an elfin knight.

For the purposes of the present study, the most significant observation regarding the changeling episodes is that they serve to problematize how we read the individual fairy characters in *The Faerie Queene*. The episodes predicate a far

---

[21] The process of assigning meaning to St. George was continued, with conscious allusion to Spenser, in Gerard de Malynes's 1601 *Saint George for England, allegorically described*; Cummings, *Spenser*, pp. 115-16, extracts the most relevant passages.

more writerly conception of fairy: Spenser's encouragement of interpretative play invites the reader to participate in the process of identifying and deconstructing fairies. They establish a potential interpretative framework with which the other characters in the *fabula* who are identified as fairies might be scrutinized. This is not to say that we are offered a key to unlocking the meaning of each fairy knight, but we are again shown what to do (or what *may* be done) when reading Spenser's fairies and there is implicit encouragement to decode them for ourselves. By deconstructing several of the characters that are frequently referred to as being fairy knights Spenser forces his readers to continually question what they are reading, to remain alert for suggestions that the likes of Guyon, Satyrane, Marinell, or Calidore might equally be more than they at first appear.[22] Attention is also drawn back to the poem's performative level through the way in which both Contemplation and Merlin momentarily act as surrogates for the narrator as they similarly, if only implicitly, lead us to distrust a literal reading of fairy.

The subsequent critical attempts by Greenlaw, Rathborne, and others to solve the problem of what Spenser's fairies 'are', or what they represent, are initiated by the fact that the poet is so suggestive, and yet leaves so much unsaid, concerning exactly how he intends the individual fairy characters to be read. At the very least, the reception history of Spenser's use of fairy has demonstrated some of the different ways in which one can respond to the poet's compelling general encouragement of a vigilant, active reading of *The Faerie Queene*. Such vigilance is particularly demanded by Spenser's presentation of the fairy queen herself.

---

[22] Satyrane and Marinell are identified as fairies at I.vi.47.1 and III.viii.39.9, respectively.

Chapter 5

The Fairy Queen

Just as fairyland and fairy characters function as a rhetorical device stimulating further interpretative and critical engagement with the text, so does the figure of the fairy queen herself. As we have seen, Spenser's use of fairy in *The Faerie Queene* as a whole centres upon the identification between Elizabeth and Gloriana, and it is this that provides the point of origin for all other elements of fairy in the text. But equally nowhere is the presence of fairy more a cause for interpretative difficulty than in Spenser's use of the fairy queen as his central conceit for Elizabeth. The identification made between the fairy queen and Elizabeth generates far more interpretative problems than similar allegorical identifications made for characters in *Orlando Furioso* or *Gerusalemme Liberata*. We are returned to the same kind of intuitive difficulty that Lewis expressed in a passage from *The Discarded Image* concerning the complex web of associations and connotations that fairy carries, and how

> within the same island and the same century Spenser could compliment Elizabeth I by identifying her with the Faerie Queene and a woman could be burned at Edinburgh in 1576 for 'repairing with' the fairies and the 'Queen of Elfame'.[1]

There has certainly been no shortage of critics prepared to address the difficulties implied by Lewis's observations on Spenser's use of the fairy queen. The imperative to deconstruct the fairy queen is present from the 'Letter to Raleigh' onwards and many theories have been advanced attempting to explain exactly how she 'means' glory in accordance with Spenser's 'generall intention' and to solve the problem of Gloriana's ontological status in *The Faerie Queene* as a whole. Neoplatonism has been by far the most common recourse adopted in approaching the question of Gloriana's (non)presence and informs many of the arguments put forward to explicate the meaning of the fairy queen.[2] In particular Gloriana has

---

[1] Lewis, *Discarded Image*, p. 124. The woman referred to was Bessie Dunlop; see Normand and Roberts, *Witchcraft*, pp. 79-81.

[2] C. S. Lewis, *Studies in Medieval and Renaissance Literature*, ed. Walter Hooper (Cambridge: Cambridge University Press, 1966), p. 159, compares Arthur's encounter with Gloriana to the 'soul's new-kindled raptures at its first meeting with a transcendent or at least incorporeal object of love'. Lewis identifies a Platonic basis for what Spenser's overall story 'was to have been' - a picture of the soul endlessly seeking that perfect beauty of which it has seen dim premonition but which cannot be found, only seen in shadows and blurred images in the realm of Nature (p. 144). See also Alastair Fowler, 'Emanations of

been interpreted as the representative or 'shadow' of heavenly glory as it is manifested in the form of sovereignty.[3] Such a reading is supported in the text through stories of the fairy queen told by Arthur and Guyon. The projected final union of Arthur and Gloriana would thus see the Briton prince wedded to the ideal embodiment of sovereignty. Specific details of exactly how this would take place, however, are much harder to establish and require us ultimately to complete the remaining books of *The Faerie Queene* for ourselves and second-guess Spenser's intentions concerning the relationship of Arthur and Gloriana. Such a method might attempt to establish what Gloriana means by projecting what she will become. Analysis in the present chapter, however, will remain focused on the fairy queen as she is presented within the text.

The overwhelming tendency in criticism of Spenser's fairy is to address the problem of Gloriana's insubstantial presence in the text by subjecting her to a kind of 'security clearance': an often elaborate critical attempt to construct the fairy queen as an unproblematic figure and to locate her within the imagined grand narrative of Tudor orthodoxy and celebration. This reveals as much about what we expect to encounter in *The Faerie Queene* as it does about what we actually find upon a close reading of the poem. We can indeed locate and establish an unproblematic, innocuous reading of Gloriana in Spenser's poem with relative ease if, because the fairy queen at least in part represents Elizabeth, we assume that the poet in no way intends to present an ambiguous, subversive, or negative representation of Elizabeth. But as the work of recent critics has shown, this is by no means the case. Spenser is no longer viewed exclusively as (to use Marx's indelicate term) the 'arse-kissing' poet of Tudor orthodoxy and the 'old' historicism. The present chapter is not intended as an exposure of a wholly negative, politically oppositional fairy queen, but as an examination of the ambiguity and specific hermeneutic difficulties that Spenser introduces through his decision to use the fairy queen as his central figure for Elizabeth. It will be shown below that the fairy queen resists any kind of straightforward, uncompromised interpretation, and how difficult it is to ever definitively 'find' the fairy queen in Spenser's poem. In the first chapter I called for attention to be focused upon the specifically textual ontology of fairy: how fairy is represented within texts as a narrative or rhetorical device. Likewise, I am interested here in examining what the fairy queen *does* within the text. I shall explore the ways in which she functions as a rhetorical device and focus upon the effect that she has upon the relationship between reader and text, both in the stories that comprise the *fabula* of *The Faerie*

Glory: Neoplatonic Order in Spenser's *Faerie Queen*', in J. M. Kennedy and J. A. Reither, eds, *A Theatre for Spenserians* (Manchester: Manchester University Press, 1973), pp. 53-82.
[3] Rathborne, *Meaning*, p. 225; Lewis, *Studies*, p. 145; Rosemond Tuve, *Allegorical Imagery: Some Medieval Books and Their Posterity* (Princeton: Princeton University Press, 1966), p. 347. The first associations made between Elizabeth and the embodiment of glory itself are found in a Latin poem *Regina Literata* presented to the queen in a visit to Cambridge University in August 1564; see John Erskine Hankins, *Source and Meaning in Spenser's Allegory* (Oxford: Clarendon Press, 1971), pp. 52-3.

Queene and, at the performative level of the poem, upon our own conceptions of Spenser's ongoing project of mythologizing Elizabeth.

The Ambiguity of the Fairy Queen in Spenser's Immediate Sources

The third Spenserian fairy story that I wish to consider is the seminal episode of the entire *Faerie Queene* where Arthur tells of his encounter with Gloriana, an episode that commonly attracts far less critical attention than the rest of the otherwise self-contained allegory of the Legend of Holiness in which it is located. Arthur's story of his encounter with Gloriana in I.ix.9-16 is the natural starting point for examination of the fairy queen. Spenser provides the basic details of the encounter in the 'Letter to Raleigh', explaining that he 'conceives' or imagines Arthur

> to haue seene in a dream or vision the Faery Queen, with whose excellent beauty rauished, he awaking resolued to seeke her out, and so being by Merlin armed, and by Timon throughly instructed, he went to seeke her forth in Faerye land.

The brevity of Arthur's own recitation of the incident belies the importance of this episode for the thematic and structural focus of the whole poem and mirrors the central and yet marginal presence in the text of the fairy queen herself. As we saw earlier, the story of telling the story of Arthur's search for Gloriana forms the basis of *The Faerie Queene*'s framing narrative. The questions that the episode raises concerning fairy resonate throughout *The Faerie Queene*.

The visitation of a fairy mistress to a mortal hero is a common motif in medieval romance, as was discussed in chapter two. Though Spenser could have drawn his overall conception for the encounter between Arthur and Gloriana from many different sources, his debt to Chaucer's 'Tale of Sir Thopas' for the particular details of the fairy encounter has long been recognized.[4] The questions raised by the figure of the fairy queen together with the rhetorical effect that she has in 'Sir Thopas' are just as important elements as narrative detail in terms of what Spenser takes from Chaucer. There are many parallels to be drawn between Chaucer's tale and Arthur's narrative in *The Faerie Queene*: the comparison of Sir Thopas's and Arthur's 'pricking forth' at the outset of their encounters; the characters' weariness and lying down to rest; and of course the respective visions of the fairy queen.[5] In Chaucer the fairy queen only 'appears' to Sir Thopas within an elliptical moment between two stanzas:

> Sire Thopas eek so wery was
> For prikyng on the softe gras,

---

[4] The 1590 edition of *The Faerie Queene* bears a trace of Spenser's other great debt to 'Sir Thopas' in a reference to how (in III.vii.48) the giant Ollyphant wrought 'great wreake to many errant knights of yore/ Till him Chylde *Thopas* to confusion brought'.

[5] Bennett, *Evolution*, pp. 10-14.

So fiers was his corage,
That doun he leyde him in that plas
To make his steede som solas,
And yaf hym good forage.

'O Seinte Marie, benedicite!
What eyleth this love at me
To bynde me so soore?
Me dremed al this nyght, pardee,
An elf-queene shal my lemman be
And slepe under my goore. ('Sir Thopas', VII 778-89)

As we shall see, Arthur's entertainment of the fairy queen is far more detailed than that found in 'Sir Thopas', though his response to (and reading of) the encounter is fraught with uncertainty and a measure of anxiety. Both Sir Thopas and Arthur are equally resolved to pursue the object of their dreams and initiate a search that forms the underlying matrix of their subsequent adventures. Arthur sets off to 'seeke her forth in Faerye land', and Sir Thopas equally:

Into his sadel he clamb anon,
And priketh over stile and stoon
An elf-queene for t'espye. ('Sir Thopas', VII 797-9)

Detailed study of 'Sir Thopas' reveals the many ways that Chaucer parodies the language, the conventions of description and content, the metre, and the generic expectations of the romance tradition; though, as Helen Cooper writes, whilst the potential body of romance sources for the tale is vast, we cannot pinpoint a single, discrete source or model.[6] Again it might be useful to suggest a more intertextual pattern of sourcing. In *The Canterbury Tales* as a whole, to tell a tale of fairy is to evoke a bygone age and a set of beliefs now past. By the time Chaucer assigns his 'elvyssh' persona the tale of 'Sir Thopas', fairies are seen to exist only in the narratives that are told about them. In 'The Wife of Bath's Tale' it was only in the 'olde dayes of the Kyng Arthur' that the land was 'fulfild of fayerye' (III 857-81), and in which the events of her tale can take place. The comment readily plays off a natural location of fairies and elves (without distinction) within the imaginative landscape of Arthurian romance. Those days, says the Wife, are gone: 'But now kan no man se none elves mo'. The blessings and visitations of the fairies have been displaced by the wandering friars, Chaucer making an ironic comparison between the superstitious abuses of fairy belief and the contemporary abuses of the ubiquitous friars. A similar comment upon the place of fairy within out-dated superstition is suggested in the 'Miller's Tale' when John the carpenter encounters the 'entranced' Nicholas (I 3479-85). John's immediate recourse to charms and formulae (the 'nyght-spel' and 'white *pater-noster*') to ward off 'elves' and

---

[6] Helen Cooper, *The Canterbury Tales*, Oxford Guides to Chaucer (Oxford: Oxford University Press, 1989), p. 301.

'wightes', is used to compound the portrait of parochialism and provincial unlearnedness.[7] The pilgrim-narrator describes his tale as 'a rym I lerned longe agoon' (VII 709) and indeed the stock descriptions and scenes that he sets out in his jog-trot 'dogerel' are certainly employed to leave one feeling that we have heard this all before somewhere else - in a far better form. The fairy episode in 'Sir Thopas' is therefore already part of an old story, a 'mouldy' tale.

The parody in 'Sir Thopas' was clearly noted by the time of the sixteenth century, as is evidenced by imitative parodies of the poem and character by William Dunbar, John Lyly, and Michael Drayton.[8] Sir Thomas Wyatt recognized the parodic nature of Chaucer's poem as he explains in 'Mine own John Poynz' how he rejects the dull wits at court that 'Praise Sir Thopas for a noble tale/ And scorn the story that the knight told'.[9] Until relatively recently there has been an enduring resistance to the idea that Spenser was aware of, and actively embraced, the element of parody and comedy when he came to read 'Sir Thopas'.[10] Whilst Spenser may have adapted the elf queen episode from Chaucer to provide 'a fitting representation of the moment when a young knight's inchoate longings for love and glory fix on a definite object, foreseen but achievable only with difficulty', the construction of a wholly 'sage and serious', moral Spenser is only half of the story.[11] It is far more likely that Spenser, as a most attentive reader of Chaucer, *was* attuned to the burlesque of 'Sir Thopas', the self consciousness of Chaucer's narrative, and the possibilities that such self-conscious burlesque offered. This is not to suggest, conversely, that *The Faerie Queene* is wholly parodic or that there is a joke in every stanza, but it opens up the possibilities for a level of play that is very much in concert with the polysemy provided by the allegory of the text. Mikhail Bakhtin highlights the interrogative function that parody can play through the provision of another voice or reading (etymologically, 'another song': *para-ode*) within a text that fragments the possibility of a unitary understanding of a

---

[7] E.K. makes reference to the 'Nightspel' in the gloss to 'March' and ascribes these kinds of verses or charms to 'elder tymes'; see *Shorter Poems*, p. 57.

[8] See John A. Burrow, '*Sir Thopas* in the Sixteenth Century', in Douglas Gray and E. G. Stanley, eds, *Middle English Studies Presented to Norman Davies in Honour of his Seventieth Birthday* (Oxford: Clarendon Press, 1983), pp. 69-91.

[9] Sir Thomas Wyatt, *The Complete Poems*, ed. R. A. Rebholz (Harmondsworth: Penguin, 1978), p. 187.

[10] See William Nelson, 'Spenser *ludens*', in Kennedy and Reither, eds, *Theatre for Spenserians*, pp. 94-6; Judith Anderson, '"A Gentle Knight was pricking on the plaine": The Chaucerian Connection', *ELR* 15 (1985), pp. 166-74; Harry Berger, Jr., '"Kidnapped Romance": Discourse in *The Faerie Queene*', in Logan and Teskey, eds, *Unfolded Tales*, p. 215.

[11] John A. Burrow, 'Chaucer, Geoffrey', in *Spenser Encyclopedia*, p. 146. Burrow, '*Sir Thopas*', pp. 81-8, assumes that Spenser was unaware of the burlesque element in 'Sir Thopas'.

text's 'meaning', engendering a form of play and plurality.[12] In a parody such as 'Sir Thopas' we have the notional orthodox form of what a romance 'ought' to be - Chaucer's sources, the 'romances of prys' with which the narrator compares his tale - together with the manipulation of the principal characteristics of that form. It is the interaction between the form and the manipulation of that form that, for Bakhtin, produces the element of linguistic and literary self-consciousness. Parody thus presents the reader with a multiplicity of possible meanings.[13] Spenser may well have taken up and treated Chaucer's parodic story of fairy as a consciously polysemic narrative.

Spenser's self-conscious awareness to the ways in which his work may be read is clearly evident in *The Faerie Queene*, as well as in *The Shepheardes Calender*. The conscious evocation of Chaucer's mouldy tale as the source for the central fairy episode of *The Faerie Queene* has implications for how Spenser uses fairy to engage the reader. Spenser's source is self-consciously literary and the parodic elements call attention to this fact. The story of Sir Thopas's search for the elf queen itself is not meant to be taken entirely seriously. One's response to the text is continually checked by reminders as to the artificiality of what we are reading, and indeed the effect that the story creates (on the pilgrims and on Chaucer's audience) is more important than the *fabula* presented. The metanarrative is an inseparable part of the tale. An element of play, critique, and possible interrogation is perforce imported when Spenser adopts the story of the fairy queen's visitation from Chaucer's burlesque. In his attempt to continue and complete Chaucer's 'Sir Thopas', as he does for 'The Squire's Tale' in book four, Spenser addresses, though does not definitively answer, those questions left by Chaucer as to the whereabouts and ontology of the fairy or elf queen, and the function of such a figure who plays a simultaneously central and marginal role in the text.

Similar ambiguity surrounds the presence and appearance of the fairy queen found in the fourteenth-century French romance *Petit Artus de Bretagne*, a further possible source for Arthur's vision of Gloriana. Spenser most likely knew the romance through the English version translated by Lord Berners as *Arthur of Little Britain*.[14] As in Spenser's poem, the adventures of the hero in *Arthur of Little Britain* (the son of the Duke of Brittany, not Arthur, son of Uther Pendragon) are initiated by a vision of a lady resembling the fairy queen. In *Arthur of Little Britain*, however, the vision is a contrivance devised by the fairy queen, Proserpine. The

---

[12] M. M. Bakhtin, 'From the Prehistory of Novelistic Discourse', *The Dialogic Imagination: Four Essays*, ed. Michael Holquist, tr. Caryl Emerson and Michael Holquist (Austin: University of Texas Press, 1981), pp. 60-61, 75-6.

[13] Gordon Teskey, *Allegory and Violence* (Ithaca: Cornell University Press, 1996), pp. 56-76, discusses the similarities that irony bears to allegory, in its capacity to engender a form of doubleness through the problematization of literal readings.

[14] Sarah Michie, '*The Faerie Queene* and *Arthur of Little Britain*', *SP* 36 (1939), p. 106. Michie offers the earliest comparative analysis of the two texts, though the first suggestion that *Arthur of Little Britain* is the source of Arthur's dream is made by Edwin Greenlaw, 'Britomart at the House of Busirane', *SP* 26 (1929), pp. 124-7.

image and identity of the fairy queen are continually problematized throughout the text: Arthur's initial vision is actually of the fairy queen's human ward Florence, and there are many points in the narrative where Proserpine is mistaken for Florence, as when they swap roles to confound the suit of the Emperor of Ynd. Florence is consciously constructed as a simulacrum of the fairy queen, a doubling of her image, as Proserpine declares:

> I wyll that this chylde be named Florence, and that she shall be floure of beautie of all other creatures as long as ever she shall live. And properly I wyl she shal resemble to me both in face, in body, in countenance, in goinge, and commynge; and in all other thynges so lyke, that whoso ever se us bothe together shall not consyder nor dyscerne the one fro the other.[15]

The fairy queen in *Arthur of Little Britain* exhibits far more of a direct influence upon the hero's adventures than Gloriana does upon the Arthur of Spenser's poem. Indeed, part of Proserpine's role in the text is to test Arthur's prowess, and she performs a similar role to the fairy queen who tests the hero of *Tristan de Nanteuil* (discussed below). A large part of this testing process in *Arthur of Little Britain* centres on Arthur's ability to distinguish between the fairy queen and her earthly look-alike, Florence. Proserpine's repeated amorous advances threaten the ultimate fulfilment of Arthur's quest/ test (to complete the adventures of Porte Noyre and thus to win Florence's hand in marriage) by offering an amenable alternative to continued questing, comparable with the wooing of Guyon by the fairy damsel Phaedria.[16]

The point to stress concerning both 'Sir Thopas' and *Arthur of Little Britain* is that the fairy queen is presented as an interpretative challenge and a potentially problematic presence. A questioning of fairy is effectively already built into the episode of Arthur and Gloriana in book one and initiates a wider interrogation both of the presence and role of fairy within the story or *fabula* of *The Faerie Queene*, and of what fairy represents within the text that the reader has before them.

Prince Arthur's Reading of the Fairy Queen

Any reading of the fairy queen is obviously framed by Spenser's declaration in the 'Letter to Raleigh: 'In that Faery Queene I meane glory in my generall intention, but in my particular I conceiue the most excellent and glorious person of our soueraine the Queene, and her kingdome in Faery land.' Spenser points here to the gap between sign and meaning, and to the capacity for fairy to operate at several levels and to signify something other than that implied by the literal level of the narrative. But whilst Spenser draws attention to how fairy is used to register the

---

[15] *The History of the Valiant Knight Arthur of Little Britain*, tr. from the French by John Bourchier, Lord Berners, ed. E. V. Utterson (London, 1814), p. 47.
[16] *Arthur of Little Britain*, pp. 297-312; Michie, '*Faerie Queene*', p. 113.

presence of 'secret meaning', the Letter forestalls further explication as to exactly how signification is to take place, and indeed introduces the possibility of multiple interpretations of the fairy queen by distinguishing between Spenser's general and particular intentions. Following the principles of Teskey's 'poetics' of allegory we may argue that the fairy queen regulates the 'loop of interpretative play' by fostering the suggestion that definitive meaning (of both the fairy queen and *The Faerie Queene*) can be found within the text itself. What the Letter sets out to establish and, I argue, as the episode featuring Arthur's encounter with Gloriana demonstrates, is that provision of any kind of definitive, uncompromised 'meaning' for fairy in *The Faerie Queene* is subordinate to the stimulation of critical engagement with the text that the appearance of the fairy queen may initiate. My focus in this section is not restricted therefore to what the fairy queen may signify, but considers also how the fairy queen functions as a sign and the effect that this has within the text.

My third Spenserian fairy story in fact constitutes the first extended treatment of fairy that readers encounter in *The Faerie Queene* following the introduction to the adventures of the would-be 'Elfin knight' Redcrosse. In reading through the episode of Gloriana's visitation as a whole we encounter many of the difficulties with reading Spenser's fairies examined in the previous two chapters. The doubts that Arthur expresses concerning the exact nature of his encounter with Gloriana are amplified and replicated by the kind of interpretative questions that Spenser's fairy presents to readers of *The Faerie Queene* as a whole. The text draws the reader into a quest to discover Gloriana analogous to the 'labour' and 'long tyne' of the Briton prince himself. The details of Arthur's oneiric encounter with the fairy queen are placed within a story told to Una and Redcrosse at Orgoglio's castle shortly before they are due to part company. Once again fairy is presented to us at several removes: the image of the fairy queen made all the more distant and ambiguous as her 'appearance' is mediated through a layered series of stories within the narrator's story. Canto nine opens with the narrator's vocative address to the 'Goodly golden chaine' linking all of the virtues that bring together the 'noble minds of yore... In braue poursuitt of cheualrous emprize', (I.ix.1). This is one of many points in *The Faerie Queene* where narratorial exordia serve to create an immediate pose of temporal distance between the 'now' of the performative level (the narrator's present) and the 'antique times' forming the subject of the story that the narrator sets forth. The opening stanza's concluding simile applies the general concept of the 'golden chayne' to the particular situation of the present action (Arthur's rescue of Redcrosse), and in so doing serves as a subtle discourse marker registering the division between the two temporal contexts of *The Faerie Queene*. This is not quite a 'once upon a time' formula but adds an extra reminder of the narrator's presence as an intermediate stage through which Arthur's fairy story is transmitted. A corresponding marker of temporal distance is established, setting a similar tone of nostalgia, when the narrator once again celebrates the chain of concord in III.i.13, as Arthur, Guyon, and Britomart are united. The fact that fairy in *The Faerie Queene* is largely presented through a layered series of stories within a story serves to highlight the provisional nature of any given presentation of fairy in the text, and Arthur's story of Gloriana is no exception. Arthur's fairy story is presented as a reading of fairy: he takes up an interpretative stance as he engages in the attempt to make sense or understand the meaning of his fairy vision.

Una's enquiry as to Arthur's 'name and nation' prompts the first occasion for the prince to tell of matters of which he possesses only partial knowledge. His answer, that he is ignorant of his lineage and the identity of his father and that he was delivered to the fairy knight Timon to be raised and educated, is clearly presented with the implication that further knowledge will be forthcoming but that it is somehow 'hidden yit' awaiting discovery. Arthur's frequent questioning of Merlin meets the same answer: 'That [he] was sonne and heire vnto a king,/ As time in her iust term the truth to light should bring' (I.ix.5). Yet the initial exchange is just as important for what it does not say, and for the questions that it leaves open. It sets out the basic terms of the epistemological terrain of *The Faerie Queene*, the pattern for how knowledge is revealed in the poem: questions are raised but the text actively frustrates the provision of straightforward answers or easy readings.

The same kind of epistemological structure frames Una's second question as she asks what adventure brought Arthur to fairyland. The reader of the 'Letter to Raleigh' is already furnished with the basic answer to this question: Arthur had a 'dream or vision' of the fairy queen and upon waking resolved to 'seeke her forth in Faerye land'. Arthur's reply to Una, however, is an exercise in periphrasis. Rather than simply answering the question with 'well, it all started with a vision of the fairy queen...', Arthur makes a circumlocutionary leap by questioning the first cause of the said vision. That is to say, the short answer to Una's enquiry would be the 'fresh bleeding wound' occasioned by Arthur's encounter with Gloriana, itself a Petrarchan shorthand employed to side-step direct description of the motive force behind Arthur's quest. Instead, Arthur's rhetorical questioning as to the first cause of the 'wound' goes one stage further by making the first attempt to ascribe some form of meaning to the initial vision of the fairy queen long before Gloriana is ever mentioned. He does so by entertaining the possibility that his 'wound' might be understood within a providentially ordained framework:

> Full hard it is (quoth he) to read aright
> The course of heavenly cause, or vnderstand
> The secret meaning of th'eternall might,
> That rules mens waies, and rules the thoughts of liuing wight.
>
> For whether he through fatall deepe foresight
> Me hither sent, for cause to me vnghest,
> Or that fresh bleeding wound, which day and night
> Whilome doth rancle in my riuen brest,
> With forced fury following his behest,
> Me hether brought by wayes yet neuer found,
> You to haue helpt I hold my selfe yet blest. (I.ix.6-7)

Arthur's function in the rescue of Redcrosse and Una as an agent of heavenly grace is certainly suggested from the opening of the canto in which he first makes an appearance (I.viii.1), but the chain of divine causation is reconstructed to explicitly incorporate Arthur's 'wound' and Gloriana. Arthur's response to Una is, in effect, the very first reading of fairy in *The Faerie Queene*, a first attempt to interpret the significance of what Arthur describes five stanzas later.[17] The fairy encounter is 'read' here as a sign of heavenly 'secret meaning'. In his interpretation of the encounter Arthur suggests that fairy acts as the temporal manifestation of divine providence. Arthur adduces in II.ix.7 that it is heaven that similarly frustrates the realization of his quest to see the fairy queen:

> Certes (then said the Prince) I God auow,
> That sith I armes and knighthood first did plight,
> My whole desire hath beene, and yet is now,
> To serue that Queene with al my powre and might.
> Seuen times the Sunne with his lamp-burning light,
> Hath walkte about about the world, and I no lesse,
> Sith of that Goddesse I haue sought the sight,
> Yet no where can her find: such happinesse
> Heuen doth to me enuy, and fortune fauourlesse. (II.ix.7)

Following Spenser's announcement that 'In that Faery Queene I meane glory in my generall intention', Arthur's quest for Gloriana reads therefore specifically as a representation of a providentially ordained quest for fame and glory.

The important feature of Arthur's reply to Una in book one is that there is no doubt that fairy must be seen to signify *something*: to function as the sign of something other than its surface appearance. Arthur's reply provides us with an implicit statement of the fairy queen's function, and this is echoed each time the text forces us to consider what the fairy queen means. As is the instinctive recourse of modern commentators on Spenser's fairy, Arthur immediately foregrounds consideration of the first cause or ultimate signification of the fairy queen. But it is important to remember that the question of function (i.e. what the fairy queen does in the text and the effect that her presentation has upon the reader) precedes that of what the fairy queen means. The search for the meaning of the fairy queen is initiated by the rhetorical effect that she has upon the relationship of reader and text and the kind of questions that are generated by her problematic presence in the poem.

Explication of the 'secret wound' prompted by Una's request (I.ix.7) introduces an additional component into the chain of causation that brought Arthur to fairyland. After Spenser calls on his muse to lay forth the antique rolls 'Of Faerie knights and fayrest *Tanaquill*' in the opening proem of *The Faerie Queene*, the

---

[17] 'Read' in the first line of the quoted passage denotes not simply the apprehension of script or text, but a wider sense of perception and comprehension, as is consonant with Spenserian usage; see Anne Ferry, *The Art of Naming* (Chicago: University of Chicago Press, 1988), pp. 23-39.

petition to 'the most dreaded impe of highest *Ioue*' to lay aside his bow makes reference to the 'cruell dart' that wounded Arthur and the 'glorious fire' that it kindled in his heart, and clearly affords Cupid a vital role as agent within the poem's overall heroic plot (I.proem.3). Arthur affirms this as he likewise apostrophizes 'Ah Loue, lay down thy bow, the whiles I may respyre' (I.ix.8) before embarking on his narrative proper. The sense of temporal distance is suggested once more by the initial reminiscence in the past tense: 'It was in freshest flowre of youthly yeares' (I.ix.9). He then proceeds to tell of how, like Chaucer's Troilus, he once commonly scorned the idle lot of the 'louers life' and for a time successfully evaded Cupid's darts. The chain of causation is finally made explicit in I.ix.12 as he refers to himself as now being 'mated' by the fairy queen - Cupid's darts having finally done their work - and then at last proceeds to relate the specific details of the encounter. Arthur carefully constructs the first cause of his encounter with the fairy queen, and then affirms Cupid's providential role here by establishing him as the intermediate agent through which God operates. Before we even get to hear about the fairy queen we are offered a provisional first reading of what the ensuing encounter may mean. Arthur's interpretative forays provide a model for our own critical reactions to the centre-piece of his fairy story, instilling encouragement that the fairy queen may be deconstructed.

The description of Gloriana's visitation in the 'Letter to Raleigh' provides, on the whole, an unequivocal, uncomplicated statement of events that bear a clear similarity to the basic details of Sir Thopas's dream. Arthur's version in *The Faerie Queene* proper is, however, far more problematic. Whilst Arthur's dream provides the immediate starting point for his quest in fairyland, his actual description of the encounter with the fairy queen is made secondary to the questions and problems that it raises. The attempt to 'decode' and understand the fairy queen displaces her actual appearance in the narrative. Many readers voice their frustration when, upon reading this passage of *The Faerie Queene* in the hope of a one-stop, simple representation of Gloriana, they are confronted instead with problems and further questions. Within the text itself core questions pertaining to who it was, what actually happened, and what the episode means, are deployed around the details of the encounter like a nest of Chinese boxes. Arthur's story of the fairy queen is already prefaced by an immediate questioning of what happened and an attempt to read and make sense of the encounter. The prefatory reading of fairy provided by Arthur performs a similar function to that of Spenser's narrator in the proem to book two: both figures will present a fairy story about Arthur and the fairy queen; both figures are compelled to explain and decode their respective fairy stories in various ways; and, by constructing their stories as verbal objects actively requiring some form of explanation, both figures imply the presence of imagined readers (realized in Arthur's case in the form of Redcrosse and Una) to whom explanation must be made. In the narratives of both Arthur and the narrator the issue of the effect upon the reader that telling a fairy story may produce is a vital, unavoidable consideration.

Arthur's story yields many hermeneutic loose ends. Ambiguity is introduced after Arthur describes how, wearied with riding, he falls asleep and whilst in this state:

> [Me] seemed, by my side a royall Mayd
> Her daintie limbes full softly down did lay:
> So fayre a creature yet saw neuer sunny day. (I.ix.13)

Spenser's use of 'seemed' here denotes a certain measure of subjectivity. He uses 'seem' to suggest an outward manifestation veiling an inner nature. In this passage it specifically denotes perception and interpretation, a subjective response to how things appeared to Arthur. Whereas Sir Thopas clearly 'dremed' of an elf queen, the precise nature of Arthur's encounter is far more open to question. Equally opaque is the question of the visitor's identity. Initially perceived and described as a 'royall Mayd', it is only as she departs that she names herself as the 'Queene of Faries'. Even within the space of the single stanza describing Arthur's night with the fairy queen revelation of her identity is deferred until the very end of their encounter. It should not be forgotten that prior to this point in book one there have been several instances of mistaken identity where a character misreads another, as when it 'seemed' to Redcrosse that Una visited him in the night (I.i.47) or when he accepts Duessa as his 'new Lady'. It also becomes something of a stock feature of *The Faerie Queene* that any sight of an earthly beauty is promptly assigned a heavenly provenance, as when Belphoebe first appears both to Trompart (II.iii.33) and Timias (III.v.35), or when Artegall first sees Britomart's face (IV.vi.22).

There are a number of literary precedents that present a character misreading or misidentifying the fairy queen upon their first encounter. Thomas of Erceldoune believes the fairy queen is the Virgin Mary when they first meet, though he is swiftly corrected; the same mistake is made in the later ballad version, 'Thomas Rymer'.[18] In the alliterative *Wars of Alexander* (c.1450), the seemingly otherworldly riches of Queen Candace's palace lead the eponymous hero to mistake her for an 'elfe out of anothire erde'.[19] There are also those examples cited earlier where individuals are deliberately tricked into believing that they have seen and met with the fairy queen (as in *The Alchemist*, or the cases of Judith Phillips and John and Alice West), and whose encounter is with one who merely says that she is the fairy queen, not unlike the way in which Gloriana names herself after her night with Arthur (I.ix.14). Note also that the key moment at which the fairy queen first

---

[18] *The Romance and Prophecies of Thomas of Erceldoune*, ed. J. A. H. Murray. EETS OS 61 (London, 1875), pp. 4-5; Francis James Child, *The English and Scottish Popular Ballads*, 5 vols. (Boston, 1882-98; repr. New York: Dover, 1965), 1: 325. Similar confusion arises when Ogier first encounters Morgan le Fay and mistakes her for the Virgin Mary; see *Ogier le Dannoys: roman en prose du XVᵉ siècle*, Facsimile ed. Knud Togeby (Copenhagen: Munksgaard, 1967), pp. 270-71.

[19] *The Wars of Alexander*, ed. Hoyt N. Duggan and Thorlac Turville-Petre. EETS SS 10 (Oxford: Oxford University Press, 1989), p. 167, line 5384.

reveals her identity to Arthur constitutes an additional layer of utterance. Identification of the motive agent of Arthur's quest takes the form of something 'said' to Arthur, who in turn tells his fairy story to Redcrosse and Una. This event is then placed within the 'famous antique history' set forth by the narrator.

The point at which Arthur falls asleep is registered by a shift from sensual luxuriance - 'The verdant gras my couch did goodly dight,/ And pillow was my helmett fayre displayd' - into what Hamilton terms a 'yielding of the senses to love' (I.ix.13.5-6n). As with the narrator's 'famous antique history', Arthur's fairy story might be misinterpreted simply as 'th'aboundance of an ydle braine'. Dreams in *The Faerie Queene* have both positive and negative connotations, and range from Britomart's dream at Isis Church that 'did appeare vnto her heauenly spright' and which 'did close implie/ The course of all her fortune and posteritie' (V.vii.12), to the 'ydle dreame' with which Archimago abuses Redcrosse's fantasy (I.i.46) and the 'blandishment' offered by the false Una (I.i.49). Arthur's dream clearly bears affinities to each of these. Again the question of provenance is crucial. Just as the narrator labours to convince us that his 'famous antique history' is not simply a product of the imagination or fantasy, something drawn from Phantastes's fly-infested chamber, so too do we find a tension concerning the provenance of Arthur's dream. For all Arthur's prefatory attempts to eschew such a reading, the possibility is never fully removed that the fairy queen only exists as part of a story, as a product of the imagination. The closest that Arthur comes to a reprise of his dream (including similar provision of improvised 'couch' and 'pillow') yields only the 'thousand fancies' of an 'ydle brayne' and the 'sights of semblants vaine', as he is momentarily led to desire that the elusive Florimell might be, or at least resemble, his fairy queen (III.iv.53-54). Care should be taken that Arthur's dream of Gloriana is not simply legitimized or 'made safe' by comparing it solely with its positive analogues in the text, not least because the doubleness and ambiguity of this particular episode are an integral product of Spenser's decision to use fairy mythology. One of the difficulties faced in reading Arthur's fairy story is the fact that the most important 'appearance' made by Spenser's central figure for Elizabeth in the entire *Faerie Queene* bears an uncomfortable similarity to the 'idle thoughtes and fantasies' of Phantastes's chamber: 'Deuices, dreames, opinions vnsound,/ Shewes, visions, sooth-sayes, and prophesies;/ And all that fained is, as leasings, tales, and lies' (II.ix.51). Arthur's story invites criticisms concerning evidence similar to those expressed by the narrator in the second proem. Indeed, the fear voiced through the narrator in II.proem.1 that the hypothetical reader might question the legitimacy of *The Faerie Queene* 'sith none, that breatheth liuing aire, does know,/ Where is that happy land of Faery', is compounded by comments such as Arthur's observation that 'So fayre a creature yet saw neuer sunny day' (I.ix.13) which, whilst stressing the fairy queen's singularity and rarity, still elicits questions concerning her presence as a whole.

As with the pastoral and beast fable genres, the dream vision operates as a device for 'speaking the other' - for simultaneously encoding and revealing. The Book of Revelation is an inescapable presence in book one of *The Faerie Queene* and obviously provides the ready model of a form that actively invites and requires interpretation beyond the literal level of the narrative. It is into just such a formal and hermeneutic framework that Spenser places his fairy queen. Her only appearance placed within a 'dream or vision', the fairy queen is naturally established as an object to be deconstructed. She functions here as a sign used to signify or point to something else. Arthur himself (in I.ix.14.5) is aware of the ontological uncertainty surrounding the fairy queen and of the ambiguity concerning what actually happened: was it merely a delusive dream? Did the encounter really take place? It is equally unclear as to whether the intercourse that takes place between Arthur and the fairy queen is simply verbal ('Ne liuing man like wordes did euer heare'), or of a more sexual nature - a common component of the fairy mistress motif. Spenser deliberately evades further reference to the royal maid's virginity and the particular stimulus of Arthur's desire, though we can certainly interpret the reference in I.ix.12 to being 'mated' by the fairy queen as a punning allusion to a sexual encounter. Spenser's use of the word 'blandishment' to describe the pleasures shared between Gloriana and Arthur further carries sexual connotations and indeed is earlier used in book one in reference to the lecherous overtures made to Redcrosse by the false Una (I.i.49).

The most problematic point of the entire episode is where Arthur awakes to find 'her place deuoyd/ And nought but pressed gras, where she had lyen', (I.ix.15). Elsewhere in *The Faerie Queene* 'troden gras' or the beaten path are evident signatures of human presence, as at I.iii.10.4-5. The imprint of where the fairy queen had spent the night also clearly serves as a sign denoting some kind of temporal, somatic presence and forces us to consider that the encounter may be more than just a dream. Once again, the text raises more questions than it answers. The pressed grass functions in fact as a marker both of the presence and absence of the fairy queen in the text, plainly denoting that she occupied a physical 'place' (and Arthur explicitly refers to 'her place' twice in the first four lines of I.ix.15), and yet signalling also that this place is now empty, 'deuoyd'. That empty space on the grass is the starting point both for Arthur's quest, and for our own attempts to, in some way, find or 'discover' the fairy queen. In the meantime, hopes for a further, less equivocal moment of discovery are raised by the purported promise made by the fairy queen herself that her appearance is to be delayed until indeterminate 'iust time' has expired. Arthur's fairy story records an attempt to read the encounter with the fairy queen as being more than simply an idle tale. His interpretation or reading of the fairy queen models the kind of response that the reader of *The Faerie Queene* should have and the hermeneutic procedures that should be undertaken in confronting Spenser's fairy. The episode models what to do when reading Spenser's text. Spenser puts to the reader those difficulties with reading the fairy queen that are present in the likely sources for this episode and that Arthur in turn takes up. Fairy needs to be placed into a structure of meaning in order to make sense of exactly what takes place.

We are led in this direction from the very opening of Arthur's fairy story and his providential reading of the episode. He uses his story as an 'ensample' that 'Nothing is sure, that growes on earthly grownd' and as a short homily on the folly of pride, comparable to the lessons gained from Redcrosse's tribulations at

Orgoglio's castle (I.ix.11-12). Arthur's fairy story is clearly assigned a utilitarian, didactic function, not unlike Spenser's fairy story as a whole. Likewise Arthur's story receives a favourable reading by Redcrosse as he makes an explicit connection between the fairy queen and Una's 'heauenly light' (I.ix.17), and their respective loves are worthy matter for further 'discoursing' in the following stanza (I.ix.18). Coupled with the critical impetus provided in the 'Letter to Raleigh', the whole episode of the encounter constitutes a clear inducement that we have to place the fairy queen within a structure of meaning and to engage exactly how fairy functions as a sign. But what Arthur's own exposition also illustrates, aside from the general comment on the impossibility of ever fully revealing the workings of providence, is that interpretation of fairy is by no means final or unequivocal. Access to an unconditional direct interpretation of the fairy encounter is impaired by the either/ or structure of I.ix.7, and perhaps we might also read the 'wayes yet neuer found' as a figurative, rather evasive reference to the recondite provenance of Arthur's 'fresh bleeding wound'. The fairy queen must be read therefore as a 'writerly' construction. She is, and remains, a problematic figure within Spenser's text and is open to multiple different interpretations.

'Now white, then blacke, your frende the fayrey Queene'

Interpretation of Gloriana is complicated by the number of negative portrayals of fairy queens that can be identified in the poem. Spenser's employment of fairy mythology draws upon an eclectic range of sources and associations, and Gloriana is not the only fairy queen that we can identify. Spenser's presentation of fairy includes several other figures who are either specifically identified as fays or that exhibit similar kinds of features and powers as fays: Acrasia, Phaedria, Agape, and even Duessa. Again Spenser has not sought to establish a rigid, consistent taxonomic framework for his use of fairy mythology and we have seen how his continually shifting use of the terms 'fairy' and 'elf' (and their adjectival equivalents) can signify a broad range of associations and attributes. It is difficult therefore to make categorical statements concerning the precise ontology of individual characters in *The Faerie Queene* and to draw a hard and fast line distinguishing the fairy queen Gloriana from other female fairy characters in the text. The field of potential analogues of Gloriana is thus further broadened. (Gloriana is referred to as both a fairy and an 'Elfin' queen (II.i.1), though never explicitly as a 'fay'.)

Etymologically 'fay' is an anglicization of OF *fae* or *fée*, from which the word 'fairy' itself derives.[20] The word 'fay' is commonly used to denote the fairy mistresses of Celtic myth and medieval romance (from which tradition Spenser

---

[20] Noel Williams, 'The Semantics of the Word '*Fairy*': Making Meaning Out of Thin Air', in Peter Narváez, ed., *The Good People: New Fairylore Essays* (New York: Garland, 1991), pp. 462-4.

derives Gloriana), as well as those individuals designated as humans who practice magic powers as an art, an enchantress or sorceress. The fay Agape, we are told,

> had the skill
> Of secret things, and all the powres of nature,
> Which she by art could vse vnto her will,
> And to her seruice bind each liuing creature,
> Through secret vnderstanding of their feature. (IV.ii.44)

One finds an increasing rationalization of the fairies in medieval romance of the twelfth and thirteenth centuries; creatures that would once be presented as supernatural beings from another world (or the Otherworld), or as some form of deity, are shown more as humans with enhanced powers operating through craft rather than any sense of innate abilities.[21] Briggs uses several examples from the French Vulgate cycle of romances to illustrate how 'fairy' was used to describe the kind of illusions conjured up by human enchantresses; she quotes a translation from *Lancelot du Lac*: 'In those days all maidens that knew enchantments or charms were called fays, and there were many of them at this time, and more in Great Britain than in other lands.'[22] Certainly by the time of Malory's *Morte D'Arthur* Morgan le Fay is presented as a mortal 'put to scole in a nonnery... [where] she lerned so moche that she was a grete clerke of nygromancye'.[23] The rationalization of fairy also informs Spenser's description of Mertia in '*Briton moniments*':

> A woman worthy of immortall praise,
> Which for this Realme found many goodly layes,
> And wholesome Statutes to her husband brought;
> Her many deemd to haue beene of the *Fayes*,
> As was *Aegerie*, that *Numa* tought;
> Those yet of her be *Mertian* lawes both nam'd and thought. (II.x.42)

The comparison of Mertia's mortal powers to those of a fay is not found in Spenser's chronicle sources but appears to be an addition of his own modelled on the descriptions of the tutelary spirit '*Aegerie*' (to whom Mertia is also compared)

---

[21] On the rationalization of fairy see Paton, *Fairy Mythology*, p. 165n1; Lucienne Carasso-Bulow, *The Merveilleux in Chrétien de Troyes' Romances* (Geneva: Librairie Droz, 1976), pp. 54-5, 83-4; Kathryn S. Westoby, 'A New Look at the Role of the Fée in Medieval French Arthurian Romance', in Glyn S. Burgess and Robert A. Taylor, eds, *The Spirit of the Court: Selected Proceedings of the Fourth Congress of the International Courtly Literature Society (Toronto 1983)* (Cambridge: Brewer, 1985), pp. 373-85; and Harf-Lancner, *Les Fées*, pp. 377-432.

[22] Katharine Briggs, *Fairies in Tradition and Literature* (London: Routledge, 1967), pp. 4-5, 9.

[23] Sir Thomas Malory, *Complete Works*, ed. Eugène Vinaver (Oxford: Oxford University Press, 1971), p. 5.

found in contemporary mythological handbooks (II.x.39.6n).[24] There is perhaps also a male example of a rationalized fairy in '*Antiquitee* of *Faery* lond' in the reference to the magic skill or 'art' through which Elfinor built 'vpon the glassy See/ A bridge of bras' (II.x.73). The rationalized fays and fairies that Spenser could have found in Malory and elsewhere are witness to the potential elasticity of fairy ontology and only serve to further complicate our reading of Gloriana.[25]

Rathborne has attempted to establish Gloriana and Acrasia in a binary relationship of 'good fairy' and 'bad fairy'. She goes about this by exploring the particular resemblance of Gloriana to a fairy specifically named as Gloriande who appears in *Huon of Burdeux* and in two fourteenth-century French romances, *Tristan de Nanteuil* and *Charles le chauve*. In each romance, argues Rathborne, Gloriande is presented as the bestower of the fairy gifts of fame and glory and, in keeping with her thesis that fairyland is the land of fame, Rathborne goes on to argue that for the figure of Gloriana Spenser combines Gloriande's traditional bestowal of fame with the bestowal of love said to be commonly associated with Morgan le Fay. As a hybrid figure who bestows a love that glorifies, Gloriana is contrasted with the figure of the love that destroys glory, the 'rival' fay Acrasia.[26] Whilst I have some reservations about the particular chain of reasoning by which Rathborne constructs the Gloriana-Acrasia binary (not least her reading of Morgan le Fay), her analysis rightly demonstrates that the fairy queen figure can signify both positive and negative associations.[27] It is perfectly possible to argue that the good fairy-bad fairy model is in keeping with what Alastair Fowler calls the 'natural law' of Spenser's fairyland, that 'at least one corresponding evil image precedes a virtuous image'.[28] Defining the benign through contrast with the malign is a central feature of Spenserian epistemology and part of the learning process to

---

[24] Harper, *Sources*, pp. 98-9. Mertia later appears in a list of 'wemen valorous' at III.iii.54. Mertia (or Martia) also appears in the entry celebrations for Elizabeth's visit to Norwich in 1578 (see p. 41 above).

[25] Greenlaw, 'Spenser's Fairy Mythology', p. 108, demonstrates just how much of *The Faerie Queene* can be read as rationalized fairy lore as he suggests that Artegall's captivity by Radigund is 'unquestionably related to the large number of legends in which a mortal is captured by a *fée* who offers him her love, with imprisonment as a penalty for refusal'.

[26] Rathborne, *Meaning*, pp. 214-18. A further polarization of good and bad fairy queens is also suggested by the antagonism between the Lady of the Lake and Morgan le Fay in Malory.

[27] Rathborne has a tendency to highlight those aspects of medieval romance fairies that relate to fame and glory and to discard everything else. If one actually reads through *Tristan de Nanteuil* (and Rathborne appears to have worked largely from nineteenth-century prose summaries) we find that Gloriande is associated more with the specific 'donation' of valour and courage than with fame *per se*. For a modern edition, see *Tristan de Nanteuil: chanson de geste inédite*, ed. K. V. Sinclair (Assen: Van Gorcum, 1971). Rathborne's observations on Gloriande (pp. 211-14) also imply a certain consistency in the character and allegiance of fairy personnel from text to text, which is a somewhat limiting way of reading fairy; witness, for example, the complexity of a figure such as Morgan le Fay.

[28] Fowler, 'Emanations of Glory', *Theatre for Spenserians*, p. 71.

which the text leads us to grow accustomed as we read through *The Faerie Queene*. The worldly vainglory of Lucifera is typically read, for example, as a parody of Gloriana, the gilded walls of the House of Pride, at least superficially, resembling those found around Cleopolis (II.x.72).[29] Again we might seek to place Gloriana within a neoplatonic framework, with false or negative presentations of the fairy queen set in contrast with the ideal.

There is a danger, however, that rigid hierarchies between ideal and type - or clear-cut divisions of positive and negative value - may be ultimately reductive and fail to fully account for seeming contradictions in Spenser's use of an image, or those occasions where interpretation of an individual figure is clearly ambiguous. Carol Kaske's study of Spenser's biblical poetics seeks to address such points of contradiction and inconsistency by arguing that Spenser follows the practice found in medieval and early modern exegesis of repeating a given image both in an honorific and a derogatory sense, *in bono et in malo*. The image of the sorceress, for example, is presented thus in *The Faerie Queene*: *in bono* in the form of Cambina, instructed in 'Magicke leare,/ And all the artes, that subtill wits discouer', by her mother Agape (IV.iii.40), and bearing a cup of Nepenthe (IV.iii.42-45); *in malo* as Duessa, whose Circean cup 'replete with magic arts' represents a form of debased eucharist (I.viii.14).[30] As Kaske demonstrates, Spenser's repetition of images *in bono et in malo* in *The Faerie Queene* is a far more commonly found practice than any comparable hierarchical models of ideal and type or parody. But can we fit the figure of the fairy queen into the same kind of polarized structure as we might apply for other representations of Elizabeth in *The Faerie Queene*? Tellingly, Kaske herself does not locate fairy within her exegetical binary.[31] Despite the fact that Spenser's identification of Gloriana with Elizabeth may suggest we should only find ways by which to read the fairy queen as wholly unproblematic or honorific, Gloriana *is* a site of ambivalence and contested signification. Spenser presents Gloriana in such a way that she is open to both positive and negative readings. The ambiguity surrounding her does little to limit the possibility of a negative reading.

Contemporary representations of fairy mythology certainly provide enough examples of the negative associations connected with the fairy queen (and, indeed, negative representations of the fairy queen) that only serve to forestall the

---

[29] Douglas Brooks-Davies, 'Lucifera', in *Spenser Encyclopedia*, p. 441.

[30] Suggested in Carol V. Kaske, *Spenser and Biblical Poetics* (Ithaca: Cornell University Press, 1999), pp. 43-51.

[31] Kaske, *Spenser and Biblical Poetics*, pp. 91-7, addresses the apparent contradiction raised by the way that the New Jerusalem and Cleopolis are explicitly contrasted at I.x.57-59, and yet the latter is still clearly endorsed (by Contemplation) and in no way presented *in malo*. The positive values of each city are stated and Contemplation refuses to definitively place one above the other. The relationship between the cities, argues Kaske, is ultimately founded upon the difference between two distinct discourses - Protestant piety and chivalric romance - and two social groups: 'godly Protestants and the court as it was constructed by romances, courtesy books, and many classical texts' (p. 96).

possibility of an unproblematic, unambiguous reading of Gloriana. Despite the appearance of explicitly Christian fairies in medieval romances such as *Huon* and *Melusine*, infernal associations of fairies remain a consistent feature in poetry, drama, and demonological treatises in England until well into the seventeenth century. This is in addition to the appearances that the fairy queen makes in contemporary Scottish witchcraft texts, both popular and elite, as noted by Lewis.[32] The fairy mistress of the ballad tradition is also frequently presented as a sinister figure.[33] One certainly finds plenty of examples of 'bad fairies' amongst the *fate* of Spenser's Italian romance sources: Boiardo's Dragontina, Morgana, and Falerina; Ariosto's Alcina; Trissino's Acratia; and Tasso's Armida.[34] Gloriana's encounter with Arthur is also suggestive of stories concerning *succubae*, demon-lovers or the Devil himself in a female guise that appear to a mortal man and engage in sexual intercourse. Attributes of *succubae* (and their male equivalent *incubi*) frequently elide with elements from fairy lore, and contemporary works by demonologists and theologians went into inordinate detail on the sexual proclivities and generative powers of demons.[35] As stated earlier, there is perhaps a conscious gesture of amelioration in the presentation of the fairy queen in the 1575 Woodstock entertainment, as she addresses Elizabeth: 'This loue hath caused me transforme my face,/ and in your hue to come before your eyne,/ now white, then blacke, your frende the fayrey Queene'.[36]

More problematic still is the essential doubleness of the figure of the fairy queen in the romance and popular traditions: her capacity to both reward and punish, and to occupy an uneasy liminal space between heaven and hell, as is seen for example in the ballad of 'Thomas Rymer'.[37] Spenser's response to this doubleness is to present a composite image of the fairy queen figure formed from both Gloriana and Acrasia. The presentation of Acrasia in the Bower of Bliss and the imprisonment of her lovers sets forth a negative, perhaps precautionary, version of the ultimate end of Arthur's quest. We are invited to compare Gloriana and Acrasia as much as we are to distinguish them. Arthur, like the imprisoned knight Verdant, is seemingly captivated under the spell of a fairy queen. The image of the *succuba* is played upon once again as Acrasia 'did sucke his spright' through her lover's eyes (II.xii.73). Verdant's entertainment by Acrasia in II.xii.72-80 offers an elaborate, sensuous display of what the 'blandishment' of a fairy queen may be like. It is tempting to use the episode to supplement Arthur's elliptical reference to what took place in the encounter described in I.ix.13-16. Mary Ellen Lamb writes that

---

[32] See above, pp. 26-7.

[33] Briggs, *Anatomy*, p. 39; Purkiss, *Troublesome Things*, pp. 68-70.

[34] Rathborne, *Meaning*, pp. 215-17; James Nohrnberg, *The Analogy of The Faerie Queene* (Princeton: Princeton University Press, 1976), p. 508.

[35] Nicolas Kiessling, *The Incubus in English Literature: Provenance and Progeny* (Pullman: Washington State University Press, 1977), pp. 43-5, 24-9.

[36] Cunliffe, 'Queenes Majesties Entertainment', p. 98.

[37] The road to 'Elfland' in 'Thomas Rymer' is located between the way to heaven and the way to hell; see Child, *English and Scottish Popular Ballads*, 1: 324-5.

Acrasia registers lurking anxieties over Arthur's fate, as a means of representing Spenser's ambivalence regarding the domination of a female sovereign over her subjects.[38] One might elaborate upon Lamb's conclusions and see Guyon's apprehension and capture of Acrasia as a means of disempowering the figure of the fairy queen, or rather of reasserting male control over her. Guyon's binding of Acrasia in the Palmer's net (II.xii.81-82) is another, albeit subtle analogue of the assertions made by Spenser's narrator of his powers to control how the fairy queen appears in the text.

I am not suggesting that in writing of the fairy queen Spenser is slavishly bound to a predetermined conception of fairy established by previous or contemporary representations. But Spenser's 'writerly' presentation of the fairy queen necessarily requires the reader to supplement what is found in the text, to complete the process of signifying fairy that Spenser initiates. In doing so our reading of Gloriana may be affected by negative associations connected with fairy suggested in sources outside of the text that are by no means excluded by the ambiguous presentation of fairy within Spenser's text itself. As with many other mythological figures employed as part of Elizabeth's representational vocabulary, the fairy queen functions as a site of interpretative struggle and contested signification. The figure of Gloriana undoubtedly 'means' Elizabeth within Spenser's allegory, but, as I have endeavoured to demonstrate, the implications of such an identification are by no means unproblematic.

The ambiguity of the figure of the fairy queen proleptically returns us to the narrator's intentions expressed in the proem to book two. There, as in Arthur's story of Gloriana, the problematic presence of fairy acts as a stimulus for further critical engagement with the text, breaking any kind of mimetic surface and introducing the possibility that fairy operates as a method of concealment. Spenser's choice of fairy mythology plays a particularly significant role in initiating and perpetuating the cycle of interpretative play throughout the poem. As has been shown, fairy mythology as a whole has a peculiar, though enduring resistance to structures requiring any form of absolutes, be it concerning questions of appearance, ontology, or moral value. Listen to or read a story of fairy - in medieval romance, popular lore, hagiography, or demonological and pneumatological treatises - and it is difficult not to encounter the same kind of questions about presence and ontology, meaning and function that we find in *The Faerie Queene*. We should not be surprised therefore that there are questions in Spenser's text regarding whether the fairy queen appears or not, and uncertainty surrounding what her presence may mean. The act of writing of fairy goes beyond simply the employment of a consciously literary device that is indistinguishable from classical nymphs or satyrs; rather, it involves embracing the issue of textual production and epistemological boundaries as part of the text's direct subject matter. It is this aspect in particular that marks out the use of fairy mythology in *The Faerie Queene* from every other mythological source employed in Spenser's

---

[38] Lamb, 'Gloriana', pp. 86, 92.

allegory. Part and parcel of a story of fairy is always this reflexive concern with fiction and story-telling itself, with the provenance and utility of those fictions or stories, and with the attendant questions and doubts that the presence (or absence) of fairy may generate. A common motif in stories of fairy is the concept of fairy glamour, of unseen forces and powers, and of a hesitancy or reticence towards disclosure and equivocal revelation. Couple this with the ontological instability of fairy examined in chapter one, and we repeatedly find that the reflexive imperative to question forms an integral thematic component of a fairy story.

Similarly, Gloriana is presented here as a problem to be solved, a sign to be decoded. She functions in the poem as an interpretative faultline, a means of initiating critical engagement between reader and text. In so doing she acts in an analogous way to the narratorial apostrophes of *The Faerie Queene* through forcing the reader back to the performative level of the poem to reflect upon and perhaps renegotiate their own engagement with the text. The problematic presence of the fairy queen draws attention to how one goes about reading Spenser's poem as a whole. The encounter detailed in I.ix.13-16 does not come close to providing the kind of direct, comparatively unmediated presentation of Gloriana that we find with the other figures of Elizabeth in *The Faerie Queene*, such as Una, Belphoebe, Britomart, and Mercilla. Rather than ever getting to see the fairy queen in person, as it were, we find that she is presented as a story or text. At the moment where we might hope to find Spenser's eponymous figure for Elizabeth attention is drawn to the matter of how Spenser chooses to represent Elizabeth and how we should go about interpreting this - exactly the same kind of preoccupations that form the basis of the poem's framing narrative. Not only is Spenser engaged in a process of creating and perpetuating (as well as in part rewriting) a mythological figure or schema for Elizabeth, but he simultaneously draws attention to that very process. The employment of fairy mythology carries with it an implicit metacommentary through inherently incorporating and foregrounding the reflexive interrogative impulse noted above. The choice of fairy builds an active questioning of presence and ontology into the subject matter of *The Faerie Queene*. Spenser's subject in *The Faerie Queene* is not just Elizabeth, but the process of representing and mythologizing Elizabeth. Fairy plays an important role in calling attention to Spenser's function in the myth-making process through repeatedly drawing our focus back to the poem's performative level, that moment of engagement between reader and text. It serves to remind us of the 'performance' of the text through foregrounding the model of a reading system of producer and receiver, never letting us ignore the presence of the poet in the playing out or setting forth of the fairy queen and *The Faerie Queene*.

Writing about Writing about Elizabeth

Spenser uses the figure of the fairy queen in such a way as to heighten the consciousness of his readers towards the process of representing Elizabeth by raising questions as to the actual presence of her central figure in the text and providing a record of the difficulty of ever de-textualizing Elizabeth. In particular I want to suggest that Spenser's representation of Gloriana serves as a way of speaking about the necessary textualization of Elizabeth within the discourse of Elizabethan myth-making. We have already looked at the background of such myth-making and at both the general and particular representational strategies that form the ultimate source of Spenser's project in writing *The Faerie Queene*. Elizabeth is repeatedly constructed as a fiction, a story, a text - both aesthetically and constitutionally - by herself and her subjects. Making a story for and about the queen is simultaneously a process of making a story *of* or *out of* the queen. The construction and perpetuation of new artificial bodies and histories for Elizabeth is a process in which critics and historians are also equally complicit.

The framing narrative to *The Faerie Queene* provides an extended example of how the textualization of Elizabeth takes place and of Spenser's own role in the discourse of myth-making; the poem draws attention back to the process in hand. As discussed above, Spenser's narrator confronts the interpretative difficulties concerning how to read fairy in II.proem.1-5, first by his recognition of the potential for multiple readings of fairy in the poem, and then by attempting to 'fix' how fairy is read. The narrator's attempt to provide an unambiguous, unequivocal reading of fairy by, at a number of points, making the simple identification between the fairy queen and Elizabeth continues to raise more interpretative questions than it immediately solves.

Consider again the scenario established within the framing narrative: Spenser's first story of fairy is about telling a story of fairy to the queen. The narrator is constructed as a character within the framing narrative who draws his text from the 'antique rolles' and then setting forth his text to the queen. In Spenser's construction of a scenario of production and reception both the producer and receiver of the text are constructed as characters. The scenario of narrator and royal reader constructed in the framing narrative sets out a grand performative gesture comparable, as I suggested, to the playing out of a masque or entertainment. The process of writing *for* the queen is simultaneously one of writing *of* the queen. In presenting his ultimate implied reader Spenser must construct (or reconstruct) the queen as a fictional character engaged in a fictional model of interaction with his text. Just as we identify a distinction between Spenser the man or author and the constructed persona of Spenser-as-narrator, so we must identify the construction of the queen-as-reader as an artificial person within Spenser's text. The scenario of an interface between author and reader (or between reader and text) is a recurrent feature in much of Spenser's work and is modelled in many of his writings: in the presence of the glossator E.K. within *The Shepheardes Calender*; in the effect of a network of reading and response 'lately passed between two Vniversitie men' consciously contrived in the 1580 Spenser-Harvey correspondence; and in the desired reception of Spenser's 'Leaues, lines, and rymes' recreated in *Amoretti* I.

The queen-as-reader is addressed in the second person throughout, she is the implied 'thou' of the narrator's apostrophes (e.g. II.proem.4.6; II.x.4.4; III.ii.3.3). Crucially, she is the second person in the tripartite identification with fairy and fairyland made in II.proem.4.

> And thou, O fayrest Princesse vnder sky,
> In this fayre mirrhour maist behold thy face,
> And thine own realmes in lond of Faery,
> And in this antique ymage thy great auncestry. (II.proem.4.6-9)

Fairy in *The Faerie Queene* is explicitly stated to function as a signifier for the queen and her realm; this much is said in the explications of Spenser's allegory provided in the 'Letter to Raleigh' and in Hobynoll's commendatory verse. As the narrator promises in II.proem.4.1-3, through 'certein signes here sett in sundry place' we may 'find' fairyland through correctly reading and interpreting Spenser's allegory. But the equation made in the second half of the stanza explicates one patently artificial construction - the sign of fairy and the fairy queen - by reference to another, the constructed figure of the queen-as-reader. The narrator within the framing narrative creates the effect of speaking to a figure outside the text (and no doubt if Elizabeth actually read *The Faerie Queene* she would identify with the 'thou' of the narratorial addresses), whereas what actually takes place is that the narrator addresses another character placed within the text. In the reading of fairy that Spenser's narrator provides, one construction of the queen is interpreted by reference to another. The signification of the sign of fairy is deferred onto another sign in need of interpretation. But again we are faced with the issue of how to read or 'find' Elizabeth in *The Faerie Queene*. Spenser's construction of the queen in the framing narrative (the queen-as-reader) is a shadowy figure placed at the very margins of the text, implored to receive the narrator's 'history' and yet at the same time the ostensible subject of that history. Within the framing narrative the queen simultaneously maintains a central and yet marginal presence: presenting the story of 'Faerie knights and fayrest *Tanaquill*' to the queen is a central dynamic within *The Faerie Queene*, and yet her presence is registered more through narratorial expressions of distance, absence, and frustration. The concluding appeal in *The Faerie Queene* for that 'Sabaoths sight' may reiterate the desire to be brought once more to Zabeth's or Elizabeth's sight. The narrator's desire for the presence of the queen mirrors that of Arthur's desire for the fairy queen, and just as Gloriana only appears in stories and images within the *fabula* of *The Faerie Queene*, so the imagined royal reader of the text is ultimately only presented through the verbal constructions of Spenser's narrator.

Returning to the end of the second proem, the narratorial apology for using the 'couert vele' of fairy in representing Elizabeth reads not simply as the narrator begging leave for such a practice but as a concise argument for the necessity of this practice:

> The which O pardon me thus to enfold
> In couert vele, and wrap in shadowes light,
> That feeble eyes your glory may behold,
> Which ells could not endure those beames bright,
> But would bee dazled with exceeding light. (II.proem.5.1-5)

The 'couert vele' and, by extension, the overall representation of Elizabeth through the allegorical form of *The Faerie Queene*, is defended on the basis that such veiling is a necessary means of capturing and transmitting what is otherwise inexpressible to 'feeble eyes'. Allegorical veils (however inappropriate the term may actually be) are thus, the narrator argues, an inescapable part of the process of representing Elizabeth. Such a form of veiling is defended in the 'Letter to Raleigh' using a different argument: the notional appeal to a contemporary taste for 'showes' ('the vse of these dayes'). The image of the concealing veil that reveals has both a Platonic and Christian heritage, but whichever way we read it the concern is still with the practicalities of the narrator's task at hand and the signs used in the representational process.[39] Similarly in the proem to book three, the narrator's initial hesitation to use 'Forreine ensamples' from fairyland to illustrate chastity is, by the end of the proem, supplanted by an affirmation of the necessity for 'colourd showes' and shadowed representations, and a resignatory confession that he cannot 'figure plaine' the queen's 'glorious pourtraict' (III.proem.3). The proem clearly foregrounds the narrator's continued interest in the artificial means used to represent Elizabeth. The narrator presents two alternatives to the 'antique praises' from fairyland. Firstly, pointing to the 'ensample' of his 'Soueraines brest', the narrator believes that if one could behold 'the pourtraict of her hart' then the fairy allegory might be eschewed. But the ability of 'liuing art' to provide such an portrait is immediately doubted:

> But liuing art may not least part expresse,
> Nor life-resembling pencill it can paynt,
> All it were *Zeuxis* or *Praxiteles*:
> His dædale hand would faile, and greatly faynt,
> And her perfections with his error taynt:
> Ne Poets witt, that passeth Painter farre
> In picturing the parts of beautie daynt,
> So hard a workemanship aduenture darre,
> For fear through want of words her excellence to marre. (III.proem.2)

There then follows a deferential recommendation of Raleigh's portrait of the queen and the 'sweete verse, with *Nectar* sprinckeled,/ In which a gracious seruaunt pictured/ His *Cynthia*, his heauens fairest light' (III.proem.4) should the queen abjure the 'antique praises' presented by Spenser. Both alternatives to the fairy 'ensamples' point to further representational strategies and the construction of other artificial bodies with which to present the queen. The sign or series of signs 'from *Faery*' are briefly substituted with the metonymic, blazon-like anatomy performed

---

[39] Antoinette B. Dauber, 'veils', in *Spenser Encyclopedia*, p. 707. John Freccero, 'The Fig Tree and the Laurel: Petrarch's Poetics', in Parker and Quint eds, *Literary Theory/ Renaissance Texts*, p. 30, writes of the long-standing tradition of using the figure of the veil concealing a radiant face to represent the relationship of sign to referent. Jeffrey P. Fruen, '"True Glorious Type": The Place of Gloriana in *The Faerie Queene*', *SSt* 7 (1987), pp. 161-4, links the image of the veil here to biblical typology.

in considering how to represent Elizabeth's heart, and by the resort to another figure from Elizabeth's own representational vocabulary, Cynthia. One representational strategy simply replaces or displaces another.

That the fairy queen also provides a commentary on the textualization of Elizabeth becomes more apparent when we examine the presentation of Gloriana within the narrator's 'antique history'. Perhaps the most elementary point that can be made about Spenser's poem, even from a first reading, is that we never actually get to see the fairy queen. We never get to see Gloriana's annual feast nor learn of Artegall's fate at the fairy court, as is promised at V.xii.43.9. Gloriana's absence from the text has, as said, been explained using theories of neoplatonic idealism or in terms of a kind of negative capability; she plays a role through absence or indirect influence.[40] But following the principles for reading fairy established in the first chapter of this book we can also speak about the textual ontology of Gloriana. On reading through *The Faerie Queene* we do encounter Gloriana through the stories and reports of other characters, as an image upon the shields of Guyon and Satyrane (II.v.11; IV.iv.17), as the design for a stone worn above Arthur's heart that adorns his 'bauldrick braue' (I.vii.29-30), and at (and as) the culmination of '*Antiquitee* of *Faery* lond' (II.x.76). This is in addition to narratorial paraphrases of actions at Cleopolis that tell of the fairy queen initiating the quests of Redcrosse (I.i.3), Guyon (II.ii.43), Artegall (V.i.4), and Calidore (VI.x.1; VI.xii.12). Gloriana does appear, but only as a story or a text, only as something put together or 'made'. She appears as the subject of discourse when Arthur enquires after the image on Guyon's shield (II.ix.2-5), and when, at the behest of Medina, Guyon is asked the same kind of question as Una asks Arthur in I.ix.2 and 6 regarding where he is from and why he is there (II.ii.39). Guyon's reply to Medina yields an enthusiastic encomium of Gloriana that grants her the same heavenly authority as Arthur constructs in his story:

> In her the richesse of all heauenly grace
> In chiefe degree are heaped vp on hye:
> And all that els this worlds enclosure bace
> Hath great or glorious in mortall eye,
> Adornes the person of her Maiestye;
> That men beholding so great excellence,
> And rare perfection in mortalitye,
> Doe her adore with sacred reuerence,
> As th'Idole of her makers great magnificence. (II.ii.41)

Gloriana represents the highest form of temporal marker of God's power on earth, the temporal glory reified in the concept of sovereignty itself. Guyon's fairy story of Gloriana's greatness (II.ii.40-44) mirrors the overall project that occupies Spenser's narrator and draws attention back to the myth-making process

---

[40] The latter line is suggested by Nohrnberg, *Analogy*, p. 50; W. H. Herendeen, 'Gloriana', in *Spenser Encyclopedia*, p. 333.

consciously foregrounded in the framing narrative. Guyon's actions in the pursuit of glory and the service of the fairy queen will in turn be presented as a story, to be heard alongside other 'straunge aduentures' (including Redcrosse's 'aduenture of the *Errant damozell*' (II.i.19)) rehearsed at Gloriana's annual feast (II.ii.42). Spenser forestalls ever fully revealing Gloriana, constructing her instead as a purely textual entity, a story that is told both by the narrator and by the characters within the poem. In doing so Spenser appears to draw upon a pertinent attribute from fairy mythology - the ontological uncertainty or instability of fairy - as a means of representing the insubstantial nature of worldly fame and glory. We can see that by understanding the nature of Spenser's presentation of the fairy queen's ontology in the text it is possible to conceive of how the poet might go about representing glory, according to his general intention, using the figure of Gloriana. By the later books of *The Faerie Queene* Gloriana appears to exist solely through reports and injunctions as a far-off, disembodied power to whom captives and disgraced knights are dispatched. For Spenser and the New English colonial administrators in sixteenth-century Ireland, Elizabeth must have 'existed' in a similar fashion.

The Fairies at Mount Acidale

Although the fairy queen is presented through multiple layers of utterance in the episode of Arthur's dream discussed above, Arthur's fairy story is in fact typical of how Gloriana 'appears' within *The Faerie Queene*. Spenser's central representation of Elizabeth appears in *The Faerie Queene* as a fragmentary story or text. At Mount Acidale we are led to expect a comparable, albeit oblique vision of Elizabeth. From early on in book six, canto ten the narrator suggests a parity between the 'one sight' that Calidore viewed at Acidale and the 'heauenly hew' of Gloriana (VI.x.4). The use of the past tense in the reference to what Calidore 'did vew' places the narrator into a position of authority as he subtly creates the illusion that he knows exactly what transpires at Acidale and, following the rhetorical 'One day...' that opens VI.x.5, that he is imparting information about events that have already happened; he knows how the story ends. The Platonic image of the dazzling light (VI.x.4), to which the 'shadowes vaine' abjured by Calidore are incomparable, also nods to the 'beames bright' of Elizabeth's glory that necessitate the 'couert vele' of allegory in II.proem.5. Calidore's approach to Acidale is marked by evocations of fairy mythology that suggest we will indeed catch a glimpse of Gloriana here: the 'Nymphes and Faeries' protecting the stream that bounds the hill (VI.x.7); the 'troupe of Ladies' dancing to music; the sense of taboo at gazing upon and interrupting the dance (VI.x.11); and the ladies' immediate disappearance as Calidore emerges from the surrounding wood (VI.x.18). Perhaps even the 'hollow ground' of Acidale denotes a fairy hill (VI.x.10.4). The location of the episode within the structure of book six also compounds expectations that Spenser is to present another fairy story, as he had in the tenth canto of books one and two.[41]

The Acidale episode consistently foregrounds the process of textual production and conjoins many different literary topoi and mythological schemes, including more than one conception of fairy. The episode also sees Spenser taking up and adapting another Chaucerian fairy story as the ladies' disappearance clearly evokes 'The Wife of Bath's Tale' where the 'ladyes foure and twenty' vanish as the knight encroaches upon their dance, only to leave a single figure remaining (III 989-96). At the centre of the dance the Graces themselves (glossed by Colin in VI.x.21-4) encircle 'another Grace': Colin's unnamed 'lasse'. The episode makes intertextual allusions back to 'Aprill' where Spenser again foregrounded his own poetic vocation and project through Colin's lay of '*Elisa*, Queene of shepheardes all'. There also Spenser enacted a similar textualization of Elizabeth by identifying her as the daughter of Syrinx, the nymph in book one of Ovid's *Metamorphoses* who is transformed into a reed to escape Pan and forms the aetiology of piping itself ('Aprill', lines 50-51; *Shorter Poems*, p. 62). Elizabeth as the offspring of Pan and Syrinx is by implication made into a song, the product of artistic process. E.K.'s gloss decodes the very elementary genealogy contrived for Elizabeth within this allusion and anticipates a similarly transparent allusion made to the queen's parentage in '*Antiquitee* of *Faery* lond'.

At a moment where we might hope that Elizabeth or her primary avatar be revealed we find instead that Spenser's focus is once more on the matter of representing or producing a song for/of Elizabeth. Acidale is as much a place of literary production as it is a site of inspired poetry, as is clearly signalled by the presence of Spenser's literary persona Colin Clout, to whom the narrator makes special emphasis through his rhetorical apostrophe 'who knowes not *Colin Clout*?' and by his address to Colin in VI.x.16. Colin is engaged in producing a work analogous to *The Faerie Queene* itself: the kind of 'enchaunted show' that irresistibly drives Calidore seek further knowledge about what he sees, to gain a better reading of the show. Calidore has been compared to a 'well-meaning but limited reader who hungers for clear glosses and neatly packaged "significance"'.[42] In his reluctant explication to Calidore Colin fails to decode the figure at the centre of the dance, leaving exact signification open for interpretation but drawing attention back to the performative level and the context of Spenser's own literary production. In VI.x.28 the voice of Spenser's narrator persona elides into that of his persona Colin the poet-shepherd as he begs pardon from 'Great *Gloriana*, greatest Maiesty' for displacing the central figure for Elizabeth and focusing instead upon figures representing Spenser's personal poetic enterprise, Colin Clout and the 'countrey lasse' Rosalind. The gesture of deference at the end of the stanza

---

[41] Greenlaw, 'Spenser's Fairy Mythology', pp. 108-09, certainly reads this as a central fairy episode and supplements the elliptical reference to Colin's 'lasse' by suggesting that his love is indeed a fay; Calidore perhaps interrupts a similar kind of 'blandishments' to those with which the fairy queen entertains Arthur.

[42] Kinney, *Strategies*, p. 109.

promises to place praise of her 'handmayd' under Gloriana's feet, 'That when thy glory shall be farre displayd/ To future age of her this mention may be made', and echoes the sentiments of Spenser's dedication to the 1596 *Faerie Queene* that the poet's labours are an inseparable part of the 'eternal' praise and fame of the queen. When Spenser adopts his poetic persona once again in *Colin Clouts Come Home Againe*, the mutual benefits of his panegyric for Elizabeth are made explicit through the veiled observations of the shepherd Alexis: 'By wondering at thy *Cynthiaes* praise,/ *Colin*, thy selfe thou mak'st vs more to wonder,/ And her vpraising, doest thy selfe vpraise' (*Shorter Poems*, p. 354).

The Acidale episode concludes with a final gesture of narratorial control as Colin's dialogue with Calidore is explicitly reported as continuing on for a 'Long time' after the dance is interrupted, though we are never made privy to exactly what additional information their 'discourses' further reveal (VI.x.30). As when Arthur and Redcrosse are seen 'diuersly discoursing of their loues' following the story of Gloriana's visitation (I.ix.18), the effect is created that the narrator always has far more information than he ever chooses to reveal, particularly concerning the appearance of the fairy queen. The narrator is once again instrumental in 'playing out' the fairy queen when we turn to the mythical genealogy of Gloriana, '*Antiquitee* of *Faery* lond'.

Chapter 6

The Fairy Chronicle

In the previous chapter it was argued that Spenser employs the figure of the fairy queen not simply as a laudatory avatar of Elizabeth but as a means of initiating critical engagement with the reader of his text and drawing attention from the narrative surface or *fabula* of the text to its performative level where Spenser foregrounds and comments upon his ongoing mythopœic project. I now wish to consider my fourth Spenserian fairy story - the presentation of Guyon reading '*Antiquitee* of *Faery* lond' - in relation to another formal strategy that was widely employed as a part of Elizabeth's representational vocabulary and an integral part of mythopœic practices used to glorify and celebrate the queen and the Tudor line: the topos of the mythical genealogy.

Formal and Historical Contexts

It is almost customary in discussing the chronicles read by Arthur and Guyon in II.x to begin by apologizing for what may appear to modern readers of *The Faerie Queene* as tedious, digressive, or at any rate unrelated to the remaining cantos of book two.[1] But the momentous importance of the task of recounting the queen's 'famous auncestryes' is clearly signalled from the opening stanzas of II.x. It is here that Spenser repeatedly stresses the size of the 'haughty enterprise' before him and directly translates the narratorial profession of inadequacy and the call upon the muses for aid that open canto three of *Orlando Furioso*, in which Ariosto sets out the mythical genealogy of the house of Este. Spenser's doubts concerning the abilities of his 'fraile pen' to 'conceiue' Elizabeth's 'soueraine glory, and great bountyhed' (II.x.2) echo similar statements expressing the difficulty of representing the queen found in the proem to book three. The mythical British history and the 'rolls of Elfin Emperours' that are to be set out in II.x are consciously located in relation to a recognizable literary and epideictic convention found both in Spenser's classical epic and Italian romance-epic sources through the direct

---

[1] Jerry Leath Mills, 'Prudence, History, and the Prince in *The Faerie Queene*, Book II', *HLQ* 41 (1978), pp. 83-101, however, attempts to read II.x constructively as a lesson in temperance, an allegory of how to use the past for the present and the future providing instruction for the reader on the proper method of using and reading histories. See also Ruth Pryor, 'Spenser's Temperance and the Chronicles of England', *NM* 81 (1980), pp. 161-8.

incorporation of Ariosto's phrasing and the Homeric allusion to a '*Mœonian* quill'.[2] Certainly, as Jerry Leath Mills observes regarding the chronicles, 'Spenser's own estimation of their relevance may be inferred from his placing the main section in canto x, a canto generally reserved for important thematic material.'[3]

The conscious construction of an ennobling lineage or a myth of origin is a commonplace both of medieval and early modern panegyric technique. The topos of the mythical genealogy is not restricted to purely literary works; the use of the marvellous to explain an individual's greatness or singularity is found in medieval historiographical and hagiographical tradition, and provides the model for many of the more fantastic elements that Geoffrey of Monmouth incorporates into his *Historia Regum Britanniae*. The *Historia* and its distillates were then drawn upon in turn during the fifteenth and sixteenth centuries in the construction of the Tudors' mythical ancestry. In many ways this is cognate with the motif of marking out the greatness of a mortal hero through representing his relationship with a fairy mistress or incorporating fairy into one's family tree (discussed in chapter two). The most famous examples of the latter are of course the Melusine legends connected with the mythical ancestry of the Angevin dynasty and, later, with the house of Lusignan.[4] Similarly, there are examples of attempts made amongst the nobility in the sixteenth century (including both Leicester and Sidney) to actively enhance their pedigree through manipulating and forging their own genealogy.[5] Harvey's reference in the 1580 correspondence to the predicted favourable reception of Spenser's Latin *Stemmata Dudleiana* may allude to a work celebrating Leicester's lineage, perhaps along the lines of Harvey's own celebration of the Dudleys' aristocratic origins in book two of *Gratulationes Valdinenses* (1578).[6]

---

[2] Thomas H. Cain, *Praise in The Faerie Queene* (Lincoln: University of Nebraska Press, 1978), p. 125, gives further examples of national epics that employ the genealogy topos or chronicle mode: Virgil's *Aeneid*, book six; Camoëns' *Lusiads*, canto three; and Ronsard's *Françiade*, book three. Spenser further invokes the association of the genealogy topos with the third canto of contemporary panegyrics by placing the continuation of the British history related to Britomart in Merlin's cave in the third canto of the third book of *The Faerie Queene*. The topos is also used in the third instalment of the British history in III.ix.33-51, the closest analogies for which are again found in Italian romance-epic and Ruggiero, mythical ancestor of the Estense, tracing his family origins back to Troy; see *Orlando Furioso*, tr. Waldman, 36.70-74; Matteo Maria Boiardo, *Orlando Innamorato*, tr. Charles Stanley Ross (Berkeley: University of California Press, 1989), 3.5.18-37. John Watkins, *The Specter of Dido: Spenser and Virgilian Epic* (New Haven: Yale University Press, 1995), p. 133, notes that the heroes' reading of their respective histories in Eumnestes's library may also be modelled upon Aeneas and Achates's discovery of Juno's murals in book one of the *Aeneid*, as they 'feast their souls' upon depictions of the Trojan wars.
[3] Jerry Leath Mills, 'chronicles', in *Spenser Encyclopedia*, p. 151.
[4] Giraldus Cambrensis, *Opera*, 8: 301-02; W. L. Warren, *King John* (London: Methuen, 1981; repr. New Haven: Yale University Press, 1997), pp. 2-3. On the Lusignan line, *Mélusine*, ed. Roach, pp. 21-63; Le Goff, 'Melusina', pp. 205-22.
[5] May McKisack, *Medieval History in the Tudor Age* (Oxford: Clarendon Press, 1971), pp. 66-7.
[6] *Three Proper and wittie, familiar Letters*, pp. 621, 620.

Spenser himself claimed he was related to the Spencers of Althorp in the dedications to several of his works, and in *Colin Clouts Come Home Againe* (lines 536-9; *Shorter Poems*, p. 360). Within *The Faerie Queene* there are several points, extraneous to the central mythological schemes used to celebrate Elizabeth, where characters construct an ennobling lineage for themselves or evoke their genealogy in a claim to authority. Lucifera masks her illegitimate title and infernal parentage by claiming descent from Jove in an attempt to legitimize the fact that she made herself queen through usurping rightful sovereign authority (I.iv.11-12). Mutabilitie bases her claim of authority over Jove in VII.vi.26-7 on the precedence of her genealogy and argues that, like Lucifera, Jove achieved his mandate to rule the heavens through might not right - a claim that is by no means conclusively or satisfactorily negotiated and refuted by Jove's reply in VII.vi.33.

As well as relating to literary convention however, II.x, and ultimately *The Faerie Queene* as a whole, is firmly located within the context of widespread and deep-seated interest in the uses and production of history that was well established in England by the time that Spenser is writing. At least in part this is set against the background of the development of fifteenth- and sixteenth-century advances in humanist historiography and its renewed focus upon the use of history to provide lessons for the present not simply in moral precepts but through increasing study of classical texts, in natural laws, causation, and political theory.[7] An important part of this development, particularly early on, is the attention paid to the stylistic aspect of historiography and the role of rhetoric in history-writing. In their attention to the comparison of different sources and assessment of the relative value and authority of different sources, the humanists evince an implicit awareness of, and sensitivity to, the historian's role in the production of history and, by implication, the production of authority. The historian's capacity for producing history was certainly an important commodity within the system of patronage and panegyric during this early period, and many of the fifteenth- and early sixteenth-century humanists were commissioned by kings and other rulers to write official histories of a country or a locality and were often complicit in elaborating upon national foundation myths as part of their eulogistic strategy.[8] The accession of Henry VII gave a new impetus to historical writing in England towards the end of the fifteenth century. I have already discussed the political utility that the mythical history of

---

[7] There is not space here to give a full account of the complexities concerning the development, characteristics, and implications of the humanist historiography, but the standard accounts of developments in historical thought during the early modern period are: Leonard Dean, *Tudor Theories of History Writing* (Ann Arbor: University of Michigan Press, 1947); F. Smith Fussner *The Historical Revolution: English Historical Writing and Thought 1580-1640* (London: Routledge, 1962); Levy, *Tudor Historical Thought*, esp. pp. 33-78; Peter Burke, *The Renaissance Sense of the Past* (London: Arnold, 1969); Ferguson, *Clio Unbound*; Antonia Gransden, *Historical Writing in England II: c. 1307 to the Early Sixteenth Century* (Ithaca: Cornell University Press, 1982), pp. 425-53; D. R. Woolf, *Reading History in Early Modern England* (Cambridge: Cambridge University Press, 2000).
[8] Gransden, *Historical Writing*, p. 429.

Arthur had during the Tudor period and its function within celebrations and representations both of England and the Tudor dynasty itself, but we shall also see how the mythical British history and the careful contrivance of the Tudors' descent from Arthur provides the model for the fairy chronicle '*Antiquitee* of *Faery* lond'. As we see in both of the chronicles in II.x, in the case of mythopœic constructions of the origins and pedigree of the monarchical line, formulation of the individual's genealogy overlaps with a process of (re)constructing the history of the monarch's nation; the narrator, accordingly, professes to recount the 'realme and race' of his queen (II.x.4). Gloriana's genealogy is also - simultaneously - a record of the successive victories of the elfin race and civic improvements of its capital city.

From the mid-sixteenth century onwards interest in the study of national 'antiquities' - including topography, archaeology, chorography, heraldry, as well as what nowadays would be classed as local history and folklore - was fed by a new national self-consciousness occasioned in no small part by the break with Rome.[9] The antiquarian impulse was, in part, a response to the dispersal of monastic libraries and the need expressed by Leland, Bale, and Archbishop Matthew Parker to locate and preserve the collections of the dissolved houses. Bale records the retrieval process in *The Laboryouse journey and serche of Johan Leylande for Englandes antiquitees* (1549) and by this time had already produced the first edition of a vast bibliography of British authors.[10] The version of national history that Geoffrey of Monmouth constructs played an important role in asserting ecclesiastical independence from papal control. The 1533 Act in Restraint of Appeals to Rome evoked a similar form of textual authority to assert the legitimacy of its powers: 'by divers sundry old authentic histories and chronicles it is manifestly declared and expressed that this realm of England is an empire, and so hath been accepted in the world'.[11] The British history and the study of histories of the period post-Norman Conquest were employed as a means of countering Catholic claims of papal sovereignty over the English church and of asserting that Christianity was established in England long before the Roman missionaries arrived

---

[9] On the rise of antiquarianism: Robin Flower, 'Laurence Nowell and the Discovery of England in Tudor Times', *PBA* 21 (1935), pp. 47-73; A. L. Rowse, *The England of Elizabeth: The Structure of Society* (London: Macmillan, 1950), pp. 49-86; Levy, *Tudor Historical Thought*, pp. 124-66; McKisack, *Medieval History*, pp. 126-69; Joseph M. Levine, *Humanism and History: Origins of Early Modern English Historiography* (Ithaca, Cornell University Press, 1987), pp. 73-106; Stan A.E. Mendyk, *'Speculum Britanniae': Regional Study, Antiquarianism, and Science in Britain to 1700* (Toronto: University of Toronto Press, 1989).

[10] See Kendrick, *British Antiquity*, pp. 45-64; Leslie P. Fairfield, *John Bale: Mythmaker for the English Reformation* (West Lafayette: Purdue University Press, 1976), pp. 86-120. Bale's *Illustrium maioris Britanniae scriptorum... summarium* was published in 1548, and appears again in an expanded two-volume form as *Scriptorum Illustrium maioris Brytanniae... catalogus* (1557-59).

[11] Anglo, *Images of Tudor Kingship*, p. 56.

in the sixth century.[12] In successive editions of *Acts and Monuments* John Foxe constructed a virulently Protestant history of the English church that told of how Joseph of Arimathea first introduced Christianity to the Britons, but how this had ultimately been degraded and defiled by the extended influx of papal influence.[13] (Spenser refers to Joseph of Arimathea's mythical mission in II.x.53.) With similar intent, Parker and his circle of assistants undertook to collect, edit, and annotate manuscripts with the intention ultimately of publishing an affirmation of the antiquity and purity of the English church.[14] It was under Parker's aegis that the Elizabethan Society for Antiquaries was established in 1572 and as part of the Society's commitment to preserving rare books and 'monuments' repeated calls were made to establish a national library although, at least during the sixteenth century, this was never achieved.[15]

Spenser's representation of Eumnestes's chamber is written therefore within a context wherein the library, as repository of historical authority, clearly plays an important ideological role and assumes the function of a political tool. One need only witness, to give a well-known example, how John Dee's substantial library at his home at Mortlake had a vital political function in acting as a reservoir of historical precedents from which authority for the present could be drawn and constructed. Dee's library was not simply a place of withdrawal or repose but functioned as an intensely active, political space where knowledge was reconfigured and applied, not merely 'stored'. Dee was able to advise and guide the reading of visitors to his library, and to aid in the process of finding authority for the commercial and ideological projects of his correspondents and clientele, as he did in 1597, for example, with Sir Edward Dyer's negotiations with the Hanseatic league concerning the 'Sea-Jurisdiction of the British Empire'.[16] Dee himself made similar appeal to historical authority when he used Elizabeth's descent from Arthur to argue that the queen could claim imperial dominion in territory overseas on the basis that it had once been conquered by her fabled ancestor.[17] It has even been

---

[12] Levy, *Tudor Historical Thought*, pp. 79-123, provides a general overview of Reformation historiography.

[13] William Haller, *Foxe's Book of Martyrs and the Elect Nation* (London: Cape, 1963), pp. 145-6, 150.

[14] See C. E. Wright, 'The Dispersal of the Monastic Libraries and the Beginnings of Anglo-Saxon Studies. Matthew Parker and his Circle: A Preliminary Study', *Transactions of the Cambridge Bibliographical Society* 1 (1953), pp. 208-37; Levy, *Tudor Historical Thought*, pp. 114-23; McKisack, *Medieval History*, pp. 26-49; Benedict Scott Robinson, '"Darke speech": Matthew Parker and the Reforming of History', *SCJ* 29 (1998), pp. 1061-83.

[15] Levy, *Tudor Historical Thought*, pp. 127-8; McKisack, *Medieval History*, p. 168.

[16] William H. Sherman, *John Dee: The Politics of Reading and Writing in the English Renaissance* (Amherst: University of Massachusetts Press, 1995), pp. 193-6.

[17] Sherman, *John Dee*, pp. 148-200, details the extent of this project. The Arthur legend was also used to assert English territorial rights in Ireland; see Andrew Hadfield, *Edmund Spenser's Irish Experience: Wilde Fruit and Salvage Soyl* (Oxford: Clarendon Press, 1997), pp. 88-96.

tentatively suggested that Spenser himself could have used Dee's library.[18] Both the formal and the historical context of the episode concerning Eumnestes's chamber provide a framework for what takes place with the construction of '*Antiquitee* of *Faery* lond' as Spenser adapts the mythical genealogy topos used to celebrate and glorify Elizabeth and the Tudors and applies it to the mythological scheme of fairy around which his work as a whole is ostensibly structured.

Access to '*Antiquitee* of *Faery* lond'

Eumnestes's library is Arthur and Guyon's final stop on their tour around the House of Alma. Having made their way through the 'Hall' of the digestive system and stomach, the knights pause for a time in the 'Parlour' of the heart, where Arthur entertains Praysdesire, a figure emblematic of his own desire for fame and glory, an externalization of his quest for Gloriana. In like fashion Guyon courts an image of his own moderation ('modestee') and shamefastness before both knights ascend the alabaster steps leading to the 'stately Turret' that represents the head within the body-allegory of Alma's house. The description of the 'goodly Beacons' of the eyes occasions a narratorial exclamation of wonder and rhetorical admission of inadequacy at the prospect of fully recounting the 'great workemanship, and wondrous powre' of the head and brain as a whole (II.ix.46-7). Focus then turns to the three rooms or parts of the brain that contain the three higher faculties of the soul - imagination, reason, and memory - that are presented as three counsellors who guide Alma in the governance of her corporeal structure. Alma first leads the knights to Phantastes, whose chamber is 'dispainted' with the stuff of 'idle fantasies' and swarming with 'Deuices, dreames, opinions vnsound,/ Shewes, visions, sooth-sayes, and prophesies;/ And all that fained is, as leasings, tales, and lies' (II.ix.51). The knights then proceed on through the middle chamber that is occupied by the unnamed individual representing reason and decorated with depictions of the active application of rational faculties: 'Of Magistrates, of courts, of tribunals,/ Of commen wealthes, of states, of pollicy,/ Of lawes, of iudgementes, and of decretals' (II.ix.53). Whilst the knights linger briefly in the middle chamber, momentarily desirous to be the disciples of reason, it is in the hindmost part of the mind and the chamber of Eumnestes or 'good memory' that the knights (and the narrator) dwell the longest. It is in Eumnestes's chamber that Elizabeth's mythical genealogy is set out in the form of the two chronicles, '*Briton moniments*' and '*Antiquitee* of *Faery* lond'.

In locating '*Antiquitee* of *Faery* lond' within the chamber of memory Spenser repeats the gesture of authorization that he attempts to establish through the narrator within the framing narrative of the poem. The fairy chronicle is sourced from the 'antique Regesters' of Eumnestes's library and not the 'leasings, tales, and

---

[18] Read, *Temperate Conquests*, p. 26.

lies' of Phantastes's chamber.[19] The fairy story set out in '*Antiquitee* of *Faery* lond'
is located within a work that evokes the kind of volume that the narrator himself
professes to set forth. As has been shown, in the framing narrative Spenser models
and comments upon the process with which he is involved - that of setting forth a
story of fairy - through establishing his narrator figure in the role of a compilator.
The *compilatio* scenario maintained throughout *The Faerie Queene* sees the
narrator drawing forth the 'antique rolles' of his text from the muses' 'euerlasting
scryne' and claiming that what the readers have before them as *The Faerie Queene*
is the rehearsal of an earlier textual authority. The narrator explicitly places his
fairy story within a textual tradition. He eschews any element of invention on his
part, claiming instead that his 'famous antique history' is the 'matter of iust
memory', and that his role is one of putting together and allowing access to the
words or *materia* of others. In so doing the narrator stresses his own crucial role as
intermediary (or 'dispenser') in allowing access to his recondite fairy source. In the
build-up to the presentation of '*Antiquitee* of *Faery* lond' that takes place towards
the end of II.ix, the narrator's role is foregrounded once again within the story that
he ostensibly sets forth by the way in which Eumnestes's role is initially mirrored
and then quickly taken up by the narrator within the canto containing the two
chronicles.

Even before Arthur and Guyon 'chance' upon records of their respective
ancestries, attention is drawn to the means through which we will gain access to the
materials contained within and, significant for present purposes, how the history of
fairy will be played out to the reader. Eumnestes's chamber is not simply a storage
facility, occupied by a passive custodian, from which the narrator draws the two
chronicles. The depiction of Eumnestes in his chamber presents the active
application of memory, and in so doing serves to foreground the actual process
itself of constructing the kind of texts to which Eumnestes grants access at the end
of canto nine and that the narrator sets forth in II.x. In his depiction of the
functioning of memory (i.e. of Eumnestes and his boy, Anamnestes, at work),
Spenser draws attention to the means by which the written record of memory is a
subjective, positivist construction shaped and compiled from many different texts
and authorities and thus susceptible to omissions and lacunae, as represented by the
'canker holes' in the old man's parchment scrolls (II.ix.57). The description of
Eumnestes's chamber briefly sketches the operation of the historian at work, the
process by which the chronicles of II.x might well be put together:

> His chamber all was hangd about with rolls,
> And old records from auncient times deriud

---

[19] King, *The Faerie Queene and Middle English Romance*, pp. 185-8, addresses this
particular issue by arguing persuasively that '*Antiquitee* of *Faery* lond' is a representation of
the Platonic and Christian idea that human memory retained an image of the ideal,
prelapsarian condition, and that this constituted a 'recollection of knowledge which humans
possessed before souls descended into bodies, or before humans deviated from God's will'.
'*Antiquitee* of *Faery* lond' thus models this ideal conception of memory.

Some made in books, some in long parchment scrolles,
That were all worm-eaten, and full of canker holes.

Amidst them all he in chaire was sett,
Tossing and turning them withouten end (II.ix.57-8).

The reference to worm-eaten documents echoes the similarly corrupt 'mouse-eaten records' mentioned in Sidney's description of his hypothetical historian in *An Apologie for Poetry*: 'authorising himself (for the most part) upon other histories, whose greatest authorities are built upon the notable foundation of hearsay; having much ado to accord differing writers and to pick truth out of partiality'.[20] The allusion further draws attention to the role of the individual engaged in constructing and emplotting histories and the means by which history is recorded and transmitted.

The narratorial attention afforded to the workings of Eumnestes's chamber and to the individual who grants access to the texts therein momentarily creates the effect that the 'chronicle of Briton kings' and 'rolls of Elfin Emperours' will simply be works that are cut and pasted into *The Faerie Queene* that we are to read, as it were, over the shoulders of Arthur and Guyon. The narrator once more claims to set forth the 'matter of iust memory', and Eumnestes could be said to imitate the narrator's role in functioning as the means through which we are allowed access to another story of fairy: the story-within-a-story or history-within-a-history that is '*Antiquitee* of *Faery* lond'. However, what actually takes place in II.x is neither the dramatization of Arthur and Guyon's reading nor the recitation in reported speech of an 'historical' narrative such as we find with Merlin's prophecy in III.iii; it is the presentation of an editorial selection or paraphrase of the chronicles that continually foregrounds the presence of the narrator as the lens through which we get to view British and fairy history. As in the framing narrative, the narrator is shown to be drawing from and digesting works of antique history, the 'old mans booke' and 'ample volume' of '*Briton moniments*' and '*Antiquitee* of *Faery* lond' respectively, and then playing these out to his reader. For sake of clarity in the discussion below I shall refer to the two books read by Arthur and Guyon, respectively, as the British and fairy *chronicles*. The British *chronicle* is distinguished from the British *history* which refers here to the collective record of events set out in '*Briton moniments*', Merlin's prophecy, and in the pre-history of the British conquest that forms the table-talk of Britomart and Paridell in III.ix.33-51. Book two, canto ten begins with Spenser's direct translation of the first three stanzas of *Orlando Furioso* canto three and establishes, following Ariosto's model, the narratorial mediation between the *fabula* presented in the chronicles and the sixteenth-century temporal context of the poem, in what I have termed the

---

[20] Sir Philip Sidney, *An Apologie for Poetry or The Defence of Poesy*, ed. Geoffrey Shepherd (London: Nelson, 1965), p. 105.

performative level of *The Faerie Queene*.[21] In doing so, the opening of II.x
reasserts what takes place in the framing narrative as a whole and returns us to the
activities and attendant preoccupations dramatized therein. After a rhetorical
profession of inadequacy for the task of recounting his sovereign's 'famous
auncestryes', the narrator makes the explicit connection between the subject matter
of '*Briton moniments*' and his implied audience as he addresses the queen directly:

> Thy name O soueraine Queene, thy realme and race,
> From this renowmed Prince deriued arre,
> Who mightily vpheld that royall mace,
> Which now thou bear'st, to thee descended farre
> From mighty kings and conquerours in warre,
> Thy fathers and great Grandfathers of old,
> Whose noble deeds aboue the Northerne starre
> Immortall fame for euer hath enrold;
> As in that old mans booke they were in order told. (II.x.4)

This kind of mediation between the *fabula* and the performative level takes place
throughout II.x. As the canto progresses we are repeatedly led back to the
sixteenth-century temporal context (the narrator's 'now') through narratorial
apostrophes and historical allusions, together with an evident self-consciousness
towards the artifice and construction of the chronicles themselves that becomes
most apparent in '*Antiquitee* of *Faery* lond'.

The Relationship of '*Briton moniments*' and '*Antiquitee* of *Faery* lond'

The juxtaposition of the chronicles of Britain and fairyland in II.x has often been
used as the basis for examining the meaning of Spenser's employment of fairy
mythology, and upon which theories regarding ontological distinctions between
human and fairy within *The Faerie Queene* may be formed. Harry Berger, Jr., for
example, argues that the two chronicles stress the contrast between the fallen state
of humankind figured by Arthur and his line, and the unfallen race of 'Elfin man'
which, whilst representing 'a much more satisfactory state of nature than that of
postlapsarian Adam... contains a much more limited possibility of perfection and
life'.[22] Another argument commonly found in critical treatments of '*Antiquitee* of

---

[21] In the episode in *Orlando Furioso* that provides the immediate model for Merlin's
prophecy to Britomart (III.iii), narratorial mediation is adumbrated by the figure of the
sorceress from whom Bradamant learns of her destined progeny as, it is explained, the
sorceress selects a choice few of the spirits of Bradamant's descendants to present and
expound (*Orlando Furioso*, tr. Waldman, 3.23).

[22] Berger, *Allegorical Temper*, p. 108. Berger utilizes his distinction between the complex,
developing Britons and the ideal, unchanging fairy race in his subsequent essay 'The
Spenserian Dynamics', in *Revisionary Play: Studies in the Spenserian Dynamics* (Berkeley:
University of California Press, 1988), pp. 34-5.

Faery lond' is that the juxtaposed chronicles represent the dichotomy of real and ideal, of history and fiction, or of different ways of presenting history.[23] One such reading is put forward by Michael O'Connell, who argues that the labours of Eumnestes in his library depict 'the constant activity of man's cultural memory, a memory in which nothing is ever really lost altogether but in which continual searching and comparison and restoration are necessary for true understanding'.[24] Taken together, the chronicles found in Eumnestes's library provide a model of the fusion of history and myth from which cultural memory is formed. The British history materials are set out in order to evoke a familiar pattern of the past in Spenser's reader, which is then set in opposition to the obviously fictive '*Antiquitee of Faery* lond'. Spenser intends us to contrast a sense of the past with his own construction of the 'golden world' of the fairy chronicle, an idealized genealogy constructed to perform a hortative function in implicitly encouraging the 'further realisation of the ideals of peace and order'.[25]

Whilst most critics focus on the contrast between the respective meaning of each of the two chronicles, it is equally important to understand the relationship between '*Briton moniments*' and '*Antiquitee of Faery* lond'.[26] Parity between the chronicles is suggested from the opening of canto ten by the narrator's reference to the plural 'famous auncestryes' of Elizabeth that he is about to recount and the inference of their shared panegyric function in the text (II.x.1). Of particular interest to the present study is the way in which the tradition of mythopœic genealogy that lies behind Spenser's construction of '*Briton moniments*' provides the most important formal and imaginative source for the structure, detail, and method of presentation of the fairy chronicle. The model of the mythical British history found in Geoffrey of Monmouth's *Historia*, together with the 'Galfridian'

---

[23] Joanne Craig, 'The Image of Mortality: Myth and History in *The Faerie Queene*', *ELH* 39 (1972), pp. 532-5; Andrew Fichter, *Poets Historical: Dynastic Epic in the Renaissance* (New Haven: Yale University Press, 1982), pp. 183-4; Hume, *Edmund Spenser*, pp. 145-61. The concept set out in Mills, 'Prudence', that '*Antiquitee of Faery* lond' represents a model of temperance set in contrast to the intemperance of the '*Briton moniments*', has been countered by Joan Warchol Rossi, '*Britons moniments*: Spenser's Definition of Temperance in History', *ELR* 15 (1985), pp. 42-58, who argues that the British history is by no means wholly negative but presents a definition of temperance as it must operate within a fallen world.

[24] Michael O'Connell, *Mirror and Veil: The Historical Dimension of Spenser's Faerie Queene* (Chapel Hill: University of North Carolina Press, 1977), p. 69.

[25] O'Connell, *Mirror and Veil*, pp. 72, 81.

[26] An exception to this is David Lee Miller, *The Poem's Two Bodies: The Poetics of the 1590 Faerie Queene* (Princeton: Princeton University Press, 1988), pp. 201-02, who argues that both '*Briton moniments*' and '*Antiquitee of Faery* lond' are structured 'with reference to the ideal body of the sovereignty' and provide a history of the concept of sovereignty itself. Jacqueline T. Miller, 'The Status of Faeryland: Spenser's "Vniust Possession"', *SSt* 5 (1985), pp. 31-44, similarly asserts that we should consider the parity of the chronicles on the basis that Prometheus's initial act of creation, and his subsequent punishment, demonstrate that the usurpation and violence of '*Briton moniments*' are not absent from '*Antiquitee of Faery* lond'.

tradition of imitators and redactors that remained and was utilized through to Spenser's day, underlies *both* of the chronicles in II.x. In particular I want to propose that '*Antiquitee* of *Faery* lond' takes up and develops an inherent self-consciousness towards its own construction that we can identify in parts of '*Briton moniments*', and that in II.x Spenser not only constructs and sets forth a bipartite mythical genealogy for Elizabeth and the Tudors in the form of the two chronicles, but also similarly demonstrates a conscious foregrounding of the vital role that the poet plays (and thus, by implication, that Spenser himself plays) in formulating and perpetuating an idealized representation of the nation and ruling dynasty. I shall examine the ways in which this takes place in '*Briton moniments*' before moving on to consider '*Antiquitee* of *Faery* lond'.

Such a measure of self-consciousness is apparent from the outset of our engagement with the chronicles of II.x, and I noted above how the narrator establishes his own role as mediator and expositor for the materials supposedly located within the British and fairy texts. Canto ten as a whole is a masterpiece of syncretism and artifice formed from multiple layers of historical, pseudo-historical, and mythical allusion and reference. There is a certain irony inherent in the opening line of the canto, which asks 'Who now shall giue vnto me words and sound,/ Equall vnto this haughty enterprise?', in that these very words are taken directly from Ariosto in the most literal translation of *Orlando Furioso* found in the entire *Faerie Queene* (II.x.1). The extended borrowing of the opening lines certainly sets the tone for Spenser's mode of construction seen throughout '*Briton moniments*' and the British history as a whole. Carrie Harper's well-known monograph on the British history painstakingly traces the extent to which Spenser composes '*Briton moniments*' from many different sources, and identifies the principal sources as being Geoffrey of Monmouth's *Historia* for provision of the general outline of the chronicle materials, together with Raphael Holinshed's *Chronicles* (seemingly both the 1577 and 1587 editions), John Stow's 1580 *Chronicles of England* (reprinted in 1584 as *The Annales of England*), and to a lesser extent *A Mirror for Magistrates* and John Hardyng's *Chronicle.*[27] At several points in the historical narrative Spenser further supplements and embellishes his chronicle sources with extraneous allusions taken from contemporary mythological dictionaries, as noted in the comparison of the British queen Mertia to a fay (II.x.42). The 'old mans booke' from which the narrator professes to draw serves as a synecdochal image of the wider intertextual composite from which Spenser himself constructs '*Briton moniments*'. Harper indeed concludes by comparing Spenser's method of compilation and synthesis to the description of Eumnestes himself (II.ix.57-8, quoted above) and her monograph provides further evidence of what is by now a truism of *Faerie Queene* source study: that, even within the economy of a single

---

[27] Harper, *Sources*, pp. 36-7. More recently, Lisa Richardson in her thesis 'Sir John Hayward and Early Stuart Historiography', PhD. thesis. Cambridge University, 1999, has suggested a greater prevalence of this mode of imitative or assimilative, syncretic historiography as she traces and details the tissue of direct borrowings and translations from which Hayward constructs his historical works.

phrase or image, Spenser can be seen to draw and translate from many different authorities.[28] As in Spenser's use of fairy mythology in his other fairy episodes, the syncretic mode of sourcing is played upon in '*Antiquitee* of *Faery* lond', as will be shown below. Harper's study is also one of the most useful tools for examining the fairy chronicle as it provides a comprehensive record of the Galfridian tradition from which Spenser builds '*Briton moniments*' and that provides the vocabulary of motifs and images from which he goes on to construct '*Antiquitee* of *Faery* lond'.

Although Spenser does not for the most part invent the chronicle materials in '*Briton moniments*' in so far as he largely draws from a textual tradition of sources, we can identify how Spenser sought to 'authorize' his own presentation of British history through the methods by which he constructs and patterns the chronicle that Arthur reads. Harper is rightly hesitant to propose a dominant framework or rationale with which to explain why Spenser uses a particular source for any given image or episode in '*Briton moniments*', but she concludes that the pursuit of historical veracity is assuredly not the primary governing principle behind Spenser's method of construction.[29] It is clear, however, from any attempt to trace and understand the construction of '*Briton moniments*', that there is emphasis on Spenser's part to stress the great variety of his chronicle sources and his orchestration of many different texts within his own work. In part, this level of conscious variation serves as a means of stressing Spenser's own role as 'poet-historical', for a contemporary reader might be expected to know the basic details of 'received' British history and go on to appreciate the workmanship of Spenser's synthesis.[30] At least one early modern reader of *The Faerie Queene*, John Dixon, read the British history presented in books two and three most attentively, carefully noting the length of each king's reign and keying Spenser's text to other chronicle sources.[31] '*Briton moniments*' does, after all, present Spenser's unique formulation of British history. In particular, Spenser appears to pattern the historical account provided in '*Briton moniments*', intimated from the outset by the narrator's reference to how the noble deeds of Elizabeth's ancestors are to be set out in Eumnestes's book 'in order' (II.x.4). Berger has shown the extent to which such patterning can be identified and has discussed how one manifestation of said 'order' in '*Briton moniments*' takes the form of a division of the chronicle materials into three parts separated by two interregna.[32] Such a conscious form of

---

[28] Harper, *Sources*, pp. 184-5.

[29] Harper, *Sources*, p. 179.

[30] O'Connell, *Mirror and Veil*, pp. 73-4. Benjamin Griffin, *Playing the Past: Approaches to English Historical Drama, 1385-1600* (Woodbridge: Brewer, 2001), pp. 74-7, argues that Tudor historical drama and poetry was produced within a context of extensive popular knowledge of British history that would inform a contemporary audience's or reader's aesthetic appreciation.

[31] Graham Hough, *The First Commentary on The Faerie Queene* (Published privately, 1964), pp. 11-14, 17-18. Dixon is silent on the fairy chronicle.

[32] Berger, *Allegorical Temper*, p. 94. Berger, 'The Structure of Merlin's Chronicle in *The Faerie Queene* III.iii', in *Revisionary Play*, pp. 121-30, similarly identifies a tripartite patterning to Merlin's prophecy.

historiographical patterning ultimately demonstrates the extent of Spenser's concern with the potential to pattern historical narrative that can be seen within the British history as a whole. Spenser exercises the prerogative of the poet-historical, mentioned in the 'Letter to Raleigh', to fragment and reorganize the sequence of his materials as befits his needs ('euen where it most concerneth him'). We can see another example of this active reorganization of materials in Merlin's prophecy as Spenser deviates from his sources in order to play down the negative aspects of Conan, whose deposition of Arthur's nephew Constantius is effaced to preserve the integrity of the prophesied British line (III.iii.27-31).[33] Spenser modifies the chronicle sources in order to make Artegall Arthur's half-brother, and Conan Artegall's son (and hence a legitimate relation of Arthur and Constantius).[34] Elizabeth's 'derivation' from Arthur proclaimed in II.x.4 is thus a more textual, positivist, 'man-made' succession rather than a direct, lineal, biological descent.

In setting out '*Briton moniments*' Spenser's narrator adopts many features directly from Geoffrey's method of historical narration and incorporates several of the narratorial authorizing gestures found in the *Historia*. These include: periodic allusions to one's source or authority at points of conjecture or questionable testimony (e.g. II.x.5.8; II.x.53.8); reference to things that can still be seen in the narratorial present 'if sought' (Caesar's sword in II.x.49, Stonehenge in II.x.66); and the use of synchronisms to locate events in the narrative within a credible framework based on events from classical and Scriptural sources.[35] The most prominent example in '*Briton moniments*' of this latter device is in stanza 50, where the narrator cross-references the reign of Cymbeline to the Incarnation, though he deferentially adopts the topos of narratorial inability, thus heightening his subject matter but also drawing attention to the poet himself through foregrounding the narration taking place:

> Next him [Cassibalane] *Tenantius* raignd, then *Kimbeline*,
> What time th'eternall Lord in fleshly slime
> Enwombed was, from wretched *Adams* line
> To purge away the guilt of sinfull crime:
> O ioyous memorie of happy time,
> That heauenly grace so plenteously displayd;
> (O too high ditty for my simple rime.) (II.x.50)

Elsewhere in '*Briton moniments*', similar use is made of parenthesis and the vocative case for narratorial apostrophe and comment, as in the lament at the Roman invasion of Britain (II.x.47) or the narrator's extended praise of Bunduca

---

[33] Harper, *Sources*, pp. 146-7.

[34] Hume, *Edmund Spenser*, pp. 152-3.

[35] On the practice of alluding to objects or places from pseudo-history and romance that might still be found or visited, see Christopher Dean, *Arthur of England: English Attitudes to King Arthur and the Knights of the Round Table in the Middle Ages and the Renaissance* (Toronto: University of Toronto Press, 1987), pp. 50-56. Spenser adapts the same motif in I.vii.36 when it is said that Arthur's arms can still be seen in fairyland 'if sought'.

(Boadicea) that Spenser adds to the materials from his sources in stanzas 54-6 to offer further compliment to Elizabeth.[36] '*Briton moniments*' ends 'abruptly' with the narrator deliberately breaking off the progression of the narrative before he names Arthur as Uther Pendragon's successor, leaving the prince momentarily frustrated and offended. But the 'vntimely breach' is the firmest statement in the whole of '*Briton moniments*' of the narrator's total control over his materials and of his role in apportioning exactly what we get to read, marked here by the reflexive reference to the seemingly casual omission of 'th'Authour selfe' to finish his narrative. As Kenneth Gross rightly observes, 'Spenser's ironic assertion of his authority over the gaps and continuities of Arthurian history *is* justified to the extent that he founds his own account of Arthur on a void in the existing legends.'[37]

Spenser's 'ample volume'

'*Antiquitee* of *Faery* lond' incorporates many of the same core features found in the Galfridian tradition of presenting mythical history that is epitomized in '*Briton moniments*'. The chronicle that Arthur reads in Eumnestes's library establishes the basic model for what we find in '*Antiquitee* of *Faery* lond': tales of a mythical founder, of indigenous gigantic races, of wars and extensive conquests, and of civic foundations and improvements. Like the British history as a whole, '*Antiquitee* of *Faery* lond' concludes with a veiled, though clearly decipherable reference to the accession of the Tudors. The juxtaposition of the British and fairy chronicles in II.x acts as a microcosm of the relationship found in *The Faerie Queene* as a whole between Spenser's use of the 'historye of king Arthure' and his employment of fairy mythology. '*Antiquitee* of *Faery* lond' is a studied 'overgoing' of the tradition from which Spenser constructs '*Briton moniments*'. Spenser takes up the formal strategy and panegyric technique of the mythical genealogy topos used to celebrate Elizabeth and the Tudors and then produces his own parodic or 'parasitic' rendition of the form. As we shall see, with each element of the topos that Spenser adopts and manipulates, attention is drawn both to the essential fictiveness and artifice of '*Antiquitee* of *Faery* lond' and to the very process of constructing the mythical genealogy itself. That is to say, through anatomizing the use of the genealogy topos in '*Antiquitee* of *Faery* lond' Spenser deconstructs the process of constructing the kind of mythical genealogy that he exemplifies in his use of the British history.

Typical of Spenser's method of construction and compilation within *The Faerie Queene* as a whole, '*Antiquitee* of *Faery* lond' is formed from a confection of many different mythological schemes and images that are then incorporated and adapted within the overall narrative. Within the six-stanza economy of '*Antiquitee*

---

[36] Harper, *Sources*, p. 117. On the potential ambiguity of this figure in Spenser, see Jodi Mikalachki, *The Legacy of Boadicea: Gender and Nation in Early Modern England* (London: Routledge, 1998), pp. 124-5.
[37] Kenneth Gross, *Spenserian Poetics: Idolatry, Iconoclasm, and Magic* (Ithaca: Cornell University Press, 1985), p. 124.

of *Faery* lond' the incorporation of mythic and historical allusion is so pronounced as to stress the point that the matter of the fairy chronicle obviously comes from elsewhere, that it is clearly a work of studied synthesis. '*Antiquitee* of *Faery* lond' is a history that openly invites decoding through consciously signalling its own artifice. It invites the kind of response commonly registered through the footnote and the marginal gloss, and provokes the stimulus of an engagement between reader and text that we have seen initiated in earlier fairy episodes, through the invitation to deconstruct the patently derivative and transparent allusions that constitute the fairy chronicle in order to approach a greater understanding of the meaning of Spenser's fairy. '*Antiquitee* of *Faery* lond' thus returns us once more to the preoccupations of the framing narrative and to the site of our own engagement with the poem, and the fairy chronicle provides an extended restatement of the fact that Spenser's fairy forms an integral part of the allegory of his poem and a reminder of how to read (through) the fairies of *The Faerie Queene*.

The fairy chronicle is prefaced by a restatement of the narrator's function as he briefly establishes the scenario in Eumnestes's library. Guyon reads his chronicle at the same time as Arthur reads his, but whereas '*Briton moniments*' was rudely curtailed, '*Antiquitee* of *Faery* lond' overgoes the British chronicle both in completeness and, we are told, in length. The narrator therefore offers an editorial selection from the 'ample volume', subtly positioning himself as the means through which we learn of fairy history through his profession to set out, not what Guyon read, but of what the volume itself 'told' (II.x.70.5). '*Antiquitee* of *Faery* lond' first tells of the creation of the fairy race:

> how first *Prometheus* did create
> A man, of many parts from beasts deryu'd,
> And then stole fire from heauen, to animate
> His worke, for which he was by *Ioue* depryu'd
> Of life him self, and hart-strings of an Ægle ryu'd. (II.x.70)

The tale of Prometheus is the first of many references to artifice and 'making' that are in evidence, and form a dominant preoccupation, throughout '*Antiquitee* of *Faery* lond'. Adapting an image that he could have found in many contemporary mythological dictionaries and commentaries, Spenser incorporates the figure of Prometheus as archetypal artificer into the fairy chronicle to provide a very obvious statement of how the fairy race of *The Faerie Queene* is, quite literally, 'made-up'.[38] Prometheus's seminal act of 'elf-fashioning' also mirrors what takes place in the production of *The Faerie Queene* itself in Spenser's own construction of his fairies from 'many parts', from many different textual sources. The fairy creation story is also an extension of Spenser's concern with the production and reception of

---

[38] On the Renaissance conceptions of Prometheus, see Olga Raggio, 'The Myth of Prometheus: Its Survival and Metamorphoses up to the Eighteenth Century', *JWCI* 21 (1958), pp. 44-62. *Variorum*, 2: 336-7, digests some of Spenser's sources for his treatment of Prometheus as artificer.

his work seen registered throughout *The Faerie Queene* by way of the narrator and through the incorporation of many poet or artificer figures in the text (e.g. Archimago, Merlin, Busirane); Prometheus's fate forms an image of the censured artist that is echoed later with Bon-/Malfont (V.ix.25-6).

The fairy creation is followed by the myth of fairy progenesis:

> That man so made, he called *Elfe*, to weet
> Quick, the first author of all Elfin kynd:
> Who wandring through the world with wearie feet,
> Did in the gardins of *Adonis* fynd
> A goodly creature, whom he deemd in mynd
> To be no earthly wight, but either Spright,
> Or Angell, th'authour of all woman kynd;
> Therefore a *Fay* he her according hight,
> Of whom all *Faryes* spring, and fetch their lignage right. (II.x.71)

The garden of Eden had already been placed within a romance matrix in book one of *The Faerie Queene* in the tale of Una's parents and their benighted kingdom (I.vii.43-51), and it is clearly evoked once again within '*Antiquitee* of *Faery* lond' with the fairy equivalents of Adam and Eve. This stanza has provided the natural focus for Berger's speculation concerning the absence of a fairy 'fall', but what is striking here, more than anything, is that the fairy progenesis is presented as a series of constructions and interpretations. Any information offered pertaining to elfin and fairy 'kind' is subordinate to the presentation of a number of subjective, positivist acts of definition. Prometheus first names Elfe using the etymology of 'Quick' contrived by Spenser, meaning 'living'. Elfe then encounters a creature within the gardens of Adonis - a location that is also a work of Spenser's own creation - and his response echoes that of Arthur in I.ix.13-14 as he attempts to interpret this seemingly supernatural being before him. Elfe then names her in turn as 'Fay' or as 'a Fay'. Whilst '*Antiquitee* of *Faery* lond' is said to have included 'Th' off-spring of Elues and Faryes' (II.ix.60), suggesting perhaps some form of essential difference between the two, the presentation of the fairy Eden in II.x.71 is one of only two points in *The Faerie Queene* at which Spenser pointedly distinguishes 'elf' and 'fay'. (The other is III.iii.26, see below.) The twin terms from fairy mythology provide a convenient moietal patterning for the respective 'authours' or ancestors of elfin and fairy kind. In the opening line of the next stanza ('Of these a mighty people shortly grew') there is some ambiguity concerning to whom exactly 'these' refers, given that the previous line describes how 'all *Faryes*' fetch their 'lignage' from Fay. But the reference to 'these' is more likely to both of the figures detailed in stanza 71 (following, obviously, the Edenic analogy) and therefore, to use the parlance of horse-breeding, the 'lignage' of Spenser's fairies derives from Elfe 'out of' Fay. The same formula is articulated in III.iii.26 to describe Artegall's imagined parentage: 'he by an Elfe was gotten of a Fay'. The contrived conjunction of the two terms provides a rationale within Spenser's narrative, should one be needed, for the interchangeability of the use of 'elf' and 'fairy' throughout the rest of *The Faerie Queene*.

The pose of narratorial selection adopted in the presentation of '*Antiquitee* of *Faery* lond' moves us on to such time within fairy history when the foundation of the ruling line is firmly established, subtly withholding any reference to the elliptical time in which 'mighty people shortly grew'. The success of the fairy race from the very outset of the chronicle set forth and epitomized in the 'puissaunt kinges, which all the world warrayd,/ And to them selues all Nations did subdew' (II.x.72), underpins the theories of many of those critics who maintain that '*Antiquitee* of *Faery* lond' represents a Tudor fantasy of control and order, an idealized exemplary chronicle set in contrast to '*Briton moniments*'. Following the regnal structure of the British chronicle, '*Antiquitee* of *Faery* lond' then sets out the order and achievements of the early monarchs of fairyland.

> The first and eldest, which that scepter swayd,
> Was *Elfin*; him all *India* obayd,
> And all that now *America* men call:
> Next him was noble *Elfinan*, who laid
> *Cleopolis* foundation first of all:
> But *Elfiline* enclosd it with a golden wall.
>
> His sonne was *Elfinell*, who ouercame
> The wicked *Gobbelines* in bloody field:
> But *Elfant* was of most renowmed fame,
> Who all of Christall did *Panthea* build:
> Then *Elfar*, who two brethren gyauntes kild,
> The one of which had two heades, th'other three:
> Then *Elfinor*, who was in magick skild;
> He built by art vpon the glassy See
> A bridge of bras, whose sound heuens thunder seem'd to bee. (II.x.72-3)

As the descendants of Elfe and Fay are recounted, each individual in the elfin succession is marked out from their progenitor by a modification of inflection added to the basic nominal stem 'Elf-'; thus, Elfin, Elfinan, Elfiline, and so on. Spenser repeats the technique of onomastic inflection in Paridell's account of his descent from Trojan Paris via Parius and Paridas (III.ix.36-7). At each stage of the fairy chronicle Spenser takes up a marker of progress and development found within the expanse of the British history materials and provides his own fairy analogue. The account of the elfin kings further demonstrates how Spenser's fairies are written to appear as familiar and yet different. The actions of the successive elfin kings bear clear similarities to those of several of the individuals found in the preceding '*Briton moniments*', inviting comparison between the two chronicles as a means of decoding each part of Gloriana's genealogy.

The enticement to deconstruct fairy, at least in II.x.72-4, appears to be more pronounced than any attempt to provide exacting identifications between British and fairy history.[39] The appeal once more is to a 'play' of interpretation. Rathborne takes up the interpretative challenge by suggesting varying historical and mythical identifications for each of the elfin kings and by initially establishing a form of fairy 'universal history' based around figures from Egyptian, Trojan, and Roman history tabulated with analogues from the Old Testament and Babylonian history.[40] These identifications have been modified and reconfigured in the exchange of letters to the *Times Literary Supplement* in 1948 between Rathborne, Kendrick, and Yates.[41] For the sake of clarity, the identifications can be tabulated as follows:

Elfin ruler	Rathborne's original identifications	Kendrick in *TLS*	Rathborne in *TLS*
Elfin	Osiris-Bacchus	Osiris-Bacchus	Osiris-Bacchus
Elfinan	Hercules	Brutus	Brutus
Elfiline	Tros	Belinus	Lud
Elfinell	Assaracus	Gurguntius Brabtruc	Locrine
Elfant	Aeneas	Lucius	Belinus
Elfar	Postumus	Constantine Chlorus	Constantine the Great
Elfinor	Brutus	Constantine the Great	Constantine II

Kendrick's main modification of Rathborne's original set of identifications is to argue that '*Antiquitee* of *Faery* lond' represents a line of specifically British, not Trojan, rulers. In terms of establishing any form of rationale for such intended identifications it must be concluded that the fairy chronicle thus further demonstrates Spenser's abilities as an antiquary through offering another, rewritten form of the British history. Guyon therefore, like Arthur, reads a form of British history. Kendrick's interpretation of '*Antiquitee* of *Faery* lond' offers a further demonstration of the parity between the chronicles in Eumnestes's library. Yates accepts Kendrick and Rathborne's readings but goes on to suggest that the elfin rendering of British history may be influenced by the 1570 edition of *Acts and Monuments* in which Foxe attempted to rewrite British and English history from Lucius onwards as a continued struggle against the papacy.[42] Yates's suggestion that '*Antiquitee* of *Faery* lond' is a 'religious story' is more of an intuitive response, founded primarily upon the intended identification made between Oberon and Henry VIII, than it is a programmatic scheme of interpretation. But Yates's letter is useful in that it begins to draw comparisons between the way in which

---

[39] There have also been a number of attempts to understand how Spenser structures the elfin genealogy and identify the employment of a numerological patterning; see Jerry Leath Mills, 'Spenser and the Numbers of History: A Note on the British and Elfin Chronicles in the *Faerie Queene*', *PQ* 55 (1976), pp. 281-7; and Maren-Sofie Røstvig, 'Canto Structure in Tasso and Spenser', *SSt* 1 (1980), 186-97.

[40] Rathborne, *Meaning*, p. 77.

[41] Thomas Kendrick, Letter, *TLS*, 7 February 1948, p. 79; Isabel Rathborne, Letter, *TLS*, 24 April 1948, p. 233. Kendrick, Letter, *TLS*, 15 May 1948, p. 275, accepts Rathborne's modifications.

[42] Frances Yates, Letter, *TLS*, 3 July 1948, p. 373.

successive writers in the Elizabethan period, Spenser included, respond to and rewrite British history. It further suggests that the sources for '*Antiquitiee* of *Faery* lond' may be found in contemporary, frequently imaginative, reworkings of national history. Yates might also have considered Bale's elaborate attempt to construct a Biblical basis for British history that he appended to his catalogues of British authors. Bale contrives a line of early British rulers that extended from Samotheus, son of Noah's son Japhet, via Osiris and Isis, through to Neptune and his son Albion whose giant 'saluage nation' were finally displaced by Brutus.[43] The interweaving of figures from Biblical, classical, and British mythology that Spenser would have found in Bale's *Scriptorum Illustrium maioris Brytanniae*, and various other contemporary constructions of universal history, appears to be the most likely source for Spenser's '*Antiquitee* of *Faery* lond'.

The reference to Elfin's conquest of India and America offers the fairy equivalent of contemporary claims to world-wide imperium made by the Tudors based on the contrivance that Elizabeth's ancient progenitor Arthur held dominion over America, as is argued in Dee's *General and Rare Memorials Pertayning to the Perfect Arte of Navigation* (1577).[44] Once again Spenser adopts an image from Tudor panegyric and applies it to his own particular mythological scheme. A similar appeal to historical precedent for sixteenth-century political dominion is made in the river catalogues set out in the Thames-Medway marriage episode, and the narratorial exhortation to Britons in IV.xi.22 regarding their 'right' to conquer the land of the Amazons to gain 'immortall glory'. The foundation and development of Cleopolis provides a compact fairy analogue to the foundation of London (or Troynovant) and the details of piecemeal improvements made over the much wider course of the British history.[45] Again, each British achievement is exceeded by a fairy equivalent and London itself is said to be surpassed (only) by Cleopolis (III.ix.51).

The roll-call of fairy achievements has not progressed far before the narrator once more voices his inadequacy in digesting '*Antiquitee* of *Faery* lond' and his hesitancy at the prospect of recording the seven hundred princes descended ('in order') from Elfinor. In addition to stressing the vast scope of the fairy chronicle and the wealth of 'braue ensamples' to be found within, the narrator draws us back to the performative level of the poem by foregrounding his own role as editor of the materials set forth. This is then followed by one of the most transparent historical allegories in the whole of *The Faerie Queene* as the more recent rulers of fairyland are recounted in such a way that the analogy to the Tudor dynasty is made explicit:

---

[43] John Bale, *Scriptorum Illustrium maioris Brytanniae catalogus* (Basle, 1557), sig. a1-a4; see also Kendrick, *British Antiquity*, pp. 69-72.

[44] Cain, *Praise*, pp. 99, 114.

[45] Several critics have focused on the evolution of Cleopolis in their studies of how Spenser's fairyland represents an ideal of humanist, civic perfection; see Thomas P. Roche, Jr., *The Kindly Flame: A Study of the Third and Fourth Books of Spenser's Faerie Queene* (Princeton: Princeton University Press, 1964), pp. 37-8, 43; McCabe, *Pillars*, pp. 101-02.

After all these *Elficleos* did rayne,
The wise *Elficleos* in great Maiestie,
Who mightily that scepter did sustayne,
And with rich spoyles and famous victorie,
Did high aduaunce the crowne of *Faery*:
He left two sonnes, of which faire *Elferon*
The eldest brother did vntimely dy;
Whose emptie place the mightie *Oberon*
Doubly supplide, in spousall, and dominion. (II.x.75)

Elficleos (Henry VII) has two sons representing Arthur and Henry Tudor (Henry VIII) and in the next stanza the identification is made explicit between Tanaquill and Gloriana, and through the allegory, between Gloriana and Henry VIII's daughter Elizabeth.[46] The fairy chronicle closes with a final reference to construction and artifice as Gloriana is literally 'made' queen through the edict of Oberon's 'last will', clearly echoing how Elizabeth was made queen through Henry VIII's will of 30 December 1546. Henry's final will stated that the crown was to go to Elizabeth if her elder sister Mary died childless, and if there were no male heirs remaining of any of his lawfull wives. The succession as it is presented through the transparent veil of '*Antiquitee* of *Faery* lond' effaces any sense of obstruction to a direct line of descent from Oberon to Gloriana, Henry to Elizabeth. It thus removes all suggestion of the troublesome reigns of Edward VI and Mary I, simultaneously affirming an idealized (fairy) version of Elizabeth's immediate title and genealogy but also allowing the difficult question of Elizabeth's succession to remain in focus.[47] The closing stanzas of '*Antiquitee* of *Faery* lond' (II.x.75-6) encourage a final, simple decoding of fairy through the transparency of the historical allusions made and provide a very obvious demonstration of how Spenser uses fairy mythology as a way of telling his own story of the queen and the Tudor lineage. The encouragement to read fairy as a sign for something else, for something beyond the literal level of the narrative, is reiterated once more.

The final stanzas of '*Antiquitee* of *Faery* lond' provide a measure of symmetry to II.x as a whole in drawing us back to the kind of interaction with the implied reader established at the beginning of the canto. There the narrator openly implored the queen to trace her 'realme and race' from the genealogy set out in '*Briton moniments*' before outlining the succession in detail. The canto comes to a close with a similar appeal made to the sixteenth-century temporal context of the poem and to a thinly veiled royal audience that still lives and breathes. The narrator mediates between the fairy chronicle and the implied audience, firstly, through describing Tanaquill in the present tense ('Fairer and nobler liueth none this

---

[46] Margaret Christian, '"The Ground of Storie": Genealogy in *The Faerie Queene*', *SSt* 9 (1988), p. 76, attempts to decode more of '*Antiquitee* of *Faery* lond' as references to Tudor history; she sees, for example, Elfinell's victory over the 'wicked *Gobbelines*' as a figure for the defeat of the Armada, and Elfant's construction of Panthea as the establishment of the English church.
[47] Miller, *Poem's Two Bodies*, pp. 207-08.

howre'), and then by paying a figurative compliment to Elizabeth by addressing Gloriana directly: 'Long mayst thou *Glorian* liue, in glory and great powre' (II.x.76). The final image of canto ten is of both Arthur and Guyon's enraptured response to their respective 'antiquities' and a necessary closure brought to their 'studies' by the figure of Alma as she bids them come to supper.

In '*Antiquitee* of *Faery* lond' Spenser takes up the genealogy topos used to authorize and celebrate the Tudor dynasty and applies it to the mythological scheme that he has employed to represent Elizabeth. But the function of the fairy chronicle is not solely one of panegyric; celebration of the queen is by no means the exclusive object of Spenser's use of the genealogy topos in II.x. Attention is drawn just as much to the poet's role in celebrating Elizabeth using this topos and the means through which that topos is employed. This is brought about through a conscious foregrounding of the narrator's role in setting forth the chronicles of II.x and relating them explicitly to the poem's implied audience, and an attendant concern to stress the element of artifice and craftsmanship with which both chronicles are put together. It is for this reason that I have treated '*Briton moniments*' and '*Antiquitee* of *Faery* lond' in concert here, for the fairy chronicle anatomizes the process of constructing the kind of mythical genealogy epitomized in '*Briton moniments*' through highlighting its own patent fictiveness and inviting us to decode each stage of elfin history. It is as if Spenser endeavours to say 'this is how one goes about creating an ideal genealogy, and these are the key ingredients that one requires; this is what I am doing here'. '*Antiquitee* of *Faery* lond' offers an important analogue to *The Faerie Queene* as a whole in that it provides within the text itself a model of a book about fairy and the fairy queen - a model both of the kind of book from which the narrator professes to draw, and of that which he ultimately sets forth. '*Antiquitee* of *Faery* lond' acts therefore as another reflexive site where, through foregrounding the action of telling, constructing, or setting forth a story of fairy, Spenser includes within his text a model of his own role in producing *The Faerie Queene*.

Conclusion

It may be observed, both from the distribution of those episodes that receive the greatest attention in this study and from *The Faerie Queene* itself, that there is a marked decrease in Spenser's use of fairy mythology following book two. Such an observation might intuitively prompt claims that the poet changes his mind concerning the overall 'invention' of *The Faerie Queene*, that he simply runs out of ideas for what to do with fairy mythology, or that fairy ultimately plays an increasingly subordinate role in the poem. It has been widely noted how Spenser's attitude to his task and his material changes during the course of the poem: how he exhibits a growing lack of optimism concerning his myth-making project, resulting in its final abandonment; and how there is a perceptible development of a 'personal voice' that reaches a terminus with the final, solo appeal for a 'Sabaoths sight'.[1] There is an increasing sense both of the failure of fairyland to represent an ideal world, and of the distance between the world of the poem and the golden world set out in '*Antiquitee* of *Faery* lond'.[2]

The growing disillusionment with the Virgilian mythopoeic trajectory is registered in the framing narrative by a noticeable shift in the narrator's attitude as to how he will use his materials. References to the narrator's doubts and anxieties about the great project of laying forth the rolls of fairy for the queen are seen to escalate, even after only the first book. In the proem to book three the narrator professes to present a 'mirrour' in which Elizabeth might see herself depicted but now also offers the caveat that this is to be a distortion, not a straightforward reflection.[3] The narrator's response to the feared 'bad reader' of IV.proem.1 is to restrict his intended audience to those that truly understand the ways of love. In doing so he restates his claim to 'sing' for the queen, though the model of presentation established in the earlier books of *The Faerie Queene* is now modified subtly in that direct identifications between the narrator's 'history' and his ultimate implied reader are placed at one remove. The narrator's text is presented as a

---

[1] See Harry Berger, Jr., 'The Prospect of Imagination: Spenser and the Limits of Poetry', *SEL* 1 (1961), pp. 93-120; Richard Neuse, 'Book VI as Conclusion to *The Faerie Queene*', *ELH* 35 (1968), pp. 329-53; Judith Anderson, *The Growth of a Personal Voice: Piers Plowman and The Faerie Queene* (New Haven: Yale University Press, 1976); Cain, *Praise*, pp. 131-85. On the abandonment of Spenser's Virgilian career, see Richard Helgerson, *Self-Crowned Laureates: Spenser, Jonson, Milton, and the Literary System* (Berkeley: University of California Press, 1983), pp. 82-9.

[2] Miller, 'Status of Faeryland', pp. 40-41.

[3] DeNeef, *Spenser and the Motives of Metaphor*, p. 112.

'lesson' for the queen, suggestive more of how she *might* be than of how she actually *is*. By the proem to book six even the narrator's homiletic role is subordinate to a growing introspection, as recourse to the 'delightfull land of Faery' is presented more as a means of private distraction or escape than of public instruction.[4]

Nevertheless, there is a consistency in the narrator's overall performative function: the setting forth of a fairy story to the queen. As I have demonstrated, the ongoing fairy story of the framing narrative is maintained throughout the poem, even in the fragmentary Mutabilitie cantos. Similarly, the outward texture of the fairy allegory is still maintained after book two through episodes featuring Agape the fay, the would-be fairy Artegall, and Calidore and the fairies of Mount Acidale. At the very least, each individual reference to a fairy or an elf serves in some way as a minute reminder of the central identification between Elizabeth and the fairy queen. The decrease in extended references to fairy may be explained as being one aspect of the wholesale change in tone, presentation, organization, and overall outlook that becomes more observable as the poem progresses. That there is less of an overt focus upon fairy as a means of representing Elizabeth in the 1596 *Faerie Queene* may be a factor of Spenser's disillusionment with his overall project, but it also demonstrates that fairy constituted a central role in his initial conception of that project. Ultimately attempts to make definitive statements concerning fairy in *The Faerie Queene* are once again frustrated by the fact that the poem is unfinished, and I have not sought to ground my study upon extensive conjectures of what Spenser's final intentions for fairy may have been. It is clear from references directly made in the text, however, that fairy was to play a vital, constitutive role in the projected ending of the poem: at Gloriana's 'yearely solemne feast' (referred to in the 'Letter to Raleigh' and in II.ii.42); in the final battle between the forces of the fairy queen and the 'Paynim king' in 'Briton fields' (I.xi.7; I.xii.18); and in the *telos* of Arthur's union with the fairy queen, implied not least by the reference to Gloriana having brought the prince's arms back to fairyland after his death (I.vii.36).

The aim of the present study has been to reassert the importance of fairy in *The Faerie Queene* by demonstrating how Spenser places fairy at the very centre of his mythopœic project, both by his seminal identification of Elizabeth with the fairy queen, and by maintaining the fictional scenario in the poem's framing narrative whereby the narrator figure is engaged in setting forth a fairy story for the queen. The literary and political background to using fairy as a panegyric device has been discussed, and I have addressed the question as to why Spenser specifically uses fairy mythology for his poem. It has been shown how Spenser, through the framing narrative, comments upon the overall process with which he is employed in *The Faerie Queene* and how the fairy stories located within the poem's *fabula* (the story or 'history' professedly set out by the narrator) not only provide analogues to the *fabula* itself and to the central action of the framing narrative, but present surrogate

---

[4] Kinney, *Strategies*, p. 85.

figures for Spenser's own role within the poem as a whole. The poem does not offer simply a straightforward, unmediated representation of Elizabeth as Gloriana, but provides a more reflexive commentary on the process of using fairy to represent the queen, and crucially foregrounds the poet's own role within this process. It is my intention that this book also offers something of a bibliographic resource for subsequent scholars wishing to study any aspect of Spenser's use of fairy.

From the 1570s until well after the death of James in 1625 there was very much a literary vogue for fairy mythology. A number of reasons for this continuing aesthetic fashion have been suggested: the use of fairy in entertainments for Elizabeth during the 1570s (discussed above); the enduring popularity of medieval romances throughout the sixteenth century, many of which feature some aspect of fairy mythology; an interest in using native mythology for aesthetic purposes in an analogous manner to the employment of classical demigods; and perhaps, in similar fashion, 'the growing number of poets from the lower classes, fresh from the country and from the smaller villages and towns... who put the fairies into poems and plays as naturally as had the classical poets, the nymphs and satyrs'.[5] The specific influence of Spenser's fairies upon such a vogue remains, however, a fertile area for further critical examination, and has a much wider remit than a simple appendix could hope to provide here if one is to maintain the close textual focus upon the rhetoric of fairy that I have advocated in the present study. The hunt for Spenserian fairies is by no means straightforward. Any attempt to trace specific details of the 'afterlife' of Spenser's fairies is complicated from early on, for example, by the pervasive influence of Shakespeare's presentation of fairy, particularly in *A Midsummer Night's Dream*. In his 1607 play *The Whore of Babylon*, Thomas Dekker consciously evokes Spenser's use of fairy mythology and casts Elizabethan England as a Spenserian fairyland, peopled by characters from *The Faerie Queene* and governed by a line of rulers that are clearly based on the thinly veiled allegory found in the fairy genealogy '*Antiquitee* of *Faery* lond'.[6] Yet even here Dekker chooses to make the far more Shakespearean gesture of naming his fairy queen Titania. The fairies in Jonson's masque *Oberon* (1611) are a curious synthesis of chivalric and classical influences, as is illustrated in Inigo Jones's drawing of the costume for Prince Henry's role as Oberon, and the text is 'Spenserian' only in as much as it employs fairy mythology within a work of royal panegyric.[7] One can do little more than conjecture, based on the title, that Dekker and John Ford's lost play *The Fairy Knight*, licensed by Master of Revels Sir Henry Herbert on 11 June 1624, was based upon a Spenserian, rather than

---

[5] Latham, *Elizabethan Fairies*, p. 18n47.
[6] Thomas Dekker, *Dramatic Works*, ed. Fredson Bowers. 4 vols. (Cambridge: Cambridge University Press, 1953-61), 2: 509-10.
[7] See Stephen Orgel, *The Illusion of Power: Political Theater in the English Renaissance* (Berkeley: University of California Press, 1975), p. 68, figure 11.

Shakespearean theme.[8] Even the fairies found in the works of consciously Spenserian poets such as Michael Drayton and William Browne bear far more resemblance to the occupants of the miniature world suggested in Mercutio's Queen Mab speech than they do to the denizens of Gloriana's realm, and there is a tendency by this point towards far more of a burlesque use of fairy.[9]

Spenser in the 'Letter to Raleigh' promised that if he found that the proposed first twelve books of *The Faerie Queene* were 'well accepted' he might be encouraged to write a further twelve. In a similar spirit I shall conclude the present work by proposing that a subsequent critical study might go on to examine in much greater detail the legacy of the identification made between Elizabeth and Gloriana, its impact upon the use of fairy in the drama of Shakespeare, Jonson, and Dekker, and its influence upon Jacobean and Caroline masques and royal entertainments.

---

[8] Julia Gasper, *The Dragon and the Dove: The Plays of Thomas Dekker* (Oxford: Clarendon Press, 1990), p. 214.
[9] Michelle O'Callaghan, *The 'Shepheard's Nation': Jacobean Spenserians and Early Stuart Political Culture* (Oxford: Clarendon Press, 2000), pp. 226-7.

Bibliography

Primary Sources

Ariosto, Ludovico. *Ludovico Ariosto's Orlando Furioso*, tr. Sir John Harington (1591), ed. Robert McNulty. Oxford: Clarendon Press, 1972.

—— *Orlando Furioso*, tr. Guido Waldman. Oxford: Oxford University Press, 1974.

Armin, Robert. *The Collected Works of Robert Armin*. Facsimile edn. 2 vols. New York: Johnson Reprint, 1972.

[*Arthur of Little Britain*]. *The History of the Valiant Knight Arthur of Little Britain*, tr. John Bourchier, Lord Berners, ed. E. V. Utterson. London, 1814.

Ascham, Roger. *English Works*, ed. William Aldis Wright. Cambridge: Cambridge University Press, 1904.

Augustine, St. *De Doctrina Christiana*, ed. and tr. R. P. H. Green. Oxford: Clarendon Press, 1995.

Bale, John. *Scriptorum Illustrium maioris Brytanniae catalogus*. Basle, 1557.

Blenerhasset, Thomas. *A Revelation of the True Minerva*, intr. J. W. Bennett. New York: Scholars' Facsimiles and Reprints, 1941.

Bodin, Jean. *On the Demon-Mania of Witches* (1580), tr. R. A. Scott, intr. Jonathan L. Pearl. Toronto: Centre for Reformation and Renaissance Studies, 1995.

Boiardo, Matteo Maria. *Orlando Innamorato*, tr. Charles Stanley Ross. Berkeley: University of California Press, 1989.

Chaucer, Geoffrey. *The Riverside Chaucer*, gen. ed. Larry D. Benson. Oxford: Oxford University Press, 1987.

Chestre, Thomas. *Sir Launfal*. ed. A. J. Bliss. London: Nelson, 1960.

Child, Francis James. *The English and Scottish Popular Ballads*. 5 vols. Boston, 1882-98; repr. New York: Dover, 1965.

Churchyard, Thomas. *A Discourse of the Queenes Maiesties Entertainment in Suffolk and Norfolk*. London, 1578.

Cunliffe, J. W. 'The Queenes Majesties Entertainment at Woodstocke'. *PMLA* 26 (1911), pp. 92-141.

Davenant, Sir William. *Gondibert*, ed. David F. Gladish. Oxford: Clarendon Press, 1971.

Dee, John. *General and Rare Memorials Pertayning to the Perfect Arte of Navigation*. Facsimile edn. New York: Da Capo Press, 1968.

Dekker, Thomas. *Dramatic Works*, ed. Fredson Bowers. 4 vols. Cambridge: Cambridge University Press, 1953-61.

Elizabeth I. *Collected Works*, ed. Leah S. Marcus, Janel Mueller, and Mary Beth Rose. Chicago: University of Chicago Press, 2000.

Generydes: A Romance in Seven-Line Stanzas, ed. W. A. Wright. EETS OS 55, 70. 2 vols. London: Oxford University Press, 1873-78.

Geoffrey of Monmouth. *The History of the Kings of Britain*, tr. Lewis Thorpe. Harmondsworth: Penguin, 1966.

[Gervase of Tilbury]. *Des Gervasius von Tilbury Otia Imperialia.* ed. Felix Liebrecht. Hannover, 1856.

Giraldus Cambrensis. *Giraldi Cambrensis Opera*, ed. J. S. Brewer, J. F. Dimock, and G. F. Warner. RS 21. 8 vols. London, 1861-91.

Harsnet, Samuel. *A Declaration of Egregious Popish Impostures.* London, 1603.

Holland, Henry. *A Treatise of Witchcraft.* Cambridge, 1590.

Le Huon de Bordeaux en prose du Xvème siècle, ed. Michel J. Raby. New York: Lang, 1998.

[*Huon of Burdeux*]. *The Boke of Duke Huon of Burdeux, done into English by Lord Berners*, ed. S. L. Lee. EETS ES 40, 41, 43, 50. London, 1882-87.

James VI and I, *Daemonologie* (with *Newes from Scotland*), ed. G. B. Harrison. London: Bodley Head Quartos, 1924; repr. Edinburgh: Edinburgh University Press, 1966.

Jonson, Ben. *Ben Jonson*, ed. C. H. Herford, and Percy and Evelyn Simpson. 11 vols. Oxford: Oxford University Press, 1925-52.

Kirk, Robert. *The Secret Commonwealth of Elves, Fauns and Fairies*, intr. R. B. Cunninghame Graham, commentary Andrew Lang. Stirling: Mackay, 1933.

—— *The Secret Common-wealth*, ed. Stewart Sanderson. Cambridge: Brewer, 1976.

—— *Walker Between Worlds: A New Edition of The Secret Commonwealth of Elves, Fauns and Fairies*, ed. R. J. Stewart. Shaftesbury: Element, 1990.

Langham, Robert. *A Letter*, ed. R. J. P. Kuin. Leiden: Brill, 1983.

Lavater, Ludwig. *De Spectris, lemuribus et magnis atque insolitis fragoribus.* Geneva, 1570.

—— *Of Ghostes and Spirits Walking by Nyght*, tr. R[obert] H[arrison] (1572), ed. J. Dover Wilson. Oxford: Oxford University Press, 1929.

Layamon's Brut, ed. G. L. Brook and R. F. Leslie. EETS OS 250, 277. 2 vols. Oxford: Oxford University Press, 1963-78.

Le Loyer, Pierre. *IIII Livres des Spectres ou Apparitions et Visions d'Espirits, Anges et Demons se monstrans sensiblement aux hommes.* Angers, 1586.

—— *A Treatise of Specters or straunge Sights, Visions and Apparitions appearing sensibly vnto men*, tr. Zachary Jones. London, 1605.

[Lydgate, John]. *Lydgate's Fall of Princes*, ed. Henry Bergen. EETS ES 123. London: Oxford University Press, 1924.

Malory, Sir Thomas. *Complete Works*, ed. Eugène Vinaver. Oxford: Oxford University Press, 1971.

Map, Walter. *De Nugis Curialium (Courtier's Trifles)*, ed. and tr. M. R. James, rev. ed. C. N. L. Brooke and R. A. B. Mynors. Oxford: Clarendon Press, 1983.

Melusine, ed. A. K. Donald. EETS ES 68. London, 1895.

Melusine: Roman du XIVe Siècle par Jean D'Arras, ed. Louis Stouff. Dijon: Bernigaud et Privat, 1932.

Middleton, Christopher. *The Famous Historie of Chinon of England*, ed. W. E. Mead. EETS OS 165. London: Oxford University Press, 1925.

Migne, Jacques-Paul. *Patrologiae Cursus Completus: Series Latina.* 221 vols. Paris, 1841-64.

Nashe, Thomas. *Works*, ed. R. B. McKerrow, rev. ed. F. P. Wilson. 5 vols. Oxford: Blackwell, 1958-66.

Nichols, John, ed. *The Progresses and Public Processions of Queen Elizabeth.* 3 vols. London, 1823.

Ogier le Dannoys: roman en prose du XVe siècle, Facsimile ed. Knud Togeby. Copenhagen: Munksgaard, 1967.

Olaus Magnus. *Description of the Northern Peoples*, tr. P. Fisher and H. Higgens. 3 vols. London: Hakluyt Society, 1996-98.

Paracelsus, *Liber de nymphis, sylphis, pygmaeis et salamandris et de caeteris spiritibus*, ed. Robert Blaser. Bern: Francke, 1960.

Partonope of Blois, ed. A. T. Bödtker. EETS ES 109. London: Oxford University Press, 1912.

Plato. *Republic*, tr. F. M. Cornford. New York: Oxford University Press, 1945.

Pollard, A. W. *The Queen's Majesty's Entertainment at Woodstock, 1575*. Oxford: n.p., 1910.

Puttenham, George. *The Arte of English Poesie*, ed. Gladys Doidge Willcock and Alice Walker. Cambridge: Cambridge University Press, 1936; repr. 1970.

Radulphi de Coggeshall. *Chronicon Anglicanum*, ed. J. Stevenson. RS 66. London, 1875.

Rémy, Nicholas. *Demonolatry*, ed. Montague Summers. London: Rodker, 1948.

Le Roman de Mélusine ou Histoire de Lusignan par Coudrette, ed. Eleanor Roach. Paris: Klincksieck, 1982.

The Romans of Partenay, or of Lusignen, ed. W. W. Skeat. EETS OS 22. London, 1866.

Scot, Reginald. *The Discoverie of Witchcraft*, ed. Brinsley Nicholson. London, 1886.

Segar, Sir William. *Honor Military and Civil* (1602), Facsimile edn. Delmar, NY: Scholars' Facsimiles and Reprints, 1975.

The Several Notorious and Lewd Cozenages of John West and Alice West, falsely called the king and queen of fairies. London, 1613.

Shakespeare, William. *A Midsummer Night's Dream*, ed. Harold Brooks. London: Methuen, 1979.

—— *The Norton Shakespeare*, gen. ed. Stephen Greenblatt. New York: Norton, 1997.

Sidney, Sir Philip. *An Apologie for Poetry or The Defence of Poetry*, ed. Geoffrey Shepherd. London: Nelson, 1965.

—— *The Countess of Pembroke's Arcadia*, ed. Maurice Evans. Harmondsworth: Penguin, 1977.

Spenser, Edmund. *Poetical Works*, ed. J. C. Smith and Ernest de Selincourt. Oxford: Oxford University Press, 1912; repr. 1970.

—— *The Works of Edmund Spenser: A Variorum Edition*, ed. Edwin Greenlaw, et al., 11 vols. Baltimore: Johns Hopkins University Press, 1932-57.

—— *A View of the Present State of Ireland*, ed. W. L. Renwick. London: Partridge, 1934.

—— *The Shorter Poems*, ed. Richard A. McCabe. Harmondsworth: Penguin, 1999.

—— *The Faerie Queene*, ed. A. C. Hamilton. 2nd edn. London: Longman, 2001.

[Sprenger, Jacobus and Heinrich Kramer]. *Malleus Maleficarum*, tr. and intr. Montague Summers. London: Rodker, 1928.

Taillepied, Noel. *A Treatise of Ghosts* (1588), tr. Montague Summers. London: Fortune, 1933.

Tasso, Torquato. *Discourses on the Heroic Poem*, tr. Mariella Cavalchini and Irene Samuel. Oxford: Clarendon Press, 1973.

—— *Godfrey of Bulloigne: A Critical Edition of Edward Fairfax's Translation of Tasso's Gerusalemme Liberata, together with Fairfax's Original Poems*, ed. Kathleen M. Lea and T. M. Gang. Oxford: Clarendon Press, 1981.

[*Thomas of Erceldoune*]. *The Romance and Prophecies of Thomas of Erceldoune*, ed. J. A. H. Murray. EETS OS 61. London, 1875.

Tristan de Nanteuil: chanson de geste inédite, ed. K. V. Sinclair. Assen: Van Gorcum, 1971.

The Wars of Alexander, ed. Hoyt N. Duggan and Thorlac Turville-Petre. EETS SS 10. Oxford: Oxford University Press, 1989.

Weyer, Johann. *Witches, Devils, and Doctors in the Renaissance*, tr. John Shea. intr. George Mora. Binghampton, NY: Medieval & Renaissance Texts and Studies, 1991.

William of Newburgh. *Historia Rerum Anglicarum*, ed. Richard Howlett. RS 82a. London, 1884.

Wyatt, Sir Thomas. *The Complete Poems*, ed. R. A. Rebholz. Harmondsworth: Penguin, 1978.

Secondary Sources

Adams, Robert P. '"Bold Bawdry and Open Manslaughter": The English New Humanist Attack on Medieval Romance'. *HLQ* 23 (1959-60), pp. 33-48.

Albright, Evelyn May. '*The Faerie Queene* in Masque at the Gray's Inn Revels'. *PMLA* 41 (1926), pp. 497-516.

Alpers, Paul J. *The Poetry of The Faerie Queene*. Princeton: Princeton University Press, 1967.

—— ed. *Edmund Spenser: A Critical Anthology*. Harmondsworth: Penguin, 1969.

Anderson, Judith. *The Growth of a Personal Voice: Piers Plowman and The Faerie Queene*. New Haven: Yale University Press, 1976.

—— '"In liuing colours and right hew": The Queen of Spenser's Central Books', in Maynard Mack and George DeForest Lord, eds, *Poetic Traditions of the English Renaissance*. New Haven: Yale University Press, 1982, pp. 47-66.

—— '"A Gentle Knight was pricking on the plaine": The Chaucerian Connection'. *ELR* 15 (1985), pp. 166-74.

—— 'The Antiquities of Fairyland and Ireland'. *JEGP* 86 (1987), pp. 199-214.

—— 'Arthur, Argante, and the Ideal Vision: An Exercise in Speculation and Parody', in Christopher Baswell and William Sharpe, eds, *The Passing of Arthur: New Essays in the Arthurian Tradition*. New York: Garland, 1988, pp. 193-206.

—— '"Myn auctour": Spenser's Enabling Fiction and Eumnestes' "immortall scrine"', in George M. Logan and Gordon Teskey, eds. *Unfolded Tales: Essays on Renaissance Romance*. Ithaca: Cornell University Press, 1989, pp. 16-31.

—— 'Narrative Reflections: Re-envisaging the Poet in *The Canterbury Tales* and *The Faerie Queene*', in Theresa M. Krier, ed., *Refiguring Chaucer in the Renaissance*. Gainesville: University Press of Florida, 1998, pp. 87-105.

Anglo, Sydney. 'Evident Authority and Authoritative Evidence: The *Malleus Maleficarum*', in Sydney Anglo, ed., *The Damned Art: Essays in the Literature of Witchcraft*. London: Routledge, 1977, pp. 1-31.

—— 'Reginald Scot's *Discoverie of Witchcraft*: Scepticism and Sadduceeism', in Sydney Anglo, ed., *The Damned Art: Essays in the Literature of Witchcraft*. London: Routledge, 1977, pp. 106-39.

—— *Images of Tudor Kingship*. London: Seaby, 1992.

—— *Spectacle, Pageantry and Early Tudor Policy*. 2nd edn. Oxford: Clarendon Press, 1997.

—— ed. *The Damned Art: Essays in the Literature of Witchcraft*. London: Routledge, 1977.

Ankarloo, Bengt, and Gustav Henningsen, eds. *Early Modern European Witchcraft: Centres and Peripheries*. Oxford: Clarendon Press, 1993.

Arestad, Sverre. 'Spenser's "Faery" and "Fairy"'. *MLQ* 8 (1947), pp. 37-42.

Axton, Marie. *The Queen's Two Bodies: Drama and the Elizabethan Succession*. London: Historical Society, 1977.

Baker-Smith, Dominic. 'Uses of Plato by Erasmus and More', in Anna Baldwin and Sarah Hutton, eds, *Platonism and the English Imagination*. Cambridge: Cambridge University Press, 1994, pp. 86-99.

Bakhtin, M. M. *The Dialogic Imagination: Four Essays*, ed. Michael Holquist, tr. Caryl Emerson and Michael Holquist. Austin: University of Texas Press, 1981.

Baroja, Julio Caro. 'Witchcraft and Catholic Theology', in Bengt Ankarloo and Gustav Henningsen, eds. *Early Modern European Witchcraft: Centres and Peripheries*. Oxford: Clarendon Press, 1993, pp. 19-43.

Barry, Jonathan. 'Introduction: Keith Thomas and the Problem of Witchcraft', in Jonathan Barry, Marianne Hester, and Gareth Roberts, eds. *Witchcraft in Early Modern Europe: Studies in Culture and Belief*. Cambridge: Cambridge University Press, 1996, pp. 1-45.

Baskervill, C. R. 'The Genesis of Spenser's Queen of Faerie'. *MP* 18 (1920-21), pp. 49-54.

Bates, Catherine. *The Rhetoric of Courtship in Elizabethan Language and Literature*. Cambridge: Cambridge University Press, 1992.

Beckwith, Sarah. 'The Power of Devils and the Hearts of Men: Notes Towards a Drama of Witchcraft', in Lesley Aers and Nigel Wheale, eds, *Shakespeare in the Changing Curriculum*. London: Routledge, 1991, pp. 143-61.

Bellamy, Elizabeth J. 'The Vocative and the Vocational: The Unreadability of Elizabeth in *The Faerie Queene*'. *ELH* 54 (1987), pp. 1-30.

—— 'Spenser's Faeryland and "The Curious Geneaology of India"', in Patrick Cheney and Lauren Silberman, eds. *Worldmaking Spenser: Explorations in the Early Modern Age*. Lexington: University Press of Kentucky, 2000, pp. 177-92.

Belt, Debra. 'Hostile Audiences and the Courteous Reader in *The Faerie Queene*, Book VI'. *SSt* 9 (1988), pp. 107-135.

Bender, John. *Spenser and Literary Pictorialism*. Princeton: Princeton University Press, 1972.

Bennett, Josephine Waters. *The Evolution of 'The Faerie Queene'*. Chicago: University of Chicago Press, 1942.

—— 'Britain Among the Fortunate Isles'. *SP* 53 (1956), pp. 114-40.

Berger, Harry, Jr. *The Allegorical Temper: Vision and Reality in Book II of Spenser's Faerie Queene*. New Haven: Yale University Press, 1957.

—— 'The Prospect of the Imagination: Spenser and the Limits of Poetry'. *SEL* 1 (1961), pp. 93-120.

—— *Revisionary Play: Studies in the Spenserian Dynamics*. Berkeley: University of California Press, 1988.

—— 'The Spenserian Dynamics', in Harry Berger, Jr., *Revisionary Play: Studies in the Spenserian Dynamics*. Berkeley: University of California Press, 1988, pp. 19-35.

—— 'The Structure of Merlin's Chronicle in *The Faerie Queene* III.iii', in Harry Berger, Jr., *Revisionary Play: Studies in the Spenserian Dynamics*. Berkeley: University of California Press, 1988, pp. 121-30.

—— *Second World and Green World: Studies in Renaissance Fiction-Making*, ed. John Patrick Lynch. Berkeley: University of California Press, 1988.

—— '"Kidnapped Romance": Discourse in *The Faerie Queene*', in George M. Logan and Gordon Teskey, eds. *Unfolded Tales: Essays on Renaissance Romance*. Ithaca: Cornell University Press, 1989, pp. 208-56.

Bergeron, David. *English Civic Pageantry 1558-1642*. London: Arnold, 1971.

Berry, Philippa. *Of Chastity and Power: Elizabethan Literature and the Unmarried Queen*. London: Routledge, 1989.

Bietenholz, Peter G. *Historia and Fabula: Myths and Legends in Historical Thought From Antiquity to the Modern Age*. Leiden: Brill, 1994.

Biow, Douglas. *Mirabile Dictu: Representations of the Marvelous in Medieval and Renaissance Epic*. Ann Arbor: University of Michigan Press, 1996.

Bishop, T. G. *Shakespeare and the Theatre of Wonder*. Cambridge: Cambridge University Press, 1996.

Bord, Janet. *Fairies: Real Encounters with Little People*. London: O'Mara, 1997.

Bowman, Mary R. '"she there as Princess rained": Spenser's Figure of Elizabeth'. *RenQ* 43 (1990), pp. 509-28.

Briggs, Katharine. *The Anatomy of Puck: An Examination of Fairy Beliefs among Shakespeare's Contemporaries and Successors*. London: Routledge, 1959.

—— *Pale Hecate's Team: An Examination of the Beliefs on Witchcraft and Magic among Shakespeare's Contemporaries and His Immediate Successors*. London: Routledge, 1962.

—— *The Fairies in Tradition and Literature*. London: Routledge, 1967.

—— *A Dictionary of Fairies*. Harmondsworth: Penguin, 1977.

Briggs, Robin. *Witches and Neighbours: The Social and Cultural Context of European Witchcraft*. London: HarperCollins, 1996.

Brill, Lesley. 'Other Places, Other Times: The Sites of the Proems to *The Faerie Queene*'. *SEL* 34 (1994), pp. 1-17.

Brooks-Davies, Douglas. 'Lucifera', in *Spenser Encyclopedia*, pp. 441-2.

Burke, Peter. *The Renaissance Sense of the Past*. London: Arnold, 1969.

Burrow, John A. '*Sir Thopas* in the Sixteenth Century', in Douglas Gray and E. G. Stanley, eds, *Middle English Studies Presented to Norman Davies in Honour of his Seventieth Birthday*. Oxford: Clarendon Press, 1983, pp. 69-91.

—— 'Chaucer, Geoffrey', in *Spenser Encyclopedia*, pp. 144-8.

Cain, Thomas H. *Praise in The Faerie Queene*. Lincoln: University of Nebraska Press, 1978.

Calin, William. *The Epic Quest: Studies in Four Old French Chansons de Geste*. Baltimore: Johns Hopkins University Press, 1966.

Campbell, Lily B. *Shakespeare's History Plays: Mirrors of Elizabethan Policy*. San Marino: University of California Press, 1947.

Carasso-Bulow, Lucienne. *The Merveilleux in Chrétien de Troyes' Romances*. Geneva: Librairie Droz, 1976.

Carroll, Clare. 'Spenser and the Irish Language: The Sons of Milesio in *A View of the Present State of Ireland*, *The Faerie Queene*, Book V, and the *Leabhar Gabhála*'. *IUR* 26 (1996), pp. 281-90.

Chambers, E. K. 'Appendix A: The Fairy World', in William Shakespeare, *A Midsummer Night's Dream*, ed. E. K. Chambers. London, 1897, pp. 134-52.

—— *The Elizabethan Stage*. 4 vols. Oxford: Clarendon Press, 1923.

—— *Sir Henry Lee: An Elizabethan Portrait*. Oxford: Clarendon Press, 1936.

Cheney, Patrick and Lauren Silberman, eds. *Worldmaking Spenser: Explorations in the Early Modern Age*. Lexington: University Press of Kentucky, 2000.

Christian, Margaret. "'The Ground of Storie": Genealogy in *The Faerie Queene*'. *SSt* 9 (1988), pp. 61-79.

Clark, Stuart. 'King James's *Daemonologie*: Witchcraft and Kingship', in Sydney Anglo, ed., *The Damned Art: Essays in the Literature of Witchcraft*. London: Routledge, 1977, pp. 156-81.

—— 'Protestant Demonology: Sin, Superstition, and Society (c.1520-c.1630)', in Bengt Ankarloo and Gustav Henningsen, eds. *Early Modern European Witchcraft: Centres and Peripheries*. Oxford: Clarendon Press, 1993, pp. 45-81.

—— *Thinking with Demons: The Idea of Witchcraft in Early Modern Europe*. Oxford: Clarendon Press, 1997.

Clegg, Cyndia Susan. *Press Censorship in Elizabethan England*. Cambridge: Cambridge University Press, 1997.

Clifford-Amos, Terence. "'Certaine Signes" of "Faeryland": Spenser's Eden of Thanksgiving on the Defeat of the "Monstrous" "Dragon" of Albion's North'. *Viator* 32 (2001), pp. 371-415.

Cole, Mary Hill. *The Portable Queen: Elizabeth I and the Politics of Ceremony*. Amherst: University of Massachusetts Press, 1999.

Cooper, Helen. 'Location and Meaning in Masque, Morality and Royal Entertainment', in David Lindley, ed., *The Court Masque*. Manchester: Manchester University Press, 1984, pp. 135-48.

—— *The Canterbury Tales*. Oxford Guides to Chaucer. Oxford: Oxford University Press, 1989.

Craig, Joanne. 'The Image of Mortality: Myth and History in *The Faerie Queene*'. *ELH* 39 (1972), pp. 520-44.

Croker, Thomas Crofton. *Fairy Legends and Traditions of the South of Ireland*. 3 vols. London, 1825-28.

Cross, Tom Peete. 'The Celtic Element in the Lays of *Lanval* and *Graelent*'. *MP* 12 (1914-15), pp. 585-644.

Cummings, R. M. *Spenser: The Critical Heritage*. London: Routledge, 1971.

Dauber, Antoinette B. 'veils', in *Spenser Encyclopedia*, p. 707.

Dean, Christopher. *Arthur of England: English Attitudes to King Arthur and the Knights of the Round Table in the Middle Ages and the Renaissance*. Toronto: University of Toronto Press, 1987.

Dean, Leonard. *Tudor Theories of History Writing*. Ann Arbor: University of Michigan Press, 1947.

Dees, Jerome S. 'The Narrator of *The Faerie Queene*: Patterns of Response'. *TSLL* 12 (1970-71), pp. 537-68.

DeLattre, Floris. *English Fairy Poetry: From the Origins to the Seventeenth Century*. London: Froude, 1912.

DeNeef, A. Leigh. *Spenser and the Motives of Metaphor*. Durham, NC: Duke University Press, 1982.

Dixon, Michael F. N. 'Fairy Tale, Fortune, and Boethian Wonder: Rhetorical Structure in Book VI of *The Faerie Queene*'. *UTQ* 44 (1975), pp. 141-65.

Dodge, R. E. Neil. 'Spenser's Imitations from Ariosto'. *PMLA* 12 (1897), pp. 151-204.

Doran, Susan. 'Juno Versus Diana: The Treatment of Elizabeth's Marriage in Plays and Entertainments, 1561-81'. *Historical Journal* 38 (1995), pp. 257-74.

—— *Monarchy and Matrimony: The Courtships of Elizabeth I*. London: Routledge, 1996.

Dorson, Richard M. *The British Folklorists: A History*. London: Routledge, 1968; repr. 1999.

Dovey, Zillah. *An Elizabethan Progress: The Queen's Journey Through into East Anglia.* Stroud: Sutton, 1996.

Durling, Robert. M. *The Figure of the Poet in Renaissance Epic.* Cambridge, MA: Harvard University Press, 1965.

Easter, De La Warr Benjamin. *A Study of the Magic Elements in the Romans d'Aventure and Romans Bretons.* Baltimore: Johns Hopkins University Press, 1906.

Emerson, Oliver Farrar. 'Spenser's Virgils Gnat'. *JEGP* 17 (1918), pp. 94-118.

Erickson, Wayne. *Mapping the Faerie Queene: Quest Structures and the World of the Poem.* New York: Garland, 1996.

Estes, Leland L. 'Reginald Scot and his *Discoverie of Witchcraft*: Religion and Science in Opposition to the European Witch Craze'. *Church History* 52 (1983), pp. 445-56.

Fairfield, Leslie P. *John Bale: Mythmaker for the English Reformation.* West Lafayette: Purdue University Press, 1976.

Ferguson, Arthur B. *The Indian Summer of English Chivalry: Studies in the Decline and Transformation of Chivalric Idealism.* Durham, NC: Duke University Press, 1968.

—— *Clio Unbound: Perception of the Social and Cultural Past in Renaissance England.* Durham, NC: Duke University Press, 1979.

—— *The Chivalric Tradition in Renaissance England.* Washington: Folger Shakespeare Library, 1986.

—— *Utter Antiquity: Perceptions of Prehistory in Renaissance England.* Durham, NC: Duke University Press, 1993.

Ferry, Anne. *The Art of Naming.* Chicago: University of Chicago Press, 1988.

Fichter, Andrew. *Poets Historical: Dynastic Epic in the Renaissance.* New Haven: Yale University Press, 1982.

Fletcher, Angus. *Allegory: The Theory of a Symbolic Mode.* New Haven: Yale University Press, 1962.

Fletcher, Jefferson. '*Huon of Burdeux* and the *Faerie Queene*'. *JEGP* 2 (1898-99), pp. 209-11.

Fletcher, Robert Huntingdon. *The Arthurian Material in the Chronicles, Especially Those of Great Britain and France.* 2nd edn. New York: Franklin, 1966.

Flower, Robin. 'Laurence Nowell and the Discovery of England in Tudor Times'. *PBA* 21 (1935), pp. 47-73.

Fowler, Alastair. *Spenser and the Numbers of Time.* London: Routledge, 1964.

—— 'Emanations of Glory: Neoplatonic Order in Spenser's *Faerie Queen*', in J. M. Kennedy and J. A. Reither, eds. *A Theatre for Spenserians.* Manchester: Manchester University Press, 1973, pp. 53-82.

Freccero, John. 'The Fig Tree and the Laurel: Petrarch's Poetics', in Patricia Parker and David Quint, eds. *Literary Theory/ Renaissance Texts.* Baltimore: Johns Hopkins University Press, 1986, pp. 20-32.

Friedman, John Block. *The Monstrous Races in Medieval Art and Thought.* Cambridge, MA: Harvard University Press, 1981.

Fruen, Jeffrey P. '"True Glorious Type": The Place of Gloriana in *The Faerie Queene*'. *SSt* 7 (1987), pp. 147-74.

—— 'The Faery Queen Unveiled? Five Glimpses of Gloriana'. *SSt* 11 (1994), pp. 53-88.

Frye, Northrop. 'The Structure of Imagery in *The Faerie Queene*', in A.C. Hamilton, ed., *Essential Articles for the Study of Edmund Spenser.* Hamden, CT: Archon, 1972, pp. 153-70.

Frye, Susan. *Elizabeth I: The Competition for Representation.* New York: Oxford University Press, 1993.

Fussner, F. Smith. *The Historical Revolution: English Historical Writing and Thought 1580-1640*. London: Routledge, 1962.

Gasper, Julia. *The Dragon and the Dove: The Plays of Thomas Dekker*. Oxford: Clarendon Press, 1990.

Genette, Gérard. *Paratexts: Thresholds of Interpretation*, tr. Jane E. Lewin. Cambridge: Cambridge University Press, 1997.

Giamatti, A. Bartlett. *Play of Double Senses: Spenser's Faerie Queene*. Englewood Cliffs, NJ: Prentice-Hall, 1975.

Gless, Darryl. 'nature and grace', in *The Spenser Encyclopedia*, pp. 505-07.

Goldberg, Jonathan. *Endlesse Worke: Spenser and the Structures of Discourse*. Baltimore: Johns Hopkins University Press, 1981.

Graham, Timothy and Andrew G. Watson. *The Recovery of the Past in Early Elizabethan England*. Cambridge: Cambridge Bibliographical Society, 1998.

Gransden, Antonia. *Historical Writing in England ii: c.1307 to the Early Sixteenth Century*. Ithaca: Cornell University Press, 1982.

Greenblatt, Stephen. *Renaissance Self-Fashioning: From More to Shakespeare*. Chicago: University of Chicago Press, 1980.

Greene, Thomas. 'Magic and Festivity at the Renaissance Court'. *RenQ* 60 (1987), pp. 636-59.

Greenlaw, Edwin. 'Spenser's Fairy Mythology'. *SP* 15 (1918), pp. 105-22.

—— 'Britomart at the House of Busirane'. *SP* 26 (1929), pp. 117-30.

—— *Studies in Spenser's Historical Allegory*. Baltimore: Johns Hopkins University Press, 1932.

Gregory, Annabel. 'Witchcraft, Politics, and "Good Neighbourhood" in Early Seventeenth-Century Rye'. *P&P* 133 (1991), pp. 31-66.

Griffin, Benjamin. *Playing the Past: Approaches to English Historical Drama, 1385-1600*. Woodbridge: Brewer, 2001.

Gross, Kenneth. *Spenserian Poetics: Idolatry, Iconoclasm, and Magic*. Ithaca: Cornell University Press, 1985.

Grundy, Joan. *The Spenserian Poets: A Study in Elizabethan and Jacobean Poetry*. London: Arnold, 1969.

Guillory, John. *Poetic Authority: Spenser, Milton, and Literary History*. New York: Columbia University Press, 1983.

Hackett, Helen. *Virgin Mother, Maiden Queen: Elizabeth I and the Cult of the Virgin Mary*. London: Macmillan, 1995.

Hadfield, Andrew. *Edmund Spenser's Irish Experience: Wilde Fruit and Salvage Soyl*. Oxford: Clarendon Press, 1997.

Haller, William. *Foxe's Book of Martyrs and the Elect Nation*. London: Cape, 1963.

Halliwell-Phillipps, J. O. *Illustrations of the Fairy Mythology of the Midsummer Night's Dream*. London, 1845.

Hamilton, A. C. *The Structure of Allegory in The Faerie Queene*. Oxford: Clarendon Press, 1961.

—— gen. ed. *The Spenser Encyclopedia*. Toronto: University of Toronto Press, 1990.

Hankins, John Erskine. *Source and Meaning in Spenser's Allegory: A Study of The Faerie Queene*. Oxford: Clarendon Press, 1971.

Hardison, O. B. *The Enduring Monument: A Study of the Idea of Praise in Renaissance Literary Theory*. Chapel Hill: University of North Carolina Press, 1962.

Harf-Lancner, Laurence. *Les Fées au Moyen Age: Morgane et Mélusine, La Naissance des Fées*. Geneva: Slatkine, 1984.

Harper, Carrie A. *The Sources of The British Chronicle History in Spenser's Faerie Queene.* Philadelphia: Winston, 1910.

Harris, Anthony. *Night's Black Agents: Witchcraft in Seventeenth-Century English Drama.* Manchester: Manchester University Press, 1980.

Hathaway, Baxter. *Marvels and Commonplaces: Renaissance Literary Criticism.* New York: Random House, 1968.

Helgerson, Richard. *Self-Crowned Laureates: Spenser, Jonson, Milton, and the Literary System.* Berkeley: University of California Press, 1983.

Henderson, Lizanne, and Edward J. Cowan, *Scottish Fairy Belief: A History.* East Linton: Tuckwell, 2001.

Hendricks, Margo. '"Obscured by dreams": Race, Empire, and Shakespeare's *A Midsummer Night's Dream'. SQ* 47 (1996), pp. 37-60.

Heninger, S. K., Jr. *Sidney and Spenser: The Poet as Maker.* London: Pennsylvania State University Press, 1989.

Henley, Pauline. *Spenser in Ireland.* Cork: Cork University Press, 1928.

Herendeen, W. H. 'Gloriana', in *Spenser Encyclopedia*, pp. 333-4.

Highley, Christopher. *Shakespeare, Spenser, and the Crisis in Ireland.* Cambridge: Cambridge University Press, 1997.

Hinton, Stan. 'The Poet and His Narrator: Spenser's Epic Voice'. *ELH* 41 (1974), pp. 165-81.

Hintz, Howard. 'The Elizabethan Entertainment and *The Faerie Queene'. PQ* 14 (1935), pp. 83-90.

Hoopes, Robert. '"God Guide Thee, Guyon": Nature and Grace Reconciled in *The Faerie Queene*, Book II'. *RES* n. s. 5 (1954), pp. 14-24.

Horton, Ronald Arthur. *The Unity of The Faerie Queene.* Athens, GA: University of Georgia Press, 1978.

Hough, Graham. *A Preface to The Faerie Queene.* New York: Norton, 1962.

—— *The First Commentary on The Faerie Queene.* Privately published, 1964.

Hume, Anthea. *Edmund Spenser: Protestant Poet.* Cambridge: Cambridge University Press, 1984.

Jack, A. A. *A Commentary on the Poetry of Chaucer and Spenser.* Glasgow: Maclehose, 1920.

Javitch, Daniel. *Poetry and Courtliness in Renaissance England.* Princeton: Princeton University Press, 1978.

—— *Proclaiming a Classic: The Canonization of Orlando Furioso.* Princeton: Princeton University Press, 1991.

Kantorowicz, Ernst. *The King's Two Bodies: A Study in Medieval Political Theology.* Princeton: Princeton University Press, 1957.

Kappler, Claude. *Monstres, Démons et Merveilles à la fin du Moyen Age.* Paris: Payot, 1980.

Kaske, Carol V. 'Spenser's Pluralistic Universe: The View from the Mount of Contemplation (*The Faerie Queene* I.x.)', in Richard C. Frushell and Bernard J. Vondersmith, eds, *Contemporary Thought on Edmund Spenser.* Carbondale, IL: South Illinois University Press, 1975, pp. 121-49.

—— *Spenser and Biblical Poetics.* Ithaca: Cornell University Press, 1999.

Keightley, Thomas. *The Fairy Mythology; Illustrative of the Romance and Superstition of Various Countries.* London, 1828.

Kelley, Theresa M. *Reinventing Allegory.* Cambridge: Cambridge University Press, 1997.

Kendrick, Thomas. Letter, *TLS,* 7 February 1948, p. 79.

—— Letter, *TLS*, 15 May 1948, p. 275.

—— *British Antiquity*. London: Methuen, 1950.

Kennedy, J. M. and J. A. Reither, eds. *A Theatre for Spenserians*. Manchester: Manchester University Press, 1973.

Ker, W. P. 'The Craven Angels'. *MLR* 6 (1911), pp. 85-7.

Kieckhefer, Richard. *Magic in the Middle Ages*. Cambridge: Cambridge University Press, 1990.

Kiessling, Nicolas. *The Incubus in English Literature: Provenance and Progeny*. Pullman: Washington State University Press, 1977.

King, Andrew. *The Faerie Queene and Middle English Romance: The Matter of Just Memory*. Oxford: Clarendon Press, 2000.

King, John N. 'Queen Elizabeth I: Representations of the Virgin Queen'. *RenQ* 43 (1990), pp. 30-74.

—— *Spenser's Poetry and the Reformation Tradition*. Princeton: Princeton University Press, 1990.

Kinney, Clare Regan. *Strategies of Poetic Narrative: Chaucer, Spenser, Milton, Eliot*. Cambridge: Cambridge University Press, 1992.

Kipling, Gordon. *The Triumph of Honour: Burgundian Origins of the Elizabethan Renaissance*. The Hague: Leiden University Press, 1977.

Kors, Alan Charles and Edward Peters, eds. *Witchcraft in Europe, 400 - 1700: A Documentary History*, 2nd edn. Philadelphia: University of Pennsylvania Press, 2001.

Kouwenhoven, Jan Karel. *Apparent Narrative as Thematic Metaphor: The Organisation of The Faerie Queene*. Oxford: Clarendon Press, 1983.

Lamb, Mary Ellen. 'Gloriana, Acrasia, and the House of Busirane: Gendered Fictions in *The Faerie Queene* as Fairy Tale', in Patrick Cheney and Lauren Silberman, eds. *Worldmaking Spenser: Explorations in the Early Modern Age*. Lexington: University Press of Kentucky, 2000, pp. 81-100.

—— 'Taken by the Fairies: Fairy Practices and the Production of Popular Culture in *A Midsummer Night's Dream*'. *SQ* 51 (2000), pp. 277-312.

Lane, Robert. *Shepheards Devises: Edmund Spenser's Shepheardes Calender and the Institutions of Elizabethan Society*. Athens, GA: University of Georgia Press, 1993.

Laroque, François. *Shakespeare's Festive World: Elizabethan Seasonal Entertainment and the Professional Stage*, tr. Janet Lloyd. Cambridge: Cambridge University Press, 1991.

Larrington, Carolyne. 'The Fairy Mistress in Medieval Literary Fantasy', in Ceri Sullivan and Barbara White, eds, *Writing and Fantasy*. London: Longman, 1999, pp. 32-47.

Latham, Minor White. *The Elizabethan Fairies: The Fairies of Folklore and the Fairies of Shakespeare*. New York: Columbia University Press, 1930.

Le Goff, Jacques. 'Melusina: Mother and Pioneer', in *Time, Work and Culture in the Middle Ages*, tr. Arthur Goldhammer. Chicago: University of Chicago Press, 1980, pp. 205-22.

Lea, Henry Charles. *Materials Toward a History of Witchcraft*, ed. A. C. Howland. 3 vols. Philadelphia: University of Pennsylvania Press, 1939.

Lecouteux, Claude. *Les nains et les elfes au moyen age*. Paris: Editions Imago, 1988.

Lee, Judith. 'The English Ariosto: The Elizabethan Poet and the Marvelous'. *SP* 80 (1983), pp. 277-99.

Leslie, Michael. *Spenser's 'Fierce Warres and Faithfull Loves': Martial and Chivalric Symbolism in The Faerie Queene*. Cambridge: Brewer, 1983.

Levine, Joseph M. *Humanism and History: Origins of Early Modern English Historiography*. Ithaca: Cornell University Press, 1987.

Levy, F. J. *Tudor Historical Thought*. San Marino: Huntingdon Library, 1967.

Lewis, C. S. *The Allegory of Love: A Study in Medieval Tradition*. Oxford: Clarendon Press, 1936.

—— *The Discarded Image: An Introduction to Medieval and Renaissance Literature*. Cambridge: Cambridge University Press, 1964.

—— *Studies in Medieval and Renaissance Literature*, ed. Walter Hooper. Cambridge: Cambridge University Press, 1966.

—— *Spenser's Images of Life*, ed. Alastair Fowler. Cambridge: Cambridge University Press, 1967.

Logan, George M. and Gordon Teskey, eds. *Unfolded Tales: Essays on Renaissance Romance*. Ithaca: Cornell University Press, 1989.

Loomis, R. S. 'Morgain la Fée and the Celtic Goddess'. *Speculum* 20 (1945), pp. 183-203.

MacArthur, J. R. 'The Influence of *Huon of Burdeux* upon *The Faerie Queene'*. *JEGP* 4 (1902), pp. 215-38.

MacCaffrey, Isabel. *Spenser's Allegory: The Anatomy of Imagination*. Princeton: Princeton University Press, 1976.

MacCaffrey, Wallace. *Queen Elizabeth and the Making of Policy, 1572-1588*. Princeton: Princeton University Press, 1981.

MacCulloch, J. A. 'The Mingling of Fairy and Witch Beliefs in Sixteenth and Seventeenth Century Scotland'. *Folklore* 32 (1921), pp. 227-44.

—— *Medieval Faith and Fable*. London: Harrap, 1932.

Maley, Willy. *Salvaging Spenser: Colonialism, Culture and Identity*. London: Macmillan, 1997.

Marinelli, Peter V. 'Ariosto', in *Spenser Encyclopedia*, pp. 56-7.

McCabe, Richard A. *The Pillars of Eternity: Time and Providence in The Faerie Queene*. Blackrock: Irish Academic Press, 1989.

—— 'Edmund Spenser, Poet of Exile'. *PBA* 80 (1991), pp. 73-103.

—— *Spenser's Monstrous Regiment: Elizabethan Ireland and the Poetics of Difference*. Oxford: Oxford University Press, 2002.

McCoy, Richard. *The Rites of Knighthood: The Literature and Politics of Elizabethan Chivalry*. Berkeley: University of California Press, 1989.

McCullen, Joseph T., Jr., 'Conference with the Queen of Fairies: A Study of Jonson's Workmanship in *The Alchemist'*. *Studia Neophilologica* 23 (1951), pp. 87-95.

McKisack, May. *Medieval History in the Tudor Age*. Oxford: Clarendon Press, 1971.

McNeir, Waldo F. and Foster Provost, *Edmund Spenser: An Annotated Bibliography, 1937-1972*. Pittsburgh: Duquesne University Press, 1975.

Mendyk, Stan. A. E. *'Speculum Britanniae': Regional Study, Antiquarianism, and Science in Britain to 1700*. Toronto: University of Toronto Press, 1989.

Michie, Sarah. 'The Faerie Queene and Arthur of Little Britain'. *SP* 36 (1939), pp. 105-23.

Mikalachki, Jodi. *The Legacy of Boadicea: Gender and Nation in Early Modern England*. London: Routledge, 1998.

Miller, David Lee. *The Poem's Two Bodies: The Poetics of the 1590 Faerie Queene* Princeton: Princeton University Press, 1988.

Miller, Jacqueline T. 'The Status of Faeryland: Spenser's "Vniust Possession"'. *SSt* 5 (1985), pp. 31-44.

Millican, Charles Bowie. *Spenser and the Table Round: A Study in the Comparaneous Background for Spenser's Use of the Arthurian Legend*. Cambridge, MA: Harvard University Press, 1932.

Mills, Jerry Leath. 'Spenser and the Numbers of History: A Note on the British and Elfin Chronicles in the *Faerie Queene'*. *PQ* 55 (1976), pp. 281-7.

—— 'Prudence, History, and the Prince in *The Faerie Queene*, Book II'. *HLQ* 41 (1978), pp. 83-101.

—— 'chronicles', in *Spenser Encyclopedia*, pp. 151-2.

Minnis, A. J. *Medieval Theory of Authorship: Scholastic Attitudes in the Later Middle Ages*. London: Scolar, 1984.

Montrose, Louis Adrian. '"The perfecte paterne of a Poete": The Poetics of Courtship in *The Shepheardes Calender*'. *TSLL* 21 (1979), pp. 34-67.

—— '"Eliza, Queene of Shepheardes," and the Pastoral of Power'. *ELR* 10 (1980), pp. 153-82.

—— 'The Elizabethan Subject and the Spenserian Text', in Patricia Parker and David Quint, eds. *Literary Theory/ Renaissance Texts*. Baltimore: Johns Hopkins University Press, 1986, pp. 303-40.

—— '"Shaping Fantasies": Figurations of Gender and Power in Elizabethan Culture', in Stephen Greenblatt, ed., *Representing the English Renaissance*. Berkeley: University of California Press, 1988, pp. 31-64.

Murray, Margaret. *The Witch-Cult in Western Europe*. Oxford: Clarendon Press, 1921; repr. 1962.

Murrin, Michael. *The Veil of Allegory: Some Notes Towards a Theory of Allegorical Rhetoric in the English Renaissance*. Chicago: University of Chicago Press, 1969.

—— 'The Rhetoric of Fairyland', in Thomas O. Sloane and Raymond B. Waddington, eds, *The Rhetoric of Renaissance Poetry: From Wyatt to Milton*. Berkeley: University of California Press, 1974, pp. 73-95.

—— *The Allegorical Epic: Essays in its Rise and Decline*. Chicago: University of Chicago Press, 1980.

—— 'fairyland', in *Spenser Encyclopedia*, pp. 296-8.

Nelson, William. 'Spenser *ludens*', in J. M. Kennedy and J. A. Reither, eds. *A Theatre for Spenserians*. Manchester: Manchester University Press, 1973, pp. 83-100.

Neuse, Richard. 'Book VI as Conclusion to *The Faerie Queene*'. *ELH* 35 (1968), pp. 329-53.

Nohrnberg, James. *The Analogy of The Faerie Queene*. Princeton: Princeton University Press, 1976.

Norbrook, David. *Poetry and Politics in the English Renaissance*. rev. ed. Oxford: Oxford University Press, 2002.

Normand, Lawrence and Gareth Roberts. *Witchcraft in Early Modern Scotland: James VI's Demonology and the North Berwick Witches*. Exeter: Exeter University Press, 2000.

Nutt, Alfred. 'The Fairy Mythology of English Literature: Its Origins and Nature'. *Folklore* 8 (1897), pp. 29-53.

O'Brien, Dennis. 'Lord Berner's *Huon of Burdeux*: The Survival of Medieval Ideals in the Reign of Henry VIII', in Leslie Workman, ed., *Medievalism in England: Studies in Medievalism IV*. Cambridge: Brewer, 1992, pp. 36-44.

O'Callaghan, Michelle. *The 'Shepheard's Nation': Jacobean Spenserians and Early Stuart Political Culture, 1612-25*. Oxford: Clarendon Press, 2000.

O'Connell, Michael. *Mirror and Veil: The Historical Dimension of Spenser's Faerie Queene*. Chapel Hill: University of North Carolina Press, 1977.

Orgel, Stephen. *The Illusion of Power: Political Theater in the English Renaissance*. Berkeley: University of California Press, 1975.

—— 'Margins of Truth', in Andrew Murphy, ed., *The Renaissance Text: Theory, Editing, Textuality*. Manchester: Manchester University Press, 2000, pp. 91-107.

Parker, Patricia. *Inescapable Romance: Studies in the Poetics of a Mode*. Princeton: Princeton University Press, 1979.

—— and David Quint, eds. *Literary Theory/ Renaissance Texts*. Baltimore: Johns Hopkins University Press, 1986.

Parker. M. Pauline. *The Allegory of The Faerie Queene*. Oxford: Oxford University Press, 1960.

Patch, Howard Rollin. *The Otherworld: According to Descriptions in Medieval Literature*. New York: Octagon, 1970.

Paton, Lucy Allen. *Studies in the Fairy Mythology of Arthurian Romance*, enlarged by a Survey of Scholarship on the Fairy Mythology since 1903 and a Bibliography by R. S. Loomis. 2nd edn. New York: Franklin, 1960.

Patterson, Annabel. *Censorship and Interpretation: The Conditions of Writing and Reading in Early Modern England*. Madison: University of Wisconsin Press, 1984.

Pearl, Jonathan. 'French Catholic Demonologists and Their Enemies in the Late Sixteenth and Early Seventeenth Centuries'. *Church History* 52 (1983), pp. 457-67.

Platt, Peter G. *Reason Diminished: Shakespeare and the Marvelous*. Lincoln: University of Nebraska Press, 1997.

Pryor, Ruth. 'Spenser's Temperance and the Chronicles of England'. *NM* 81 (1980), pp. 161-8.

Purkiss, Diane. *The Witch in History: Early Modern and Twentieth-Century Representations*. London: Routledge, 1996.

—— 'Old Wives' Tales Retold: The Mutations of the Fairy Queen', in Danielle Clarke and Elizabeth Clarke, eds, *'This Double Voice': Gendered Writing in Early Modern England*. London: Macmillan, 2000, pp. 103-22.

—— *Troublesome Things: A History of Fairies and Fairy Stories*. Harmondsworth: Penguin, 2000.

Quilligan, Maureen. *Milton's Spenser: The Politics of Reading*. Ithaca: Cornell University Press, 1983.

Radcliffe, David Hill. *Edmund Spenser: A Reception History*. Columbia, SC: Camden House, 1996.

Raggio, Olga. 'The Myth of Prometheus: Its Survival and Metamorphoses up to the Eighteenth Century'. *JWCI* 21 (1958), pp. 44-62.

Rambuss, Richard. *Spenser's Secret Career*. Cambridge: Cambridge University Press, 1993.

Ramsey, Lee C. *Chivalric Romances: Popular Literature in Medieval England*. Bloomington: Indiana University Press, 1983.

Rathborne, Isabel E. *The Meaning of Spenser's Fairyland*. New York: Columbia University Press, 1937.

—— Letter, *TLS*, 24 April 1948, p. 233.

Read, David. *Temperate Conquests: Spenser and the Spanish New World*. Detroit: Wayne State University Press, 2000.

Richardson, Lisa. 'Sir John Hayward and Early Stuart Historiography'. PhD. thesis. Cambridge University, 1999.

Roberts, Gareth. 'magic', in *Spenser Encyclopedia*, pp. 445-6.

—— 'The Descendants of Circe: Witches and Renaissance Fictions', in Jonathan Barry, Marianne Hester, and Gareth Roberts, eds. *Witchcraft in Early Modern Europe: Studies in Culture and Belief*. Cambridge: Cambridge University Press, 1996, pp. 183-206.

Robinson, Benedict Scott. '"Darke speech": Matthew Parker and the Reforming of History'. *SCJ* 29 (1998), pp. 1061-83.

Roche, Thomas P., Jr. *The Kindly Flame: A Study of the Third and Fourth Books of Spenser's Faerie Queene*. Princeton: Princeton University Press, 1964.

Rosen, Barbara, ed. *Witchcraft*. London: Arnold, 1969.

Rossi, Joan Warchol. '*Britons moniments*: Spenser's Definition of Temperance in History'. *ELR* 15 (1985), pp. 42-58.

Rossi, Marguerite. *Huon de Bordeaux et l'évolution du genre épique au XIIIᵉ siècle*. Paris: Champion, 1975.

Røstvig, Maren-Sofie. 'Canto Structure in Tasso and Spenser'. *SSt* 1 (1980), pp. 177-200.

Rovang, Paul R. *Refashioning 'Knights and Ladies Gentle Deeds': The Intertextuality of Spenser's Faerie Queene and Malory's Morte Darthur*. Cranbury, NJ: Associated University Presses, 1996.

Rowse, A. L. *The England of Elizabeth: The Structure of Society*. London: Macmillan, 1950.

Royster, James. 'E.K.'s *Elf<Guelph, Goblin<Ghibelline*'. *MLN* 43 (1928), pp. 249-52.

Russell, Jeffrey Burton. *Witchcraft in the Middle Ages*. Ithaca: Cornell University Press, 1972.

Sanderson, Stewart. 'A Prospect of Fairyland'. *Folklore* 75 (1964), pp. 1-18.

Sands, Kathleen R. 'The Doctrine of Transubstantiation and the English Protestant Dispossession of Demons', *History* 85 (2000), pp. 446-62.

Schulze, Ivan. 'Elizabethan Chivalry and the Faery Queene's Annual Feast'. *MLN* 50 (1935), pp. 158-61.

—— 'Reflections of Elizabethan Tournaments in *The Faerie Queene*, 4.4 and 5.3'. *ELH* 5 (1938), pp. 278-84.

—— 'Blenerhasset's *A Revelation*, Spenser's *Shepheardes Calender*, and the Kenilworth Pageants'. *ELH* 11 (1944), pp. 85-91.

Scott, Sir Walter. *Letters on Demonology and Witchcraft*. London, 1830.

Sherman, William H. *John Dee: The Politics of Reading and Writing in the English Renaissance*. Amherst: University of Massachusetts Press, 1995.

Sidgwick, Frank. *The Sources and Analogues of A Midsummer Night's Dream*. London: Chatto, 1908.

Sisson, C. J. 'A Topical Reference in *The Alchemist*', in J. G. McManaway, ed., *Joseph Quincy Adams Memorial Studies*. Washington: Folger Shakespeare Library, 1948, pp. 739-41.

Spalding, Thomas Alfred. *Elizabethan Demonology*. London, 1880.

Spence, Lewis. *British Fairy Origins*. London: Watts, 1946; repr. Wellingborough: Aquarium, 1981.

Starnes, DeWitt T. and Ernest W. Talbert. *Classical Myth and Legend in Renaissance Dictionaries*. Westport, CT: Greenwood, 1955.

Stocker, Margarita. *Judith, Sexual Warrior: Women and Power in Western Culture*. New Haven: Yale University Press, 1998.

Strong, Roy. *The Cult of Elizabeth: Elizabethan Portraiture and Pageantry*. London: Thames and Hudson, 1977.

—— *Gloriana: The Portraits of Queen Elizabeth I*. London: Thames and Hudson, 1987.

Summers, David A. *Spenser's Arthur: The British Arthurian Tradition and The Faerie Queene*. New York: University Press of America, 1997.

Teall, John T. 'Witchcraft and Calvinism in Elizabethan England: Divine Power and Human Agency'. *Journal of the History of Ideas* 23 (1962), pp. 21-36.

Teskey, Gordon. 'allegory', in *Spenser Encyclopedia*, pp. 16-22.

—— 'Arthur in *The Faerie Queene*', in *Spenser Encyclopedia*, pp. 69-72.

—— *Allegory and Violence*. Ithaca: Cornell University Press, 1996.

Thomas, Keith. *Religion and the Decline of Magic*. Harmondsworth: Penguin, 1973.

Thomas, Sidney. '"Hobgoblin Runne Away With the Garland from Apollo"'. *MLN* 55 (1940), pp. 418-22.

Tillyard, E. M. W. *Shakespeare's History Plays*. Harmondsworth: Penguin, 1944.

Tonkin, Humphrey. *Spenser's Courteous Pastoral: Book Six of the 'Faerie Queene'*. Oxford: Oxford University Press, 1972.

Train, Lilla. 'Chaucer's Ladyes Foure and Twenty'. *MLN* 50 (1935), pp. 85-7.

Tuve, Rosemond. *Allegorical Imagery: Some Medieval Books and Their Posterity*. Princeton: Princeton University Press, 1966.

—— *Essays by Rosemond Tuve: Spenser, Herbert, Milton*, ed. Thomas P. Roche, Jr. Princeton: Princeton University Press, 1970.

—— 'The Red Crosse Knight and Medieval Demon Stories', in Rosemond Tuve, *Essays by Rosemond Tuve: Spenser, Herbert, Milton*, ed. Thomas P. Roche, Jr. Princeton: Princeton University Press, 1970, pp. 39-48.

—— 'Spenser and Some Pictorial Conventions', in Rosemond Tuve, *Essays by Rosemond Tuve: Spenser, Herbert, Milton*, ed. Thomas P. Roche, Jr. Princeton: Princeton University Press, 1970, pp. 112-38.

Van Dyke, Carolynn. *The Fiction of Truth: Structures of Meaning in Narrative and Dramatic Allegory*. Ithaca: Cornell University Press, 1985.

Wall, Wendy. *The Imprint of Gender: Authorship and Publication in the English Renaissance*. Ithaca: Cornell University Press, 1993.

Warner, Marina. *From the Beast to the Blonde: On Fairy Tales and Their Tellers*. New York: Noonday, 1994.

Warren, W. L. *King John*. London: Methuen, 1981; repr. New Haven: Yale University Press, 1997.

Warton, Thomas. *Observations on the Fairy Queen of Spenser* (1762), Facsimile edn. 2 vols. New York: Haskell, 1969.

Waters, D. Douglas. 'Spenser and Symbolic Witchcraft in *The Shepheardes Calender*'. *SEL* 14 (1974), pp. 3-15.

Watkins, John. *The Specter of Dido: Spenser and Virgilian Epic*. New Haven: Yale University Press, 1995.

Watson, Elizabeth Porges. 'Mr Fox's Mottoes in the House of Busirane'. *SSt* 13 (1999), pp. 285-90.

Wells, Robin Headlam. *Spenser's Faerie Queene and the Cult of Elizabeth*. London: Croom Helm, 1983.

Welsford, Enid. *The Court Masque: A Study of the Relationship Between Poetry and the Revels*. New York: Russell and Russell, 1962.

Wentz, W. Y. Evans. *The Fairy-Faith in Celtic Countries*. London: Oxford University Press, 1911.

West, Robert. *Reginald Scot and Renaissance Writings on Witchcraft*. Boston: Twayne, 1984.

Westoby, Kathryn S. 'A New Look at the Role of the Fée in Medieval French Arthurian Romance', in Glyn S. Burgess and Robert A. Taylor, eds, *The Spirit of the Court: Selected Proceedings of the Fourth Congress of the International Courtly Literature Society (Toronto 1983)*. Cambridge: Brewer, 1985, pp. 373-85.

Whitaker, Muriel. *Arthur's Kingdom of Adventure: The World of Malory's Morte D'Arthur*. Woodbridge: Brewer, 1984.

White, Hayden. *Metahistory: The Historical Imagination in Nineteenth-Century Europe*. Baltimore: Johns Hopkins University Press, 1973.

—— 'The Historical Text as Literary Artefact', in White, *Tropics of Discourse: Essays in Cultural Criticism*. Baltimore: Johns Hopkins University Press, 1978, pp. 81-100.

Wilby, Emma J. 'Hobmen, Familiars and the Early Modern Visionary'. M.A. thesis. Exeter University, 1996.

Williams, David. *Deformed Discourse: The Function of the Monster in Medieval Thought and Literature*. Exeter: Exeter University Press, 1996.

Williams, Elizabeth. '"A damsell by herselfe alone": Images of Magic and Femininity from *Lanval* to *Sir Lambewell*', in Jennifer Fellows, Maldwyn Mills, and Carol M. Meale, eds, *Romance Reading the Book: Essays in Medieval Narrative Presented to Maldwyn Mills*. Cardiff: University of Wales Press, 1996, pp. 155-70.

Williams, Kathleen. *Spenser's Faerie Queene: The World of Glass*. London: Routledge, 1966.

Williams, Noel. 'The Semantics of the Word '*Fairy*': Making Meaning Out of Thin Air', in Peter Narváez, ed., *The Good People: New Fairylore Essays*. New York: Garland, 1991, pp. 457-78.

Wilson, E. C. *England's Eliza*. Cambridge, MA: Harvard University Press, 1939.

Wilson, Jean. *Entertainments for Elizabeth I*. Woodbridge: Brewer, 1980.

Woodbridge, Linda. 'Amoret and Belphoebe: Fairy Tale and Myth'. *N&Q* 231 (1986), pp. 340-42.

Woodcock, Matthew. 'The Fairy Queen Figure in Elizabethan Entertainments', in Carole Levin, Debra Barrett-Graves, and Jo Eldridge Carney, eds, *Elizabeth I: Always Her Own Free Woman*. Aldershot: Ashgate, 2003, pp. 97-115.

Woodhouse, A. S. P. 'Nature and Grace in *The Faerie Queene*'. *ELH* 16 (1949), pp. 194-228.

—— 'Nature and Grace in Spenser: A Rejoinder'. *RES* n. s. 6 (1955), pp. 284-8.

Woolf, D. R. *Reading History in Early Modern England*. Cambridge: Cambridge University Press, 2000.

Wright, C. E. 'The Dispersal of the Monastic Libraries and the Beginnings of Anglo-Saxon Studies. Matthew Parker and his Circle: A Preliminary Study'. *Transactions of the Cambridge Bibliographical Society* 1 (1953), pp. 208-37.

Wurtsbaugh, Jewel. *Two Centuries of Spenserian Scholarship (1609-1805)*. Baltimore: Johns Hopkins University Press, 1936.

Yates, Frances. Letter. *TLS*, 3 July 1948, p. 373.

—— *Astraea: The Imperial Theme in the Sixteenth Century*. London: Routledge, 1975.

Index

Lloyd-George, David 4
Lydgate, John 3
Lyly, John 14, 92

McCabe, Richard 4, 16-17, 34
magic 18, 21, 36, 38, 44, 77, 81, 103-5
magic weapons 31, 81
Malleus Maleficarum 22, 25
Malory, Sir Thomas 44, 54, 62, 103-4
masque 12, 43-4, 79, 109, 139-40; *see also* entertainments and pageants
Melusine 33, 35-8, 71, 106, 117
Mills, Jerry Leath 117
Minnis, A. J. 62
Mirror for Magistrates 126
monstrous, theories on the 71
Montrose, Louis Adrian 6
More, Thomas Sir 69, 77
Morgan le Fay 32, 99n18, 103-4
Murrin, Michael 80

Nashe, Thomas 1
neoplatonism 15n17, 40, 88, 105, 112; *see also* Plato
Norbrook, David 77
Norwich entertainment, *see* entertainments and pageants
Nutt, Alfred 13, 28, 35

Oberon
    in *Faerie Queene* 37, 133, 135
    in *Huon* 37-8
    see also Jonson, *Oberon*
O'Connell, Michael 125
Ogier 35, 99n18
Ó hUiginn, Tadhg Dall 34
Orgel, Stephen 26
Orlando Furioso, *see* Ariosto
Ovid 114

Page, William 64-5
Parker, Matthew 119-20
parody 21, 91-3, 105, 129
Partonope of Blois 33
pastoral 17, 68-9, 100; *see also* Spenser, *Shepheardes Calender*
Philips, Judith 23, 99
Plato 71, 111, 113, 122n19; *see also* neoplatonism
Praise of Folly 71
Purkiss, Diane 9

Puttenham, George 68-9

Raleigh, Sir Walter 55-6, 111; *see also* Spenser, *Faerie Queene*, 'Letter to Raleigh'
Rathborne, Isabel 2-5, 80-81, 87, 104, 133
Rémy, Nicholas 24
Robin good-fellow 11, 13-14, 22-4

St. George 83-6; *see also* Spenser, *Faerie Queene*, Redcrosse knight
Scot, Reginald 7, 11, 20-24, 28
Scott, Sir Walter 13
Shakespeare, William 13-14, 23, 28, 66, 139-40
    Midsummer Night's Dream 13-14, 139
    Merry Wives of Windsor 23
    Romeo and Juliet 66, 140
Sidney, Sir Philip 31, 43, 45, 64, 77, 117, 123
Sir Launfal 33, 37
Sir Orfeo 33
Skydmore, Sir James 31
Spenser, Edmund
    Amoretti 56, 62, 109
    Colin Clouts Come Home Againe 115, 118
    correspondence 1, 32, 49, 109, 117
    Epithalamion 19n30
    Faerie Queene
        Acrasia 34, 49, 78, 81, 102, 104, 106-7
        Agape 81, 102-3, 105, 138
        Amphisa 82
        'Antiquitee of Faery lond' 3-4, 8, 38, 50, 63, 72, 75, 77, 81, 104, 112, 114-37, 139
        Archimago 81n15, 100, 131
        Artegall 4, 54, 70, 81-2, 86, 99, 104n25, 112, 128, 131, 138
        Arthur 4, 8, 21, 30, 34-5, 49, 53, 57, 59-60, 74-6, 80-82, 89-91, 93-102, 106-7, 110, 112-16, 121-4, 127-31, 133, 136, 138; *see also* Arthur, King of the Britons
        Belphoebe 56, 72, 82, 99, 108
        Bon- / Malfont 131
        Bower of Bliss 5, 77, 106